AFRO-ARAB FRATERNITY

Volume 95, Sage Library of Social Research

Sage Library of Social Research

1 Caplovitz **The Merchants of Harlem**
2 Rosenau **International Studies & the Social Sciences**
3 Ashford **Ideology & Participation**
4 McGowan/Shapiro **The Comparative Study of Foreign Policy**
5 Male **The Struggle for Power**
6 Tanter **Modelling & Managing International Conflicts**
7 Catanese **Planners & Local Politics**
8 Prescott **Economic Aspects of Public Housing**
9 Parkinson **Latin America, the Cold War, & the World Powers, 1945-1973**
10 Smith **Ad Hoc Governments**
11 Gallimore et al **Culture, Behavior & Education**
12 Hallman **Neighborhood Government in a Metropolitan Setting**
13 Gelles **The Violent Home**
14 Weaver **Conflict & Control in Health Care Administration**
15 Schweigler **National Consciousness in Divided Germany**
16 Carey **Sociology & Public Affairs**
17 Lehman **Coordinating Health Care**
18 Bell/Price **The First Term**
19 Alderfer/Brown **Learning from Changing**
20 Wells/Marwell **Self-Esteem**
21 Robins **Political Institutionalization & the Integration of Elites**
22 Schonfeld **Obedience & Revolt**
23 McCready/Greeley **The Ultimate Values of the**
24 Nye **Role Structure & Analysis of the Family**
25 Wehr/Washburn **Peace & World Order Systems**
26 Stewart **Children in Distress**
27 Dedring **Recent Advances in Peace & Conflict Research**
28 Czudnowski **Comparing Political Behavior**
29 Douglas **Investigative Social Research**
30 Stohl **War & Domestic Political Violence**
31 Williamson **Sons or Daughters**
32 Levi **Law & Politics in the International Society**
33 Altheide **Creating Reality**
34 Lerner **The Politics of Decision-Making**
35 Converse **The Dynamics of Party Support**
36 Newman/Price **Jails & Drug Treatment**
37 Abercrombie **The Military Chaplain**
38 Gottdiener **Planned Sprawl**
39 Lineberry **Equality & Urban Policy**
40 Morgan **Deterrence**
41 Lefebvre **The Structure of Awareness**
42 Fontana **The Last Frontier**
43 Kemper **Migration & Adaptation**
44 Caplovitz/Sherrow **The Religious Drop-Outs**
45 Nagel/Neef **The Legal Process: Modeling the System**
46 Bucher/Stelling **Becoming Professional**
47 Hiniker **Revolutionary Ideology & Chinese Reality**
48 Herman **Jewish Identity**
49 Marsh **Protest & Political Consciousness**
50 LaRossa **Conflict & Power in Marriage**
51 Abrahamsson **Bureaucracy or Participation**
52 Parkinson **The Philosophy of International Relations**
53 Lerup **Building the Unfinished**
54 Smith **Churchill's German Army**
55 Corden **Planned Cities**
56 Hallman **Small & Large Together**
57 Inciardi et al **Historical Approaches to Crime**
58 Levitan/Alderman **Warriors at Work**
59 Zurcher **The Mutable Self**
60 Teune/Mlinar **The Developmental Logic of Social Systems**
61 Garson **Group Theories of Politics**
62 Medcalf **Law & Identity**
63 Danziger **Making Budgets**
64 Damrell **Search for Identity**
65 Stotland et al **Empathy, Fantasy & Helping**
66 Aronson **Money & Power**
67 Wice **Criminal Lawyers**
68 Hoole **Evaluation Research & Development Activities**
69 Singelmann **From Agriculture to Services**
70 Seward **The American Family**
71 McCleary **Dangerous Men**
72 Nagel/Neef **Policy Analysis: In Social Science Research**
73 Rejai/Phillips **Leaders of Revolution**
74 Inbar **Routine Decision-Making**
75 Galaskiewicz **Exchange Networks & Community Politics**
76 Alkin/Daillak/White **Using Evaluations**
77 Sensat **Habermas & Marxism**
78 Matthews **The Social World of Old Women**
79 Swanson/Cohen/Swanson **Small Towns & Small Towners**
80 Latour/Woolgar **Laboratory Life**
81 Krieger **Hip Capitalism**
82 Megargee/Bohn **Classifying Criminal Offenders**
83 Cook **Who Should Be Helped?**
84 Gelles **Family Violence**
85 Katzner **Choice & the Quality of Life**
86 Caplovitz **Making Ends Meet**
87 Berk/Berk **Labor and Leisure at Home**
88 Darling **Families Against Society**
89 Altheide/Snow **Media Logic**
90 Roosens **Mental Patients in Town Life**
91 Savage **Founders, Heirs, & Managers**
92 Bromley/Shupe **"Moonies" in America**
93 Littrell **Bureaucratic Justice**
94 Murray/Cox **Beyond Probation**
95 Roberts **Afro-Arab Fraternity**
96 Rutman **Planning Useful Evaluations**
97 Shimanoff **Communication Rules**
98 Laguerre **Voodo Heritage**
99 Macarov **Work and Welfare**

Afro-Arab Fraternity

The Roots of Terramedia

GEORGE O. ROBERTS

Volume 95
SAGE LIBRARY OF
SOCIAL RESEARCH

SAGE Publications Beverly Hills London

For information address:

SAGE PUBLICATIONS, INC.
275 South Beverly Drive
Beverly Hills, California 90212

SAGE PUBLICATIONS LTD
28 Banner Street
London EC1Y 8QE England

Printed in the United States of America

Library of Congress Cataloging in Publication Data

Roberts, George O
Afro-Arab fraternity.

(Sage library of social research ; v. 95)
Bibliography: p.
1. Africa--Relations (general) with Arab countries.
2. Arab countries--Relations (general) with Africa.
3. Africa--Civilization. 4. Arab countries--Civilization. I. Title.
DT38.9.A4R62 301.29'6'0174927 79-20316
ISBN 0-8039-1334-6
ISBN 0-8039-1335-4 pbk.

FIRST PRINTING

CONTENTS

To Saranen and Samuel, who never lived long enough to enjoy the Terramedian promise, and to their tenacious mother and my devoted wife, Michaela.

PREFACE

The notion of Terramedia first gained my attention in 1964, while heading a multicultural and interdisciplinary faculty at a New York college. Not only did the individual inclinations and perceptions of my coworkers pose a challenge to the task of coordinating Africa and the Middle East into one required course, but the skepticism of predominantly reluctant students (assisted by the academic myths of African and Arab irrelevance), complicated the task even more. By 1970, however, it had become clear to me that even Africans and Arabs shared in the faulty view of their distinctiveness. Not apparent to the majority of Africans and Arabs were the similarities with which geography, foreign incursions, and cultural evolutions had endowed them, and the degree to which concerted acknowledgement of them might alleviate the impediments to their viability as modern nation-states.

Regrettably, the experience which began the search for commonalities among Africans and Arabs has fallen upon bad times. Few are the colleges today that view courses dealing with these peoples as important to a sound college education, and fewer still are the scholars (and political leaders for that matter), who see any merit or purpose in pursuing a single Terramedian orbit encompassing both Africa and the Middle East. Despite these developments, it is clear that viable independence and sustained dignity can come to Africans and Arabs only through a perception of their necessary interdependence and cooperation.

The promise of a Terramedian view of things would, perhaps, have faded away were it not for the nurturing provided by a few of my colleagues. Jay Martin contributed by affording the opportunity to participate in comparative culture studies, as did those who gave substance to such studies: Pete Clecak, Jim Flink, Joe Jorgensen, Myron Simon, and Joe White. From afar, of course, Jess Shelton has been a constant friend, stimulant, and critic, as has Molefi Asante. The University of California, Irvine, was generous with resources whereby I was able to observe the constants and variables of Terramedian realities in Africa and the Middle East. My humble gratitude is hereby expressed to all of them, for encouraging an idea that might have otherwise suffered atrophy from untenable ridicule and intellectual arrogance.

The volatile nature of contemporary Terramedia necessitated occasional hasty revisions. Thanks to the patience and tolerance of my secretaries, to whom the manuscript often appeared strange and remote, such needs were readily accommodated. Let me, therefore, express my gratitude to Froke Blessum, Rosemary Johnson, and Esther Bagley, who had to endure my incessant shifts from administrative to scholarly activities.

G. O. R.

Chapter One

THE RE-EMERGENCE OF TERRAMEDIA

Introduction

Many books have been written about Africa and the Middle East, but none exist to satisfy the need for a short, useful survey of the two areas as a natural and cultural unit.[1] Although physically contiguous with Africa, the Middle East (or Near East, as some prefer to call it) had been given European and Asian attention for its presumably distinct cultural heritage, whereas Africa–particularly black Africa south of the Sahara–had been relegated to a position of "darkness" from which it could never arise into "enlightenment" except with the "help" of those from "superior" cultures.[2]

As Alioun Diop, editor of *Presence Africaine*, and others have observed, the history of Negro Africa was either ignored or deprecated by the Europeans (which in this work includes Americans, Australians, white South Africans, and all other Europeans about the world). Those who claimed black Africa was unimportant held that it was devoid of a literary heritage, thus without any civilization worthy of serious study. The few observations of early anthropologists, furthermore, arose from a romantic interest in the "noble savage," and felt needs to support theories rationalizing the "superior" race, nature, and attainment of non-Africans.[3]

Change has gradually improved perception. Not only is there much serious research being carried on (and a great amount already accomplished), but many institutes and college curricula also are committed to an objective analysis and teaching about Africa. Of course, studying and teaching about the Middle East continue. Nevertheless, there is still no uniform approach. The term *Terramedia* (see Figure 1) therefore, is used to identify the two areas of Africa and Arabia as a special unit of the Third World lying, as it were, "between" EuroAmerica and Asia and sharing many common features.

Figure 1.1 Nation States of Terramedia

GEOGRAPHY

The geographical position of Terramedia afforded it the opportunity to serve as a link between the eastern lands beyond Iran and the western lands beyond Turkey and north of Spain. Not only did overland caravans traverse these middle lands, but the subsequent construction of the Suez Canal—identifiable as both Middle Eastern and African—strengthened this historical trading link. Given the reality of a spherical world, one could argue that the strategic importance of Terramedia derived merely from historical accident. Certainly, another sector of our human universe could have provided the same combination of desert, arable land, and waterway which "encouraged" international interchange involving commerce, religious expansion, and imperialistic activities. The fact remains, however, that it was in Terramedia, rather than somewhere else, where the physical environment allowed a sustained and enduring evolution of man (from Olduvai Gorge) and the basis of contemporary civilization (from the Fertile Crescent) entailing agriculture, animal husbandry, and expansive religiosity.

Ironically, advancement in technology (in aviation, chemistry, and physics, for example) has not diminished the centripetal influence of this geographical entity. For, accidental or not, Terramedia retains its place of prominence as a region extremely endowed—even when it requires the aid of sophisticated technology developed outside of Terramedia to make them evident—with such geographical creations as petroleum, diamonds, gold, and uranium. Making geography a uniting thread must not, of course, ignore the physical and climatic variations existing within Terramedia (such as desert, savanna, and forest, or hot, mild, and cold sectors). Nor must one ignore differences in community structure and organization (town, village, or hinterland). But even in this connection, there is a "mirror-image" effect which contributes still further toward making the Middle East and Africa geographically comparable.

HISTORY

Most of the countries of Terramedia have provided, and continue to provide, a centripetal stimulus for exploitation and the pursuit of diverse self-interests. Gone are the days when the Arabs, Ottoman Turks, and Europeans extended their domination to faraway places. For sub-Sahara Africa, that mastery by others took the obnoxious form of the transatlantic slave trade, carrying away millions of Africans from the exploited womb of the "Black Mother." It also entailed the colonialization of Africa, with stern military, political, and economic control aimed at improving life in the rapidly industrializing European world. For the Middle East, on the other hand, the experience of a less overt domination did not truly save the area from equally effective control, as a careful examination of the mandate system and the European exploitation of the Middle East's major resource (petroleum and a militarily strategic location for the West) will reveal. As has been noted by Gamal Abdel Nasser,

> The Western conquest of the Middle East was mental no less than physical. Overwhelmed and unsettled, Eastern minds lost almost all national values, yet could not absorb Western values. Misapplication of Western patterns of government brought a confused mixture of political systems and philosophies. Democracy was only a veil for dictatorship. Constitutions framed in the interest of the people of the Middle East became instruments for their exploitation and domination. . . . Politicians and factions for the most part made themselves subservient to the forces that were ravaging the country—British rulers, corrupt monarchs, feudal overlords.[4]

Consequently, Middle Eastern statesmen still denounce neocolonialism and, like their darker brothers to the south, challenge the honesty and integrity of the more powerful nations that persist in imposing their conceptions of race and culture on problems of universal human equity.

Regrettably, Terramedia has failed (since its modern independence), to put this experience of inequity and exploitation to good use. While there is still the cry from its many sectors against injustice, and neocolonialism meted out presumably by "Europeans," many Terramedians inflict these same "curses" upon their own kith and kin. Aside from the fact that Terramedians were not always humane and just toward each other—Arabs had enslaved Africans, Berbers had looted Hausas, and Zulus had massacred Sothos—there is still a level of domineering, intergroup hostility and atrociousness (between economic classes, between power wielders, between nation-states, and between ideological camps), which deserves condemnation. The preponderance of military regimes, for example, is not in keeping with the historical stimulants of independence. The assessment of Kwabena Fosu-Mensah is applicable to all of Terramedia:

> Most people who appreciate the importance of political stability to the economic growth and development of a country must be wishing for the demise of the "Khaki" governments. . . . Today, countries governed by "Khaki" personnel represent about two-thirds of the entire population of independent Africa—they control almost the same proportion of its Gross National Product. A cursory look at statistics reveals that the following belong to the "Khaki 22": the four most densely populated countries (Egypt, Ethiopia, Nigeria,

> Zaire), the four most extensive countries with the highest Gross National Product (Algeria, Libya, Egypt, Nigeria). There cannot be a more eloquent testimony, though Nigeria and Ghana are happily leaving their "Khaki" friends.[5]

One only has to include the situation in Jordan, Lebanon, Syria, and Iraq (why not even Saudi Arabia?) to appreciate the seriousness of Terramedia's blindness to a valid lesson of its history. One can only hope that the advantage of perpetual fraternity and the absence of an opportunity for extraterritorial loyalty will contribute toward a hastened demise of such indigenous aberrations.

UNITY OF HUMAN EXISTENCE

The close integration of the spiritual and the temporal further binds the two geographical areas of Terramedia. In the Middle East, man has been guided by a system of beliefs and practices emphasizing the interaction between the supernatural and temporal. Islam as theocracy emphasized the integrative community of man guided by Allah and his servants. Quite similar are general African beliefs in which man is integrated with the High God, with godlings, ancestors, and with the universe itself. Even the modern presidents and kings manifest such notions of interactions between different strata of powers in their relation to their "parliaments" and "cabinets."

FAMILY STRUCTURES

In Terramedia, polygyny is widely accepted as the ideal form of marriage, which unites more than the members of the conjugal unit. Marriage thus is considered to be a means for reinforcing extensive group values, including the perpetuation of the species, rather than primarily as a means of promoting the happiness of a nuclear family or an individual. The emphasis on communality, of course, has its drawbacks. Not only does it condone unnecessary dependency at the expense of individual vitality and initiative, but the primacy of the group vis-à-vis the individual tends to reduce actions to the level of "the least common dominator."

ETHNIC RECOGNIZABILITY

Major racial and ethnic prescription also unifies much of Terramedia. With some exceptions, of course, the area is inhabited predominantly by darker peoples and their admixtures—peoples who, although not all explicitly Negroid, can be distinguished from other territorial blocks of European Caucasoids and Asian Mongoloids.

While it is true that most Middle Easterners have tended to suppress aspects of their "negroidness"—supported in part by the historical shield of European intermarriage, Islam, and "Arabness," as well as by the tradition of according esteem, prestige, and power to "whiteness"—they have never shared in the total security of non-negroid privilege. They might have escaped the certain degradation reserved for "Negroes" lacking occasional "redeeming" qualities of "whiteness"; except for differences in the degree of covert or overt acceptance of their presumed superiority to "Negroes," however, Middle Easterners had always been cast in the sphere of "Niggerdom" by status conferrees under the influence of apogean whiteness. Such contradiction between self-perception and outside-directed identification accounts for the emotional anguish which possesses an individual:

> I developed an unnatural sensitiveness which made me react with disproportionate intensity to little incidents, and see racial slights where probably no such were intended. The division of the world in which I lived into rulers and subjects burned steadily into my soul. . . . In this world in which, according to race, some people exercised, and others obeyed, authority, I belonged to the latter group. I was chained to it by the chains of blood and birth, chains which my passage through Victoria College and Oxford had, like some temporary magic, obliterated to touch and sight, but which I would now see and feel again.[6]

This discrimination of color helped potential masters to set themselves apart from potential servants and to blind even men of good will to the injustice of withholding human rights from their darker brothers. Yet this same discrimination was also destined to serve as a bond linking the oppressed, a means whereby disparate groups could realize their common racial plight and could amass strength (even if such solidarity was based on negation), to assert their rights to equality in a world community of nations. Such was the awakening of the urbane and loyal product of Oxford University, Edward Atiyah,

> No more the glories of British dominion for me; these glories did not belong to me; the manifestations of that dominion served only to humiliate me. I was on the side of the subject races, and the nationalist yearnings of the East arose before me with a new and overwhelming appeal. Philosophic conservatism, reason with its stately troop of cold and cogent arguments, the realists mistrust of theories, the tendency to scoff at popular movements, the wisdom of the ages and the belief in the beneficial mission of the British

> Empire—all the pillars of my political philosophy—shivered and crashed into the abyss of abandoned things.[7]

ECONOMICS

Relatively low living standards, as well as a low level of urbanization and of industrialization, characterize all countries in Terramedia. Terramedian economies are largely extractive, rarely productive: Petroleum is taken from the Middle East, Nigeria, and Angola; copper from the earth of Zambia and Katanga; cacao from Ghana, coffee from Uganda and tea from Kenya. Most of what is extracted through agriculture, though, is consumed; so Terramedia is still a vast subsistence economy. Even where such cash crops as coffee, ginger, oil palm, and cacao are produced, very little of the gains accrue to Terramedia.

NEITHER EAST NOR WEST

Other factors that unite Africa and the Middle East into Terramedia include the rise of national identification and especially the emergence of an independent Third World force. Until such an emergence, which began shortly after the Second World War, one accepted the existence of two major power blocs: The East (The "Second" World), and the West (The "First" World). These blocs competed for men's sympathies and for the control, sometimes indirect, of national loyalties. In this contest, the nations of the world were expected to define the nature of their self-interests and expectations, and to align themselves accordingly. But suddenly, Terramedian peoples denied the inevitability of alignment, and instead declared their positive neutralism and nonalignment. In doing so, the acknowledgement evolved that a distinction between East and West could not be made absolute. "Indeed, a great deal of what appears today to be conflicting and incompatible is in fact of Western origin. Thus, Communism, whose professors are called the 'Eastern states,' and capitalism, whose advocates are called 'Westerners,' are both, in fact, a part of the Western legacy and a product of Western thinking."[8] Nonalignment has been extolled by the majority of Terramedian countries not only during casual deliberations in the United Nations, but also during crucial confrontations with armed might, when prudence and self-interests might have otherwise dictated alignment.

Factors in Re-Emergence

Now that a case has been made, however briefly, for viewing Africa and the Middle East as a contiguous unit, we might examine its scope and limitations. Terramedia is used to refer to the land mass which includes the whole continent of Africa and Madagascar, the Arabian Peninsula, the nations of the Levant, and Iraq. It should be noted, of course, that there are certain episodes in the African and Middle Eastern heritage which cannot be treated as totally Terramedian; where these occur, they will be analyzed separately. Furthermore, the term "re-emergence" acknowledges that Terramedia once enjoyed an era of grandeur and self-determination which, however, was lost to alien incursion and domination. It is only since 1945 that the region has again experienced a measure of sovereignty, with countries enjoying a mastery over their "houses" and affairs—a mastery comparable to that enjoyed by the majority of nations in the contemporary world. After all, the last century was characterized by Caucasoid mastery of other peoples, even while non-Caucasoid nations in Arabia, Liberia, and Ethiopia claimed to be independent of outside influence and pressure. None of the countries of Terramedia, however, can be said to have enjoyed real sovereignty (after the effective infiltration of Causasoid economic, political, and religious agents into their territories and societies) until the United Nations and other agents of change reestablished and supported their recent attainment of self-rule.

Six principal factors contributed to the contemporary re-emergence of sovereignty in Terramedia:

THE UNITED NATIONS EMPHASIS ON SELF-DETERMINATION AND UNIVERSAL EQUALITY

Before 1945, the year in which the United Nations Organization was founded, there were sovereign states in Terramedia, as well as countries with a "mandate" status which implied forthcoming independence but at no specific date. The significance of the United Nations was that its public debates made it increasingly difficult for the colonial powers to justify their rights to control the affairs of less-developed, weaker countries, whether as colonies or mandates. The real examination of complaints, and the potential for ruling on specific relations among nations and peoples made the United Nations a stimulus for the pursuit and realization of nationalist aspirations, which hitherto had gone unheeded by imperialist regimes not deriving their authority to rule from the indigenous population.

DIFFUSION OF THE IDEAL OF SELF-DETERMINATION

A second factor leading to sovereignty was the widespread diffusion of the ideal of self-determination. Such diffusion can be said to have resulted from the forthright deliberations carried out under United Nations auspices, as well as from the more overt appeals of nationalists and freedom fighters of the colonialized nations. Long before 1950, the peoples in the various countries of Terramedia had either demanded self-determination or had voiced interest in participating in the administration of their territories. In many instances (e.g., Lebanon and Syria), legitimate requests were denied and the leaders of protest movements were punished. Various techniques–including religious separatism and armed suppression–were used to squelch the desire for self-determination or participation by colonialized peoples in their own government. But the climate of fair and open discussion aimed at promoting justice for all, which resulted from the establishment of the United Nations, tended steadily to reduce the threat to nationalist agitators and encouraged them to spread their gospel of indigenous redemption over a constantly widening area–and with much more militancy. Administrative modifications subsequently developed in the colonialized territories, ranging from mere toleration of damning criticism, through the establishment of local administrative units controlled by elected rather than appointed officials, to the legitimization of political parties that publicly sought mass support for independence from colonial rule.

Necessarily related to the diffusion of ideas of self-determination was the development of mass communication as part of the colonialist infrastructure (including, later, the transitor radio), and particularly the acquisition of a vehicular language by the colonialized peoples. With the vehicular language (in most cases either a form of pidgin or the actual language of the European colonial power), people could communicate across tribal linguistic barriers, even across colonial and national barriers, to plead their case before the world.

CONTRADICTIONS AND HYPOCRISY

A third factor of the growth toward Third World autonomy was the greater realization of the injustices of colonialism and the hypocrisies underlying much colonialist and Christian missionary behavior, and a more favorable climate for the overt expression of resentment against them. In part, it was the result of the accidental "enlightening" influence of colonialism and the missionary activities themselves. Under colonial administrations, the indigenous population became steadily more involved either as subordinate instruments (clerk-typists, mine workers, askaris) for realizing the vested self-interests of the colonial powers, or as the victims of such realization–the directly exploited. Missionary activities usually centered about the instruction of the people, usually in the vehicular language, so that the people might more effectively be converted and controlled. The result was glaring contradictions between educational and Christian ideals, on the one hand, and colonialist and missionary practices on the other. More and more people became aware of the meanings of Western democracy and of its limitation in practice to the metropolitan peoples and, in the colonies, to those aspects of life that could not enable the colonialized people to achieve goals disapproved by the authorities.

While Europeans resisted the spread of equality and equity for all persons, colonial subjects continued to be exposed to the principal ideas of Europe and to acquire proficiency in European technology that hitherto had been monopolized by Europeans. Private firms and missionaries, pursuing economic and apostolic goals, and clearly concerned with supporting colonial and administrative controls over the people, opened doors to the colonialized subjects that led to even further reaction against the different standards and opportunities for Terramedians than for Europeans. Equally relevant was the effect of scientists and scholars—private as well as official—in exposing the injustice of colonialism and in promoting (whether paternalistic or not) the mental and physical progress of the indigenous subjects. Examples of the potential for more scientific enlightenment can be seen in the endeavors of the International Africa Institute, the American University at Beirut and at Cairo, and some of the works of H.A.R. Gibb, Gustav von Grunebaum, Lord Malcoln Hailey, Frederick Lugard, and Margery Perham.[9]

Modernization, industrialization, and urbanization also were influential in removing people from the traditional subservience to colonial domination. Not only did this process encourage greater participation in alien ways, but it exposed people to diverse behavior and further emphasized the interelation of responsibilities and rights. Removed from the security of ethnic homogenity and consistency of behavior and values of the traditional community, the more aware Terramedian became more conscious of the need to protect himself and his values against those who would alter both for alien reasons. It became even more evident that colonialism was not only unfair in rewarding achievement or even giving more than lip service to basic human rights, but that domination itself was based on a racial dichotomy of "light" masters and disenfranchised "dark" subjects. Indeed, some of this awareness began early in the history of colonialism. For example, at the beginning of this century the *Sierra Leone Weekly News* ran a series of editorials complaining about the situation:

> The policy of repression is the same *everywhere on the Coast.* It is a policy for the abolition of Negro scope and efficiency so far as these may depend upon Government assistance, and not confined to one

place as against another. Briefly put, the policy aims at abolishing forever all black or coloured men from the higher and more remunerative services of the State. . . . The policy seems to take a twofold shape, viz.—the development of the land for the well-being of the white man, and the utter suppression of the natives of the place.

WORLD WAR II

Accelerated acculturation encouraged cultural diffusion. Although Terramedia had been involved in other wars before 1939, the greater involvement of colonial territories in Africa and Asia during World War II left an imprint that made any return to the traditional colonial situation almost unbearable. Not only had many of the returned soldiers and sailors observed patterns of comfortable living standards elsewhere, but many had been profoundly impressed by the argument that one could properly sacrifice one's life in combatting a threat against human liberty and democratic government. Hitler and his ambition for world conquest, the argument went, had to be checked; and, once the Axis threat had been successfully crushed, it seemed perfectly relevant to presume that similar undemocratic practices under colonialism could be legitimately challenged. Of course, the colonial rulers—most of whom had argued for the justice of war against Nazism and Fascism—could not easily defend their continued colonialism in Terramedia. So World War II created an atmosphere of heightened morality conducive to a re-evaluation of colonial policy and practices. The war itself had also strained the resources of the colonial powers, although not to the point where they could not have contained the sporadic demands for independence or for participation by indigenous subjects in their own government.

The wind of change which swept over all of Terramedia, ranging from the successful overthrow of Farouk's unrepresentative monarchy in Egypt in 1952, through an unsuspected granting of independence to Guinea in 1958, to the emergence of a liberated monarchy in Iraq in 1958, was partially stimulated by a shared belief in the justice of representative government. In addition, the successful challenge to white supremacy, which resulted in the independence of some territories in southern Asia and in the Middle East, served as a further stimulant for those nations whose advocates for participation or independence might have been more subtle or hesitant because of their relative weakness vis-à-vis the colonial powers. If independence for Burma, why not for Nigeria? And if for Ceylon, why not for Morocco? So the wind of change blew even stronger, encouraging the sort of daring which gave substance to the aspirations of Zionism in a new nation of Israel, as well as to seemingly reckless desires of nationalists and freedom fighters in Angola, Mozambique, Rhodesia, South Africa, and South West Africa.

THE COLD WAR

With the end of the war and the opportunity to view the peculiar nature of national vested interests deriving from varying ideologies, there soon emerged two major blocs proclaiming similar interests in universal progress, while advocating and using conflicting tactics. In their deliberate search for supporters of their different ideologies, the East and West disseminated propaganda that presumably revealed the weaknesses of one another's ideology and tactics. From such confrontation accrued several benefits to Terramedia, especially in terms of getting powerful nations to recognize the basic justice of self-determination. The East, interested in expanding its influence, first had to neutralize or to "liberate" territories which had for a long time been under domination of the West. The West, on the other hand, had to offset persistent criticism of its imperialistic tendencies by granting independence to territories for which sovereignty was merely nominal and farcical.[10]

THIRD WORLDISM

Not all of Terramedia is free today: There are still territories seeking to attain the status of masters of their own houses. Nevertheless, there is some justification to suspect that the wind of change will prove ineffectual before all of them gain independence. Witness, for instance, the continuing tension over Namibia, Palestine, Rhodesia, and South Africa. Moreover, there are some former sympathizers whose enthusiasm has waned because of the apparent tendency of military oligarchies to replace what seemed to be popular democracies. At present the feasibility of democracy in a European sense for some Terramedian countries is debatable, and one can question the justice of granting independence to such nonviable states as Botswana, Gambia, Guinea-Bissau, and Jordan. Perhaps it is unimportant to examine the prerequisites for independence, or foolish to believe that political independence will automatically bring a ready solution for all problems. What is most important, regardless, is that many Terramedian nations have regained their sovereignty and a right to determine their destinies. Although charges of undue dependence (neocolonialism) on the former colonial powers continue, these independent nations are able, nonetheless, to present a collective posture as a Third World force.

As evidence of the foregoing, one might point to the collective adherence to positive neutralism—non-involvement as partisans in world power politics. There was a time when neutralism would have been considered suicidal, and the last two decades, in fact, have witnessed attempts in American, Chinese, and Soviet foreign policy to grant benefits on the basis of alignment in the East-West power struggle. Partly because of the Cold War, but more definitely because of the "positive" character of Terramedian neutralism, world politics previously guided by gun-boat diplomacy have been modified to the extent that the efficacy of noninvolvement is grudgingly recognized by the power blocs. Other characteristics of a Terramedian Third World Force, visible amidst the more pronounced and militarily powerful Western and Eastern blocs, might be noted. Possibly because of a long period of domination by white Europeans, the Terramedian nations—at least, through their leaders—exhibit a strong sensitivity to racial discrimination. This in part explains the preoccupation with self-rule for the nonwhite groups of Southern Africa, as resolutions sponsored by Terramedian nations in the United Nations indicate.

It is important to note, of course, that in some of their own internal affairs these same Terramedian nations manifest discrimination against their own nations because of cultural, ethnic, or tribal differences. Witness, for example, intergroup relations in Iraq (Iraqi versus Kurds), Israel (Israeli versus Palestinian Arab), Nigeria (tribe versus tribe), and Uganda (Kakwa and Teso versus Baganda and Asian). Another characteristic of the Terramedian Third World force is the interest in simultaneous development of all sectors of the nation, despite the glaring lack of adequate human resources and domestic capital. That it can be pursued so feverishly, when economic plans depend so largely on outside sources (at least 25% expected from foreign aid), suggests that Terramedian countries consider aid—with no strings attached, because of the emphasis on nonalignment—to be their just reward for the many decades of exploitation and domination by foreigners.

The fact that the Terramedian countries could potentially muster the largest single bloc of votes in the United Nations is significant. But as a Third World force held together by the adherence to non-alignment, there are other noteworthy characteristics of the area. One of these is a tendency to be suspicious of persons identifiable with excolonial powers, with the result that some benefits which are well-intended are not always fully realized. The occasional diatribe by a Sadat, the emotionalism of a Sekou Toure, or the decrees of Nyerere have often resulted in curtailing necessary financial or technical aid—a situation which probably would not have arisen except for the paranoia resulting from domination.

There is also an ignorance of, or indifference to, the imperialistic potential of Communism. While this can be understood in view of the relative lack of actual contact with Communists (compared with the historical contact with capitalist exploiters), such indifference could very well undermine the preferred condition of nonalignment. As a block of nations, Terramedia further manifests a peculiar contradiction: There is, on the one hand, a great emphasis on rapid modernization and, on the other, a desire to uphold or reassert the prominence of traditional values which project an indigenous heritage worthy of universal pride. It becomes a problem for example, to urge the acceleration of education and industry, while at the same time considering the advantage of instruction in the vernacular language (even in cases where there is a decided lack of a literary or modern technological heritage), or the promotion of traditional practices which work against industrial and agricultural efficiency. Furthermore, it is a fact that Terramedia for the most part remains subject to the whims and determinations of a small corps of leaders—the new elite—who have relatively free rein to shape the destiny of a mass following whose support remains essentially emotional rather than rational. Some of the foregoing must provide concern for the rest of the world, as does the fact that as a Third World force Terramedia serves as a constant prick upon the conscience of the "have" sector of the world. For, indeed, in health, wealth, and education, Terramedia is glaringly deficient and is a prominent segment of the "have-not" nations of the world. Terramedia has reemerged! How significant sovereignty in Terramedia is today can be realized by noting its sudden catapulsion into independence. Before 1900, only Ethiopia and Liberia were independent, and only South Africa had acquired a similar status by 1920. Until the beginning of World War II, only Egypt, Iran, Iraq, and Saudi Arabia, could assert their right to the title of independent states. It took a global war, along with the various factors discussed earlier, to bring independence on a large scale. Soon after World War II, Israel, Jordan, Lebanon, and Syria attained sovereignty. During the 1950s, first Libya, then Tunisia, Morocco, Sudan, Ghana, and Guinea became free of colonial rule.

The wind of change was indeed producing results, and the 1960s were to become the decade for the wholesale and relatively bloodless liberation of most of Africa. With few exceptions, such as Algeria, which underwent a bloody revolution against French colonialization, it was assumed by the indigenous nationalists that their independence would become a reality once the necessary constitutional arrangements were concluded. So even the Belgian Congo was surprisingly granted independence in 1960, along with Cameroon, Central African Republic, Chad, Dahomey, French Congo, Gabon, Ivory Coast, Malagasay, Mali, Mauretania, Niger, Senegal, Togo, and Upper Volta. Between 1961 and 1966, other colonies attained independence: Algeria, Botswana, Djibouti, Gambia, Kenya, Kuwait, Lesotho, Malawi, Rwanda, Tanganyika, Uganda, and Zambia. There are still European-dominated countries in Terramedia, such as Rhodesia, South

Africa, and South West Africa; but the attainment of independence by so many, along with the successful projection of mastery in their own affairs (despite overt or subtle threats to their independence, as well as the serious problems remaining to be resolved), provides justification for asserting that Terramedia has indeed come of age in the family of modern nations.

What becomes of Terramedia will depend on the realities of a changing environment, including the lifestyles allowed to persist in relation to major cultural changes. The chronicles and analyses which follow will, hopefully, clarify the conditions and prospects which determine and shape Terramedian aspirations.

Treating the Middle East and Africa on a common canvas is a departure from scholarly tradition. Not since the descriptive efforts of early chroniclers has there been presented a rationale for viewing the two from a basis of commonalities. It may be that an era preoccupied with Eurocentric analysis made segmental assessment a necessity, since to do otherwise might have undermined the conquest by division upon which external incursion and overlordship depended. Moreover, leaders of the contemporary Middle East and Africa, with the exception of those in Libya and Tanzania, might prefer to be left out of the comprehensive bond implied by Terramedia. After all, the pursuit of commonalities, rather than differences, can impose a threat to newly attained sovereign grandeur. Despite such understandable barriers, the time has come to examine the threads that bind, however fragile these might be. Hence this relatively bold attempt to bring so many independent nations under the single orbit of Terramedia. Furthermore, an acceptance of the Terramedian potential, if not the reality, can accelerate the attainment of necessary adaptations attuned to the realities of existence within Terramedia, rather than according to the realities orchestrated for Terramedia by non-Terramedians. The resulting lifestyles might, in turn, reflect not unavoidable responses to unchanged nature and physical environment, or to colonial and neocolonial impositions, but conscious responses to designs created deliberately by Terramedians themselves.

In the chapters that follow attention has been given to the role of geography in shaping living patterns within Terramedia, including its effect on economic and social organization, power politics, and values. The latter have been analyzed to reveal the connections they have engendered among various religious beliefs—Animism, Christianity, and Islam—and the way they have shaped the responses of Terramedians to historical accidents and social change. Aside from examining the influential roots from which ideologies and activities designed to regain independence flowered, we shall assess the obstacles to be surmounted if Terramedian independence is to continue.

NOTES

1. It is worth noting that, until the State University College of New York, at New Paltz, decided on such a unitary treatment around 1960, no serious reason (at least pedagogical) existed for treating together such seemingly different areas of the world.

2. Cf. Dike's comments in J.F. Ade Ajayi and Ian Espie, *A Thousand Years of West African History* (Ibadan, Nigeria: Ibadan University Press, 1969), p. ix.

3. Cf. Lucy Mair, *African Societies* (London: Cambridge University Press, 1974), pp. 1-4.

4. "The Egyptian Revolution," *Foreign Affairs* (January 1955): 199.

5. "How Khaki Power Has Failed," *West Africa* (12 March 1979).

6. Edward Atiyah, *An Arab Tells His Story* (London: John Murray, 1946), p. 147.

7. Ibid., p. 148.

8. From a lecture by Abdal Rahman al-Bazzaz, cited in Jacob M. Landau, *Man, State, and Society in the Contemporary Middle East* (New York: Praeger Publishers, 1972), p. 33.

9. See, for example, H.A.R. Gibb, *Modern Trends in Islam* (Chicago: University of Chicago Press, 1947), and Margery Perham, *Native Administration in Nigeria* (London: Oxford University Press, 1937).

10. Such a posture did not, of course, negate the emphasis on vested-interests. Strategic bases and defense pacts were secured from independent regimes in Libya and Nigeria, at the same time that independence movements were being discouraged in Algeria and Angola, for example.

Chapter Two

RANDOM IMPRESSIONS OF CONTEMPORARY TERRAMEDIA

Cairo and Its Surroundings

From a terrace on the eleventh floor of the Cairo Hilton at night, one can view the famous and ancient Nile River. There are boats below. Shadows are caused by streetlights from the boulevard. Lights reflect from buildings and minarets, and many stars shine above. There are casual lovers out for a boat ride, while many, many compact cars drive along the river banks with reckless abandon. A broad sidewalk attached to the adjacent boulevard affords a promenade with flowering shrubs hanging above the water—a beautiful and relaxing sight! Another amazing realization is that in this place astride the desert, in a country where 98% of the population is concentrated in only 3% of the land mass, one can feel quite comfortable. There is a gentle breeze, making the environment as pleasant as an air-conditioned room. Another interesting realization is the extremes in temperature, ranging from a cool 65°F at night to a depressing 110°F during the day. With the desert almost at the edge of the Nile River, one is forced to wonder how so much harshness could forever threaten the green lushness protecting the farming of the people clustered along the banks of the river.

The air terminal provides a surprising experience. One who has gone through the trauma of strangeness would better appreciate what it means to be a stranger: the unintelligibility of language, the alienness of customs, the discomfort of not knowing what one is expected to do next. Even in this strangeness, though, a manifestation of kindness shows itself, albeit in the unfortunate disguise of defeat. I was helped through customs and the routine of currency exchange by an official-looking gentleman whom I presumed to be an officer of immigration. As it turned out, he was just a businessman about his task, who ended up helping me without demanding a fee or a tip; he made my initial entry into Egypt a smooth and welcome one. It was good to be among people with a different tongue and different customs, but who also shared something easily found among human beings throughout the world: a capacity for kindness, an ability to show empathy, and a propensity toward being helpful and kind without necessarily expecting a reward.

An early morning fog hangs over the River Nile. Below the hotel balcony there is a six-lane, tree-lined boulevard, almost like a California freeway, but much more attractive, with people walking and risking their lives to cross the street. Instead of a number of private cars, there are many buses and taxis. Most of the buses are crowded, indicating a widespread use of public transportation. Even the river is plyed by many barges. Some look like work-barges carrying supplies, sand, and hardware, while others are ferries carrying pedestrians and bicyclists.

The sound of the town is getting louder now, as if it is becoming more awake. More and more buses are going by. In fact, just in front of me, I can count eight buses in the space of one block, but only about ten people walking. A truck serving as a bus unloads people who now have to maneuver their way across the street in the heavy traffic. One gambles with life around here, but in a relatively nonchalant way.

On the outskirt of Cairo there is a nightclub under a huge tent in the desert, reputed to have been a favorite retreat of ex-King Farouk. The show here is diversified, but features several belly dancers representing a variety of Middle Eastern choreography. One show that I found particularly amusing was labeled the African Dance. It occurred to me that the word *African,* as used, had the same connotation of primitiveness often used by Europeans and other Westerners. To one such as I who had always argued that Egypt was a part of Africa, I found it fascinating that Egyptians themselves conceived of Africa as something below Egypt and inferior to Egypt. My conversation with different classes of Egyptians—professors, students, and working people—led me to realize that they did not ordinarily consider themselves to be Africans. There was talk of Abyssinians and Nubians, for example, and there was care taken at the

Cairo Museum of Archaeology to point out that the black color of one of the ancient Egyptian kings (about 3000 B.C.) was not to be understood as conveying negroidness; rather, he was depicted as black to suggest the angry mood in which he was perceived to be at the time of the sculpture. This lack of identity with Africans is a natural Egyptian manifestation of the universal phenomenon of ethnocentrism. As for the African dance, the costumes were predominantly depictions of South Africa and the Pacific Islands. In fact, the movements of the women, the rhythm of their hips, and the short grass skirt, suggested not as much Africa as Polynesia or Hawaii. They were good dancers, no question about it; but any one who had seen African dancers, particularly South of the Sahara, would conclude that the effort was a stage interpretation far removed from the realities of the Congo, Basutoland, or Guinea, for example.

Driving through Cairo and into the suburbs, one encounters a variety of people and different examples of the human condition. There is the highly articulate and well-travelled manager-owner of a perfume factory, for example, who enjoys all the comforts that the rewards of his profession could provide. In contrast, there are those who ride through town on platforms attached to donkeys or horses, with their feet dangling on the side of the cart. There are many others going to or from work, or merely going from one part of town to another, holding on to the overcrowded buses. In fact, many buses pass by which one would expect to tumble because of the overweight caused by people hanging on to the sides and doors. One wonders how people endure such overcrowded riding, a condition far in excess of a New York subway crowd during rush hour.

About five miles outside of Cairo, the urban, industrial-commercial picture turns into agrarian tranquility. Along the banks are square and rectangular mud huts with thatched walls—the homes of farmers, their livestock, and their children. It is soothing to the eye to see the dry, coarse sand at one side, and then green vegetables and productive fields on the other. One can only conclude that, were it not for the waters of the Nile and the irrigation canals that have been constructed, there would not be the vitality that seems so abundant in Egypt.

A visit to the great pyramid outside Cairo indicates that although the exterior of the pyramid was very smooth at one time, it no longer is today. Kings and rulers during more recent times have removed some of the huge rocks, some weighing as much as thirty tons, from the pyramids to construct buildings of their own. The serial removal has produced a step-like surface. However, a cutting into the side has been provided with metal stairs enabling people to enter the interior of the pyramid. One goes first through a series of dark, winding tunnels, until one enters a stairway which rises about 180 feet to the top platform containing the mausoleum of the particular king. Halfway to the top, there is a special platform where people are allowed to rest.

The mosque built by the great modernizer of Egypt, Muhammad Ali, is still an elegant piece of architecture. Muhammad Ali had been greatly influenced by Napoleon Bonaparte, who, toward the end of the eighteenth century, had invaded Egypt with technicians and scholars to expand the glory of France into Africa. Muhammad Ali had been a vassal of the Sultan of the Ottoman Empire, and it was not long after his being posted to Egypt as Governor, that he decided to compete for the Sultan's power, rather than remain his subject. The influence of Muhammad Ali lives on, for his name inspires reverence among Egyptians almost with the same force as the names of Nasser and Saladin the Great. The mosque is an imposing structure in the heart of what is known as the Citadel, a fort on a hill overlooking the rest of Egypt, and where today part of the modern Egyptian militia is encamped. There seems to be no extra security for entering the fort, but there are certain restricted roads off the main one leading to the entrance of the mosque (which is itself in a walled courtyard). There are roadblocks preventing access into these side streets, which, through casual observation, seemed to contain more restrictive military camps and operations.

Approaching the mosque, one is stopped by a guard and directed toward several attendants by the wall who provide clothbags which fit over shoes. This is a compromise between the propensity of non-Muslims to enter dwellings with their shoes, and that of Muslims who normally would take off their shoes at the doorway before entering a dwelling. Certainly it is improper for one to enter a holy place, such as a mosque, with one's shoes on. It would seem more appropriate to demand that shoes be taken off, rather than compromising with "shoe-covers." If, in fact, reverence requires taking off one's shoes, why are visitors allowed to keep their shoes on (and to merely project a sort of shoelessness by having little shoe-bays of cloth placed over the shoes)? This compromise, evidently, meets the expectations of Islam, in that one was now free to enter the courtyard, and to walk on the rich tapestry that covers the vast floor of the mosque.

Within the mosque, one is struck by the absence of pews and chairs; but we realize that worshipping in a mosque is done by sitting, standing, and prostrating on the floor. The interior is truly magnificant, furnished with two imposing pulpits. From the dome, which is about 180 feet from the floor, hang several circular glass lights arranged in forms of chandeliers in ever-widening circles. It is truly a beautiful sight to lift one's eyes toward the ceiling, and become immersed in the beauty of the combined reflections of variegated stained-glass and numerous crystal clear-glass lamps. Yet this is only one of four major mosques in Cairo where many Muslims worship on Fridays. There is also a reading platform, somewhat like a lower pulpit, from which important personalities of the state and the Arab world stand to recite passages of the Koran, especially during the month of Ramadan. There is a circular gallery within the mosque, which provides a podium for visiting women, since tradition does not permit them to worship in the mosque; only men are allowed to worship on the main floor of the mosque. There is, of course, a very large courtyard within the walls of the mosque, outside of the building, which can be used for praying, either by an overflow crowd or by women, if the need should arise.

The Museum of Archaeology and Antiquity is a very elegant and adequate structure. It was designed and built around 1920 by a French archaeologist and it now houses most of the statues and treasures of the important pharoahs and kings of Egypt. The ceiling is two stories high; artifacts of mummies, tombs, apparel, and jewelry have been well preserved here. Many tourists and scholars go through its doors daily, although photography within its walls is prohibited. In the courtyard one can, of course, purchase filmslides of some of the impressive artifacts within. It is simply soul-searching to ponder the techniques used in embalming, and in preserving the many evidences of this ancient civilization. Walking from artifact to artifact, from one pharoah's heritage to another, inspires one to appreciate the grandeur of Egypt, and the contribution the nation made to civilization many thousands of years ago.

Cairo is also the home of the ancient University of Alhazzar, founded in 900 A.D. The physical plant must have undergone a series of modifications and improvements since that time, for, other than the mosques and minarets, the solid cement and concrete buildings are of modern vintage. There are buildings which date to the eighteenth century; the campus comprises about 50,000 students. The atmosphere is relatively austere, not surprising for an institution whose claim to fame had always been one of excellence in theology and philosophy. The university is renowned throughout the Muslim and Arab world, and serves students from many nations. The instruction is, however, not restricted to theology and philosophy (for which Alhazzar has always been famous), but includes the natural sciences and medicine as well. Indeed, there is a university hospital adjacent to the rest of the campus, and there are those who find more confidence in physicians and lawyers trained at Alhazzar than at other well-renowned institutions of higher learning. The University of Cairo, with over 100,000 students, unlike the austerity at Alhazzar, seems vital and appealing to nonorthodox students. Activities on the Cairo campus seem comparable to what one would observe in any large university campus in the United States.

As one looks upon the Nile, and the brilliant amber sunshine that daily sets down past the ancient pyramids, one becomes invigorated with the legendary grandeur and mistique of Egypt: a land whose glory has been claimed by Europe while negating its connection, however unconsciously and inadvertently, with the rest of Africa. One cannot but be impressed with man's ability to maintain and sustain civilization, even as one experiences distress over man's propensity to enjoy comforts only for himself, and to feel scant remorse for those of his kith and kin on whom fate has not seen fit to smile as profusely. In Egypt, in the faces of the affluent and of the poor., in the bodies of the healthy and of the sick, one sees the need for leadership that can develop strategies to serve the needs and the yearnings of the many. Egypt, however, can excite in one a sense of concern and a compulsion to promote understanding among all men—to articulate an appreciation for differences and, above all, to help create an environment in which empathy may blossom.

Ethiopia Under Haile Selassie

From the terrace where I sit, I can see the majestic hills and mountains that surround the depressed plateau upon which the lovely city of Addis Ababa has been built. There is rainfall in September but it falls crisply and gently, giving a feeling of exhilaration as one beholds the variety of foliage that landscape the city of lofty buildings and simple dwellings. One gets the satisfaction of having so much room to spread out arms and legs, and to share in the instant and distant intimacy of people constantly on the move, and yet not crowded to block and interfere with each other's movement.

First impressions of Addis Ababa are highly favorable, beginning with the reception at the airport and the drive through the city. There is an aura of orderliness and relative cleanliness; beyond that, there is an overwhelming majesty imposed by the surrounding hills and mountains which lend a freshness and beauty to the city. Furthermore, there is a striking juxtaposition of elegant affluence with simple and dignified poverty. There is a casualness about life, despite the contrast between those who seem to have, and the many who seem not to have. Talking informally and observing movements and behavior, one feels a pervading serenity and calmness and an acceptance of, if not satisfaction with, the status quo. This might be due to the consistent presence of His Imperial Majesty, whose concern and paternalism are made manifest in many forms. There is, first of all, the very visible and expansive Imperial Palace, with its well-manicured lawns and gardens, and dignified guards. There are also monuments throughout the city depicting the glory and fame of the emperor. Equally impressive is the integration of the monarch with the Coptic Church. A visit to Trinity Cathedral impresses one with the way in which twentieth century Ethiopian history is embossed in the domed ceiling and walls of the Cathedral. The Emperor sits on a prominently positioned throne when he visits; and in a room to the side, but adjacent to the restricted room for the patriarch and high priest, is the vault of the late Empress. Next to this vault is another of the same design and size, which is to be the final resting place of His Imperial Majesty, Haile Selassie.

The security provided the people by the emperor is further enhanced by the flying of two flags when he is residence. It would appear that, even though he is not always visible, those of his citizens around town who wish to glance at the flag post can gain the satisfaction that all is well with the Emperor. There is another vivid evidence of his ever-present paternalism: behind the residential palace, and somewhat close by his imperial office, is a large field or park to which numerous beggars congregate to seek audience with His Imperial Majesty. The presence of the emperor himself was not always necessary during such gatherings, in view of the fact that his palace guards oftentimes circulate among the poor to hand out money—a gift from the Emperor.

It is amazing to observe the many projects that have been started and maintained mainly by the financial and other resources from the private coffers of the emperor. The administrative office of Haile Selassie University, for example, is in a palace previously used by the emperor. Indeed, the Museum of Ethnology, which is a pride of the campus, contains numerous artifacts donated by the emperor. One of the imposing segments of the museum is the Emperor's bedroom and private chambers containing many gifts from various countries he has visited, including model battleships, keys to cities, and so on. Included also are crown jewelry and other regalia of royal households and dignitaries of royal affinity. Another example of the emperor's largesse to his people is that, from time to time, gifts of buildings or of money are made to undertake a project relating to economic development and social welfare. He is fond of appearing at opening ceremonies of industrial projects. There is a dry-cell battery factory, for example, operated by a commercial corporation which he helped establish with a donation of $40,000 many years ago. An interesting objective of this particular adventure is that it seeks to provide job opportunities for physically-disabled people. In an opening ceremony statement, His Imperial Majesty reiterated his interest in seeing that citizens are not denied the opportunity to realize the dignity of labor because they are physically disabled.

Addis Ababa reveals the presence of many poor people. Yet, an observation of the countryside reveals a great potential for a healthy economy and an adequate and satisfying level of living for the majority of the people. The fact is that the country is vast, the climate is favorable, and the soil is sufficiently fertile for successful agriculture with a minimum amount of labor. As a matter of fact, it does not take too serious an observation to realize that there are many Ethiopians who derive a satisfactory livelihood from farming, with enough being produced for an exchange economy. Unlike many other African countries, especially in the tropical zone, one has to be impressed with the fact that many people who would normally be classified as lowly peasants have the ability to move about on some form of animal transport. Yet their amenities of housing, clothing, and the like, fall nearer the low scale. There is evidence of potential which can be realized through proper planning and instilling a commitment to self-development.

Within the city limits and the proximate suburban area, various factories and secondary industries have been erected. For example, one factory produces wheels in common use for the donkeys and horse drawn carts that serve as the primary mode of transportation for most of the farmers. It is supplemented, of course, by a large fleet of trucks and buses for which maintenance garages and depots for parts have been erected. There is also a vital activity in textiles, providing job opportunities for a substantial number of Ethiopian citizens. In addition, there is an iron and corrugated steel operation which meets the widespread use of corrugated metal sheets for the roofing of middle-class and lower middle-class houses. Even the well-to-do, who can afford to construct substantial concrete and brick dwellings, use the locally produced roofing material. The commercial segment of Ethiopia, therefore, is quite substantial. The presence of the headquarters and secretariat of the Organization of African Unity, furthermore, brings to Addis Ababa, rather frequently, peoples from all over the world in need of various types of services; this, in turn, has generated still more commercial and other service enterprises.

A noteworthy aside concerns a visit to a traditional Ethiopian restaurant. Operating out of a regular home, the setting is one of a livingroom with sofas and coffee tables. The relaxed atmosphere suggests a casual visit to the dwelling of a friend. Food is served in the traditional manner, and eaten by hand without utensils. The food is served on a big platter enclosed in a raffia-woven basket with an elongated bottom upon which the flattened top rests. The platter is covered with the main course, a locally prepared bread called *injera,* (which looks somewhat like a tortilla), made from the local grain called *tef*. On top of the *tef* the sauce (made usually of a combination of chicken, lamb, and boiled eggs, and highly seasoned with paprika and curry) is poured. The *injera* is pinched, a small portion at a time, and serves as the receptacle for picking up or sucking up the sauce and meat to be conveyed to the mouth. At the end of the meal, often accompanied by the local drink made from fruit or grain beer and honey, the hand is again washed. That concludes the meal.

The atmosphere of this traditional dining may be relaxed, but it also is not very sanitary, so it can lead to digestive problems. In the first place, the highly seasoned nature of the meal causes a gastronomic dilemma for persons not accustomed to such types of food. Furthermore, even though the washing of hands may suggest the pursuit of cleanliness, the fact is that one has no assurance that the hand towel, which might have been used by many other people, is at all clean. For persons accustomed to a relatively sterilized environment, the way in which dishes are washed, usually in cold water, provides an opportunity for still further germ infection. Cases have been known of well-intentioned persons desiring to have a real experience in traditional dining becoming seriously ill. A word of caution, then, is in order, perhaps applicable in all situations of cultural contact: One should not be surprised if the consequences of one's involvement in a strange culture is not entirely satisfactory or pleasant.

Addis Ababa is really a cosmopolitan community. There is, perhaps, not as much overt interchange among peoples, but the presence of so many nationalities engaged in various sectors of the economy and administration provides a sound potential for intercultural awareness and stimulates an appreciation of cultural differences. It is refreshing to observe that indigenous peoples nowadays occupy most of the top levels of management and policy formulation. This is true in the various sectors of commerce, banking, and secondary industries. An example of Ethiopian efficiency can be observed in the operation of the International Airport and the Ethiopian Airways. The pilots, crew, and airport officials are all Ethiopians, and their performance at all levels leaves nothing to be desired. Service at the airport, especially when compared with the chaotic operation at Cairo International Airport, is highly satisfactory. The activities relating to customs, immigration, and health officials, and even the various ticketing agents, are carried out with smoothness and efficiency. It is truly relaxing to go through the International Airport.

Throughout the city and in the countryside, Ethiopians are involved in small businesses and secondary industries, as well as in the few major industries. Of course, there are very few trained professional Ethiopians in certain skilled areas, so technicians and experts from the more developed countries, through bilateral or multilateral contract agreements, serve needs as agreed upon by the Ethiopian ministries and policy makers. An interesting sort of small business is the mini-taxi which is very common in

Addis Ababa. There is a bus service throughout Ethiopia into the countryside, and a railroad service as well. Within the city, however, one can hop into a mini-taxi, usually a small car such as a Fiat, Honda, or Toyota, and for a fee of only twenty-five cents get to one's destination. These taxis, of course, make frequent stops, as persons along the way wave them down. It is up to the driver to accept or reject the passenger, depending on whether the new destination is consistent with the destinations to which the driver has already committed himself.

Addis Ababa houses the headquarters of the Economic Commission for Africa (ECA) and the Organization of African Unity (OAU). These two international organs require the presence of a large number of diplomats representing the various African countries, in addition to the numerous other countries that have expressed a desire to maintain normal relations with Ethiopia. The presence of a large diplomatic corps, then, and the routine of interacting socially in the pursuit of individual or group interests, afford the chance for international communication and understanding on the soil of Addis Ababa. Addis Ababa has excellent hotel and restaurant facilities. The Hilton Hotel, for example, has a large banquet hall which is often used for social functions by the resident diplomatic corps, or by visiting representatives to formal conferences and meetings. Although the appointments at the Hilton are very comfortable and first-rate, the price for food is quite high for Africa. A normal breakfast of sausages and eggs, or of pancakes and sausage, costs about $3.00. Dinner, of course, costs a minimum of $8.00. It is to be concluded, therefore (given the level of living of the average Ethiopian), that hotels like the Hilton exist to serve only the tourist market and the upper echelon of Ethiopian society. One service rendered Ethiopian society by an establishment such as the Hilton, is the provision of lower- and middle-level job opportunities to the local citizens. The desk-clerks, for example, are all Ethiopians, as is the staff of the restaurant and the numerous shops established to serve the clientele. With a tennis court and a beautiful swimming pool and lawn, added job opportunities are provided in maintenance.

Njomo Kenyatta's Kenya

Being processed through immigration and customs upon arrival in Kenya is not annoying, for there is orderliness and a smooth flow in the operation. It does require a little patience, however, to transact currency exchange, entailing long lines and a long wait. One has no choice in this matter, since to do otherwise would make it impossible to tip and to pay for immediate services, such as getting a taxi to the hotel in town. Driving the ten-mile distance between the airport and the hotel, one is first struck by the strangeness of driving on the left hand side of the road. The land is flat for the most part, with cattle grazing and indications of an efficient agricultural system.

Entering the city is not annoying either, for the traffic of Nairobi does not appear excessive and unwieldy. There are many imposing superstructures between six and ten stories high, and people (Asian, black, white) walk casually about their apparently-appointed tasks. The streets, however, are unnecessarily dirty. Here would be one opportunity for providing jobs for some of the many unemployed who drift to the urban area. This impression, of a not too well-kept external environment, is further reinforced when one visits some of the ministerial offices. Another amazing fact is the relatively high cost of parking, at least in the central part of the city, considering the income level.

At the Hilton Hotel, an imposing looking building, one is struck immediately with the vitality and movements of all kinds of people. It comes as a surprise that entry into the hotel lobby is not an easy one. The street facing the main entrance is usually blocked by cars and taxis, and one has to struggle through an iron barricade in order to get to the entrance and into the hotel lobby.

The hotel main floor contains a wide variety of shops, although it would be reasonable to conclude that these were designed mainly to serve the tourists who go in and out of Nairobi constantly. The Safari experience is suggested clearly by the shop window displays of clothing and other supporting implements to make "trekkers" comfortable, well-attired, and properly equipped. The hotel entrance serves as one of the points where people taking pause for a few hours, or several days duration, start off on Safari. Mainly Volkwagen buses are used, and these are in such high demand that they cost around $10,000 each. Surprisingly, the supply is controlled by a foreign automobile monopoly, the Cooper Company.

The center of Nairobi is very much modernized, with several high-rise buildings and a variety of commercial and service facilities. It is highly unlikely that one will not be able to secure whatever supply or amenity one requires. The cost of goods and services, however, is quite another matter. Not far away is the impressive Museum of Nairobi. There is no question but that, in the proximity of Olduvai Gorge, the site of decades of research by Professor L.S.B. Leakey and his family, expert care has been given to the projection and interpretations of artifacts from this area. A large number of school children from outside of Nairobi visit the museum, many of them amazed by what they see, so one must be impressed by the effort being made by Kenyan educators to make the young aware of their own illustrious heritage.

Another impression is the persistence of separate, ethnic neighborhoods. Kenya's independence, which occurred in 1963, and brought Africans into political and administrative control, has not eliminated the historical residential division that characterized colonial Kenya, or at least colonial Nairobi. There are visible divisions of residential areas for Africans, Asians, and Europeans. Unfortunately, the European area is still the more affluent and expensive, suggesting that foreigners are still able to maintain a better standard of living than the indigenous peoples of Kenya. Aside from the low-cost housing units which have been provided by the government and the municipality for Africans in the African section of town, many Kenyans still reside roughly two to ten miles from the city in their traditional homelands and villages. This is a convenient arrangement, given the ease of bus and bicycles to come to work in the city. One has to wonder why a relatively long period of independence has not produced a more visible integration of residential facilities and utility.

The President, surprisingly, is not a resident of Nairobi, but lives in a private home thirty miles from the city. He does visit once or twice a week to perform official functions as he deems fit. The day-to-day management of the central government is left in the trusting hands of the Vice President of the Republic. Perhaps this is as it should be, for President Kenyatta to function as a dignified and respectful statesman; after all, he did bear the burden of evoking national consciousness as far back as 1920, and it would seem a fitting reward that after fifty years of political agony and labor, on behalf of his people, he should be able to enjoy a more relaxed pace of activity.

Nyerere's Ujamaa

It is generally believed that the presence of Chinese in Tanzania, and their support of the vital railroad development with Zambia, has influenced the attitudes of Tanzanians to the point of asserting an ultraconservative Victorian attitude. Indeed, one is cautioned about appropriate attire since the people's militia of Tanzania make no hesitation in apprehending, and sometimes prosecuting, those who are deemed guilty of indecent exposure. The dress code demands a complete covering of the chest of both males and females. This ruling is not usually taken literally, since one can observe many citizens casually strolling about with their shirts not as completely closed as is normal among the Chinese.

Going through the air terminal at Dar es Salaam is normally an experience marked by efficiency, courtesy, and honesty. As an example, the taxi driver who brought me to the Kilimanjaro Hotel in town, could very easily have demanded more than his due fare; I would not have known the difference. Instead, he charged me what was considered fair, including the patience to wait for about fifteen minutes after my arrival at the hotel so I could exchange my travelers checks for the local currency. And when I would buy a daily newspaper or take a taxi, I was able merely to present my coins and allow individuals to choose what was due them. In all instances, my subsequent checking of what had been selected proved precisely the amount they had first demanded.

Tourism has witnessed a very impressive development in Tanzania. The Tanzanian Tourist Corporation has established a series of resort hotels, all different and comfortable, for those who wish to come and share in that nation's tranquility and grandeur. Along the coast there are five hotels already in operation: New African Hotel, Kunduchi Beach Hotel, Mikumi Wild Life Lodge, Mafia Island Lodge, and Bahari Beach Hotel. All of these hotels are within thirty miles of the city of Dar es Salaam, and all have immediate access to, and view of, the beautiful beaches. The Kunduchi Beach Hotel, for example, is built close to the sight of the ruins of one of the earlier settlements of the coast, with an architecture imitating the culture that prevailed in the area between 1300 to 1400 A.D. This area, at the time, was predominantly Arabic, and the present hotel has used early drawings and engravings to permit the arches, swimming pools, and benches to reflect the type of architecture and artifacts that symbolize that period of Arabic settlement.

By the way of contrast, the Bahari Beach Hotel, about two miles further on, used the local coral rocks to provide cottages which have been thatched with the local coconut palms. The hotel gives an exotic and dignified atmosphere, and the rooms and furniture are adequate to the standards of any demanding person. The rounded concrete bungalows with thatched roofs are the most striking feature of the Bahari Beach Hotel. Even the main bar, lounge, restaurant and dance hall are located in a huge tent-shaped and thatched roof structure. The hotel's own brochure describes the facilities:

> This unique and imaginatively designed hotel is undoubtedly ideal for those seeking a restful holiday with an accent on informality. The hundred bedrooms are all air-conditioned, and have private showers, toilets, and balconies with a panoramic sea view. There are also a series of two-story round cottages, each cottage being constructed of coral rock with an attractive thatched roof and containing four bedrooms. . . . For those not wishing their children to share the same room, the design of bungalows makes them very suitable for accommodating families in adjoining rooms. The public rooms are covered by a palm thatched roof like a huge opensided tent which covers the lounge, bar, and restaurant and the whole concept

> is reminiscent of an African Village; but set in magnificent gardens of tropical plants and lawns. Just off shore, forming part of the protective coral reef is Mbudya Island which is a romantic uninhabited island where there is a beach bar; this is an ideal spot for those wishing to spend a day on a desert island, or for parties and barbeques. It is easily reached from the hotel by a short boat trip.
>
> The Kunduchi Beach Hotel, according to its brochure, is situated: on a sandy beach beside a fishing lagoon and village, fourteen miles north of Dar es Salaam. . . . The style is based on the early architecture of the coast and the magnificent carved doors were made by a Zanzibar craftsman. All bedrooms are air-conditioned, with private bathrooms and separate toilet and each room has its own balcony overlooking the Indian Ocean. Each bedroom is built on a split level and one has the opportunity of being able to sit in the bath and enjoy a panoramic view of the ocean. There is a spacious lounge and bar and meals are served either in the restaurant or on the shaded terraces. The reception area has an open tropical garden, pool and fountain, a hair-dressing salon, a shop and a tourist information office. Situated beside the ocean is a swimming pool and oasis bar. There is a variety of entertainment, ranging from dances and barbeques to volleyball and tabletennis, and facilities for all water sports and boating provided.

Dar es Salaam has always been known as a seaport, and it is a city whose history dates back to about 300 A.D. What is less known and particularly impressive today is the establishment of a variety of industrial plants which are in, or close to, the city. In cooperation with the Chinese, and in partnership with Zambia and other countries, factories to satisfy various secondary industrial needs are readily evident. There is a big engineering yard at the railroad terminal; there is also a huge textile mill to facilitate the production of the highly attractive cloth that characterizes this part of Africa. One is also able to appreciate the highly developed cooperative organization under the auspices of the Tanganyika African National Union (TANU). The cooperative union has proved to be very effective among all occupational levels in Tanzania. There are facilities for a taxi cooperative which owns a fleet of taxis and trucks, as well as a gasoline station that affords them wholesale prices for gasoline, parts, and other necessary services.

The University of Dar es Salaam sits on a hillcrest in a section of the city near the ocean. University experience is a relatively new one for Tanzanias, having had to depend during the colonial period on access to Makerere University College (Uganda) which once was responsible for the higher education of all qualified members of the East African community. Although there is no question about the serenity and architectural beauty of the campus, it will require a period of time for the university to settle down in the pursuit of a philosophy befitting the nation-building aspirations of President Nyerere and policy makers of Tanzania.

With the death of President Karumi of Zanzibar, a more moderate tone has developed in Tanzania. After all, it was President Karumi who, having overthrown the Sultan of Zanzibar following independence on that island, pursued a strict commitment to the kind of communism pursued by the People's Republic of China. It may be inferred that the current moral restrictiveness in dress and other behavior was the result of President Karumi's conservatism or radicalism, depending on one's point of view. There is no denying, however, that Tanzania as a nation, at least as espoused by the current leadership, is committed to a policy of self-reliance. Following the nationalization of the banks, President Nyerere carefully encouraged Tanzanians to live on their own resources and capabilities. Requiring university students to serve the rural environment while still enrolled in the university, for example, is the type of practice designed to promote total national integration. In line with his policy, especially as a result of the cold reception given by Western countries to Tanzania's developmental priorities, there has developed a close relationship with China. It can be said that the relationship has been beneficial to Tanzania, in that tremendous secondary industrialization has taken place.

In Dar es Salaam and the surrounding areas, there is evidence of vital manufacturing activities in shoes, textile, cement, furniture, and woodcarving. Official energy also has been directed to developing wildlife parks and the related infrastructure of hotels and transportation to make the natural wildlife resource of Tanzania accessible to tourists. One cannot but be impressed with the manner in which the tourism board has facilitated the development of ancillary requirements to use the wildlife and expansive beach resources of Tanzania.

Nigeria's Military Regime

Military rule seems to have reduced the number of pseudo-officials assisting incoming passengers, and one can now more easily avoid the many individuals who normally attempt to receive tips from strangers by rendering unnecessary assistance and guidance. Driving from the airport to the Federal Palace Hotel soon makes one realize that traffic through and around Lagos remains a grave problem. Traffic remains congested late into the night, and one would rather be caught in the morning traffic of the San Diego Freeway (in Los Angeles), than in the Lagos city traffic. Strangely enough, even though civil servants leave their offices for the day at around 3:00 p.m., traffic remains heavy as late as 7:30 p.m.

Among recent developments is the newly built stadium with a 50,000-seat capacity. The question one is left to ponder is how vehicular access to this impressive stadium is controlled when important activities are scheduled. There is public awareness of the problem and need for a solution; but the joke has become that there is no way of letting the leadership realize the gravity of the situation as long as traffic is readily cleared when the head of state has to travel from one point to another. Another impressive development is the housing boom on Victoria Island, a man-made island. The homes and apartment complexes are quite modern, indicating the continuing growth and economic vitality of Lagos and of Nigeria. There is no question but that oil and petroleum, centered in the federal capital of Lagos, have attracted an undue number of international businessmen whose needs await satisfaction.

A matter of bewilderment is the fact that Nigeria continues to impress one as being highly disorganized. There are vast and diversified natural resources, and there is evidence of commercial activity on a successful and grand scale. Moving about Lagos, the capital, however, remains a nightmare in the highly erratic traffic. To compound the matter, the restriction on automobile importation, which had been in vogue during the civil war, has now been lifted, resulting in an annual registration of 15,000-18,000 vehicles. Related to this matter of continuing increase in the volume of motor vehicles is the ingenuity of most Nigerians in being able to keep on the road vehicles which, in other situations, long ago would have been abandoned to the wrecking yard.

The impressive housing developing on the man-made Island of Victoria will contribute to further increase in the traffic volume. Yet, there seems to be no hurry in providing an alternative access to the mainland or with the other islands, to supplement the one bridge which links Victoria Island to the rest of Lagos. One can see that an attempt has been made during the past several years, at least since independence, to improve the condition of roads and to extend access and exit routes; yet the seeming lack of enforcement with regard to traffic flow and driving behavior contributes to an annoying congestion. There are so many vehicles not in road-worthy condition forming part of the traffic, that the recurrent breakdowns which inevitably occur readily contribute to bottlenecks and traffic delays.

There is also a problem of population. Lagos has always been known as a highly urbanized city. Independence has certainly brought more people to this island city, and not only has this inflow contributed to pedestrian and vehicular traffic, but it has expanded the petty trade sector for which Nigeria has always been famous. It must be annoying to merchants in the downtown commercial district, for example, to have the entrances to their business establishments blocked by large numbers of petty traders displaying their wares on the sidewalk, or in front of their business houses. People ply their trade by investing in a few pounds of onions, or sugar, or a dozen pairs of sandals; anything, for that matter, goes! Even walking through town, aside from the need to be constantly on the alert for disorganized traffic, requires a constant awareness of persons and goods that might be in the way of one's potential path.

Since 1948, when the University of Ibadan was established with a commitment to academic excellence, Nigeria has maintained quality higher education. There is still, of course, a profusion of many colleges and educational institutions—establishments which give bogus diplomas and pseudo-professional credentials. The thirst for education and the prestige value of accumulating diplomas and documents of the successful pursuit of knowledge is a popular venture among Nigerians. While these bogus institutions continue to flourish, sometimes causing problems for companies that may hire unqualified individuals on the basis of phoney documents, formal university development continues on a grand scale. There is an emphasis on developing regional universities, each of which maintains a sort of independence within the region it is meant to serve. In the North, for example, Amadu Bello University makes no bones about its commitment to people of the North. This firm commitment, the corollary of which is a negative attitude toward Nigerians from the South, is manifested in the large number of expatriates who still serve on its staff and its regional branches in Kano and Kaduna.

Ibadan University, on the other hand, an institution that has always stood as the proud national University of Nigeria, remains in the city of Ibadan among the Yorubas. A criticism of Ibadan University is that, although maintaining quality and excellence, it has persisted in pursuing a traditionalism which has not been altogether to the benefit of a new nation. The concern with maintaining a stature comparable to the Oxbridge Universities or that of Harvard, Yale, and the University of California system, has impressed many observers as giving very little room to the type of curricular innovation and reform demanded by a new and developing nation. This may, perhaps, be too harsh a criticism; yet a visit to the campus leaves no doubt about the preference for being judged along the lines of the major European and Western Universities. Indeed, a reflection of this is to be noted in the relatively stagnant enrollment figure of Ibadan University, at a time when most other African countries are finding it necessary to modify admission standards, or to conceive of other means by which applicants could be judged as being qualified to receive higher education.

About sixty miles from the University of Ibadan, there has been established a Western Regional University—The University of Ife. Ife is an example of the crucial problem of curbing regional and ethnic tendencies in favor of promoting national integration. The westerners, it would seem, were not satisfied with having Ibadan in their homeland or with seeing it develop to the point where it could serve their interest along with that of other Nigerians. When Ife, as the Western Region University, was established, this was done right in the same city of Ibadan, no more than a mile from the Ibadan campus. There is, therefore, tremendous rivalry between Ibadan as a national university, and Ife as a regional university. The Ife campus has developed on a grand scale and now operates out of a magnificent campus. It is to be noted that the institution, even though less than thirty years old, has already won international recognition, and has the primary loyalty of people of the Western Region who see it as *their* university. It would not be surprising at all if the enrollment figures at Ife indicate much more accelerated growth than Ibadan, particularly since the Ife administration has a commitment to innovation and the pursuit of admissions criteria that would open wider the doors of the university to many more of its potential clientele.

The relation between Ife and Ibadan is duplicated in regard to the other regional universities. The University of Nigeria at Nsukka, which once served the Eastern Region, was seriously damaged during the civil war. The federal government has since rendered constructive support and it is now solidly back on its feet.

Another impressive university in Nigeria is the University of Lagos. Beginning with a small physical plant and the nucleus of a library, administration building, and few classrooms about twenty years ago, there is evidence today of tremendous physical expansion to provide facilities for the large enrollment which a city like Lagos demands. Again, like the other major Nigerian universities, the University of Lagos has a solid curriculum and has already instituted most of the professional schools that good universities provide. Apart from schools of engineering and architecture, the University of Lagos has a school of law and a college of medicine. With the high population of Nigeria, and the demand for doctors, it can be asserted that this is a valuable mission in these professional areas for the University of Lagos, as well as for the University of Ibadan and Amandu Bello University which also have medical and nursing schools.

There is an apparent consciousness of the role which universities in developing nations should play. Occasionally, administrators, decision makers, and university professors expound on the directions which curricula should take, and the nature of support which should come from the public and private sectors. Most African universities, as should be the case, have already manifested their ability to pursue research in the interest of nation-building and in service to the central government. Occasionally, political philosophies and controversies get in the way of objectivity. One can conclude, nonetheless, that the future will see greater and greater participation and contribution by universities to ideas and strategies which could be used effectively by governments and nation-builders. On this matter of higher education, it should be pointed out that there is already recognition for the intensive training of high level manpower. Nigeria has an Institute of Public Administration and an African Studies Institute; the latter is, indeed, a development in most African countries with universities. The concern in this regard is to see that the heritage of African societies is reasserted to its rightful place, thus negating whatever inadvertent stereotypes might have resulted from interpretations of the colonial and early preindependence periods.

Nigeria remains one of the primary instruments for developing the African continent. Having a wide variety of natural resources (including petroleum), as well as a large cadre of professionals and skilled personnel, it should be possible for Nigeria—once a climate of cooperative Africanization has been established—to assist other nations further along the road toward achieving a better standard of living for all. It is imperative, however, that policy makers of Nigeria, and those who have assumed the mantle of leadership, develop an attitude of concern for all their citizens. Too often, one sees people succumbing to the selfishness and greed that results from the arrogance of power. There are wealthy individuals in Nigeria, as indeed there are in the other developing countries. Yet, one is forced to agonize over the seeming sense of irresponsibility and indifference to the plight of the many poor. No longer can one rationalize that foreigners have to bear the burden of reproach for the ills that continue to plague African societies. The poor, the sick, and the ignorant must no longer be pushed on the conscience of outsiders.

Africa, for the most part today, has its own destiny to shape through the hands of its own leaders. In this regard, Nigeria, being the country with the largest concentration of Africans, can begin to live the example of responsible statesmanship rather than of exploitive individualism which the continent can ill afford. It is, perhaps, a sign for the future that the current leaders of Nigeria have won the respect of other African leaders. It is to be noted, however, that there are many areas of development, both economic and social, in which Nigerian leaders can undertake a more realistic and equitable approach, in order to service the needs and aspirations of those who have chosen them to guide their future. There is hope in the fact that Africa contains leaders of stature, leaders with excellent training, who can resolve the many problems that persisted from the colonial era through the stage of independence. Only through an inner resolve to truly serve the interest of those who, like children, have entrusted their care to such leadership, can the potential hope and a life worth living begin to find fruition.

Undoubtedly, there have been advancements in most of the physical and social sectors throughout Terramedia. Progress has been made in promoting cooperation between neighboring countries, in the pursuit of improved aviation, commerce, defense, economy, and education. Recently, for example, Sierra Leone carried out an effective and realistic agreement with Nigeria and Liberia in order to meet their individual and cooperative needs in aviation and commerce. These advancements, however, especially in the face of the observed caution and skepticism among the rank and file of Terramedian citizenry (and coupled with the corruption prevailing among some top officials), give a valid reason for arguing that things could have been much better than they are at present. The potential gains of self-determination, it seems, are held in check by a lack of commitment to strategies which would serve the whole nation. One cannot but wonder how the ordinary citizen in any of the Terramedian countries can exist in dignity and with confidence in his leaders, when he has to endure an ever increasing cost of living without an opportunity to earn such a living.

Too many of the present-day policy makers and leaders are insulated from the ordinary citizen. Certainly, one could argue that written statements and parliamentary debates suggest a sensitivity to the needs of the people being led. One can further observe that there have been significant infrastructural developments in the creation, for example, of commercial banks controlled by indigenous persons and with improved facilities for extending development loans to private individuals in the pursuit of commerce, farming, transport, and select types of secondary industries. A careful examination of parallel developments, however, and of the activities of principal officials, leaves one to wonder why there is so much external travel by civil servants and members of the cabinet. One might ask if it is in the best interest of some of these countries to expend valuable foreign exchange in sending delegations to Australia or Canada or to Guinea to debate issues often not directly relevant to development. Such funds could be used to respond to clearly expressed needs in keeping with avowed policies identified in the speeches of many of these leaders. What is the need of an air force, or naval force, for example? The answer usually given is to provide an effective national defense. Yet no Terramedian country is in a position to mount a truly effective and independent defense against a major invasion. These nations would be well advised to use their defenselessness, in terms of military technology, as a moral shield, rather than use scarce resources for the acquisition of a few unnecessary, and at best relatively ineffective, components of tanks, planes, or naval patrol boats.

Chapter Three

GEOGRAPHY AS A DETERMINANT OF LIFESTYLES

Geographical Realities

It is often not realized that the exciting social and political upheavals that receive so much publicity in the world press are integrally related to geography and ecology. While it is true that modernized cultures are technologically able to modify the environment in ways that would have seemed impossible not long ago, most of Terramedia remains subject to the limitations of geography and the traditional adaptations that people made to their environment. Although industries have developed in some areas that until recently were agrarian or nomadic, at least 75% of Terramedia remains subject to the limitations of the environment. Some knowledge of the geography, as well as of the significant ecological consequences of that geography, is therefore essential for a satisfactory understanding of past, present, and future lifestyles in Terramedia.

PHYSICAL STRUCTURES

Geologically, Terramedia is a remnant of the ancient continental land mass of *Gondwanaland,* portions of which broke off and drifted away to become Australia and South America.[1] Because most of the land has been long subjected to erosion, with frequent extrusion of molten rocks from the surface, most of Terramedia possesses easily accessible minerals such as copper, diamonds, gold, iron ore, petroleum, and uranium (see Figure 3.1). Despite such erosions, Terramedia consists of an ancient basement complex that is stable and rigid and that has been spared the folding movements of other continental land masses. With minor exceptions (such as the folding revealed by the Atlas mountains and the Great Karroo), the land mass of Terramedia is a plateau at least 200 million years old.

Figure 3.1 Major Mineral Occurrences

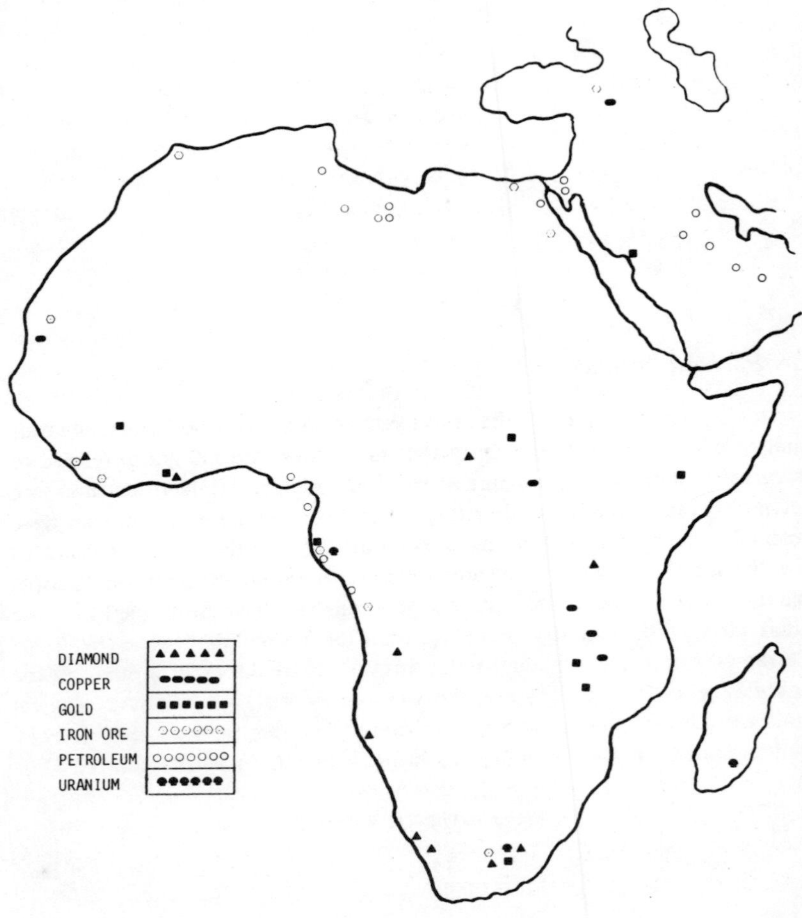

Projecting from this plateau lower in the northwest and higher in the southeast), are prominent elevations significantly influencing precipitation, temperature, and human ecology.

Northeast of Iraq, sheltering the fertile crescent of the Tigris and Euphrates valley and the *Shatt-al-Arab,* are the Elburz Mountains which rise to 19,000 feet. On the northwest are the Taurus Mountains of about 12,000 feet and the highlands of eastern Turkey, from which flow the Tigris and Euphrates rivers. Farther south, and paralleling the Levantine coast, are the mountains of Lebanon (10,000 feet) from which flow politically and agriculturally important rivers such as the Jordan, Litani, and Orentes. Because the bulk of the Middle Eastern part of Terramedia experiences very little precipitation, the irrigational potential of these rivers is vitally important in determining the degree of dependence upon outsiders for food. Largely because of this geographical reality, nomadism, and agricultural and pastoral symbiosis, are common.[2]

Other prominent elevations are the Atlas Mountains in western North Africa (13,000 feet) and in the central Sahara, and the Ahaggar and Tibesti Mountains (10,000 feet). Between the Tropic of Cancer and the Equator, in the western sector, are the Futa Djalon Mountains (4,000 feet) serving as the source of the rivers Niger, Senegal, and Gambia; the Moshi Highlands in Upper Volta and Komadugu Rivers; the Cameroon and Ubangi-Shari uplands (4,000 feet, but with Mt. Cameroon itself being over 13,000 feet), from which flow the Benue, Sanaga, and Shari Rivers, and which make inland Lake Chad possible (see Figure 3.2).

Eastern Africa is marked most noticeably by the Great Rift Valley caused by faults in the basement complex–the result of uplifts, depressions, and volcanic eruptions–which resulted in such finger lakes as Nyasa, Tankanyika, Albert, Rudolph, and the Red Sea. Accompanying the "rift" feature in eastern Africa is the impressively high (8,000 feet) plateua which dominates the area from Ethiopia southward to South Africa. Exceptions to this rather consistent elevation are the low-lying desert and coastal areas of the Somali Republic, the Congo River basin, the coastal areas of Tanzania and Mozambique, the Kalahari desert in Botswana, the Cubango and Okovango basin in south-central Angola, and the Namib desert in Namibia. Certain elevations or mountains which project from the East African and Ethiopian Highlands are noteworthy: the Ras Dashan of about 15,000 feet and the Choke Mountains–the location of Lake Tana and the source of the Blue Nile; the Ruwenzori, Elgon, Kenya, Kilimanjaro, and Meru Mountains (between 14,000 and 19,000 feet) that almost encircle lakes Victoria, Kioga, and Albert–sources of the White Nile which flow half the length of Africa into the Meditarranean Sea. The Ruwenzori,

Figure 3.2 Major Mountains, Rivers, and Dams

furthermore, gives rise to some of the tributaries of the Congo River. Several other rivers, of course, gain their existence from these impressive mountains: the Rufiji, flowing through Tanzania into the Indian Ocean; the Lualaba and the Lomami, flowing northward from the Mitumba Mountains in southern Zaire into the main Congo River; the Zambezi, flowing south then eastward through Zambia and Mozambique; and the Orange River, deriving from the Drakensberg Mountains of 10,000 feet, and flowing westward through South Africa into the Atlantic Ocean.

The many mountains, lakes, and rivers would seem to indicate that water, so vital to agriculture and human sustenance, ought not to pose a problem for Terramedia. The fact, however, is that the predominance of a desert environment in the northern sector and the characteristic tropicality of the central two-thirds of Africa make the conservation and availability of water a serious concern.[3] A great deal of redistribution effort through effective irrigation and storage has been necessary to use the heavy downpours that seasonally occur in the tropics.

CLIMATE

Although the many countries that constitute Terramedia cover so vast an area of the earth—roughly five times the size of the United States although with less than twice the population—there are certain basic climatic patterns that create much uniformity.[4] These climatic patterns, along with the nature of the topography, have significantly influenced the lifestyles that have developed in the various regions of Terramedia. Almost nowhere, except at its northerly limits and the tops of some mountains, does the temperature drop below the freezing point. With the exception of the mild temperate zone along the Mediterranean coast, the uplands of the Taurus and Elburz regions, and the coastal area of South Africa, most of Terramedia has high temperatures, normally ranging from 70 to 110 degrees during the day. Where the plateau is high, as in eastern Africa, the temperature hovers about 70 or slightly below; and where there is a predominantly desert environment, the temperature hovers around 100 degrees (although the nights are commonly very cool).

Terramedia suffers a "feast or famine" of annual rainfall: There is little or no rain in much of the Middle East, and too much rain—over 100 inches—in the tropical rain forests. Furthermore, the heavy rainfall on either side of the Equator is most often extremely seasonal, so that almost all of the "annual" rainfall occurs during a six- or eight-month period, with the remainder of the year being utterly dry.

Because of the location of the African continent somewhat evenly between the Tropics of Cancer and Capricorn, there is a "mirror image" of climate, reflected in a gradual reduction in temperature and precipitation as one moves farther away from the Equator. It is true, of course, that because of the movement of air masses—whether they are dry or moist—as well as the movement of the earth itself, there is fluctuation in the position of the intertropical convergence zone which demarcates the location of high and low pressure centers.[5] The general picture, nevertheless, is one of a tropical forest zone stretching from the westerly limits of the Rift Valley across the Guinea Coast to Guinea, with rainfall of more than 100 inches per year and consistently high temperature. This tropical zone is followed, to the north and south (hence the mirror image), by a zone of savanna grassland where rainfall and vegetation diminish from about 80 inches and heavy bush to about 10 inches and very sparse scrub vegetation. In the east, because of the high plateua, the temperature is milder and the precipitation less because the prevailing moisture-laden winds tend to blow parallel to the coast rather than overland—giving rise to the Somali Desert within the same latitudes.

North and south of the savanna are the deserts—the Sahara and Arabian to the north, and the Kalahari and Namib to the south—which are hot and dry the year round. There may occur in this zone unpredictable thunder-

Figure 3.3 Physical Environments

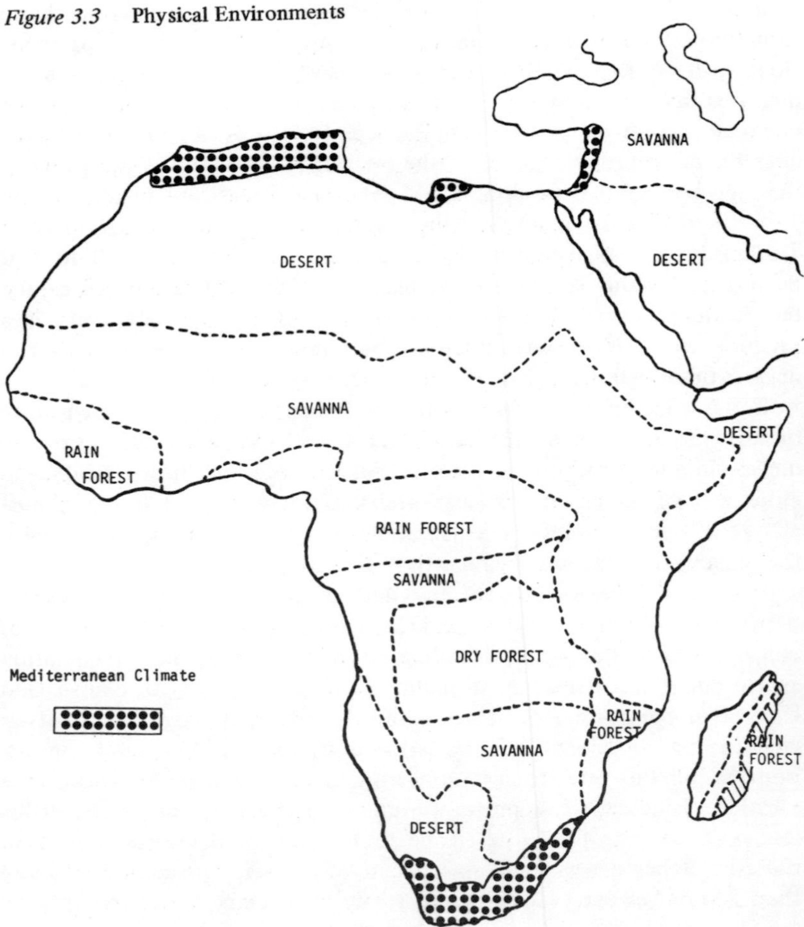

storms which give an annual rainfall of five inches or less. In the south, below the desert zone, there is the mild "Mediterranean" climate of South Africa, the eastern coast of which tends to be warmer and has more rain (about 50 inches annually) than the western. In the north, continuing along the coast of the Mediterranean to Lebanon and Syria, there is a similar mediterranean zone, with mild temperatures and winter rains (about 30 inches). Farther inland from the coast, depending on the proximity to mountains and desert, rainfall decreases radically to about 10 inches annually (see Figure 3.3).

RESOURCE

Partly because of the realities of geography (although these have from time to time been modified by improved technology and altered value systems), the economic activities of Terramedian countries reflect the influence of geology, climate, and the available natural resources. Valuable minerals are scattered throughout the continent and the Middle East, and more have been discovered since independence in areas where it was presumed either that they did not exist, or they were too scarce to exploit profitably. Terramedia has a vast hydro-electric power potential for processing its varied mineral and agricultural products. At present, however, the economy of Terramedia is basically extractive and, where it is not merely subsistence economy, is based on export of the extracted minerals or agricultural produce.

In the northern sector, expecially in the desert zone and delta region of Kuwait and Iraq, petroleum is most important. How beneficial this type of lucrative activity is to the mass "owners" of this resource is, of course, open to question since participation in the rewards is usually limited to foreign investors and despotic rulers. In areas of the Middle East with a favorable climate, barley, citrus fruits, grapes, livestock, olives, and wheat are cultivated. In the valley of the Nile River, the chief product is cotton, while the highlands of Ethiopia provide a climate suitable for mixed agriculture featuring coffee, livestock, tobacco, and wheat. The predominantly desert areas of Algeria and Libya have become sources of petroleum, whereas in the milder and moister areas—as well as in Tunisia and Morocco—citrus fruits, grape, and wheat are produced, in addition to such valuable minerals as cobalt, iron ore, phosphates, and salt. The heartland of the Sahara, in common with other deserts, produces dates and camels (although not in large quantity), mainly for the subsistence of small resident populations. The production is sufficiently meager to make life precarious in the area.

Immediately south of the Sahara, from Senegal to northern Nigeria, groundnuts (peanuts) are produced, along with cotton, millet, livestock, rice, diamonds (in Sierra Leone), and tin (in Nigeria). In the zone of the tropical forests, extending from Guinea to Zaire, there is a healthy variety of mineral and agricultural products. Numerous types of cereal, tuberous and tree crops are grown as staples–maize, millet, and rice in the savanna, and yam, cassava, cocoyam, banana, and plantain in the forested areas. The more significant crops, however, (because of their importance in international trade), are cacao, coffee, ginger, kola, oil palm, rubber, and sisal. The major mineral products are bauxite, chromite, diamonds, iron ore, and tin. Coal and petroleum are also produced in southern Nigeria. Below Zaire, especially in Zambia, Rhodesia (Zimbabwe), Angola, and Namibia, there is sufficient climatic variation to support profitable mixed farming. Beans, manioc, and wheat are produced for local consumption; but the main emphasis is on the production of citrus fruits, coffee, livestock, and tobacco. Although petroleum has become a prominent resource in Angola, the major mining activity (drastically affected by recent liberation struggles and civil wars) is in the production of asbestos, chromite, coal, copper, diamonds, iron ore, mica, and zinc.

In the east, from Uganda southward to Mozambique, both subsistence and plantation agriculture–rather than mining–dominate the economy. Some mineral deposits are known to exist, but the difficulty of working and transporting these ores has restricted activity mainly to Tanzania, where there are diamonds, gold, lead, mica, and tin. There is a wide variety of staple crops (such as cassava, maize, millet, rice, and wheat), and there is also cattle raising, although the quality of the cattle is poor owing to widespread tsetse fly infestation. The cash crops important in international trade are cloves, coffee, cotton, sisal, tea, sugar, cane, and tobacco. Malagasy, along with South Africa, has a generally healthy climate and soil, making mixed agriculture feasible. Although lacking the vast mineral resources and superior technology of South Africa, Malagasy produces–apart from rice, its major subsistence crop–a variety of tropical and semitropical crops, including cloves, coffee, pepper, sugar cane, tobacco, and livestock. South Africa has the widest variety of agricultural and mining activity. Comparatively self-sufficient as a nation, South Africa is able to emphasize the mining of diamonds, coal, chromite, copper, gold, tin, and uranium.

This brief overview suggests that Terramedia has a wide variety of agricultural and other resources to make it self-sufficient (see Map 5). But this variety at present is only potential, since many of the resources have not featured in the adjustments made by the people to their environments.

Even with modern independence, only a small number of the population of specific countries or regions realize substantial material benefits from the goods with which nature has endowed the area. The substantial foreign exchange currency derived from diamonds, for example, has not altered the extremely low level of living which has been the lot of the majority of South Africans and Sierra Leoneans. Similarly, the wealth brought by petroleum extraction and processing in Saudi Arabia, Libya, and Nigeria, for example, has not eased the burden of poverty and disease which many of the people continue to endure. Furthermore, the potentially rewarding

Figure 3.4 **Agricultural Resources**

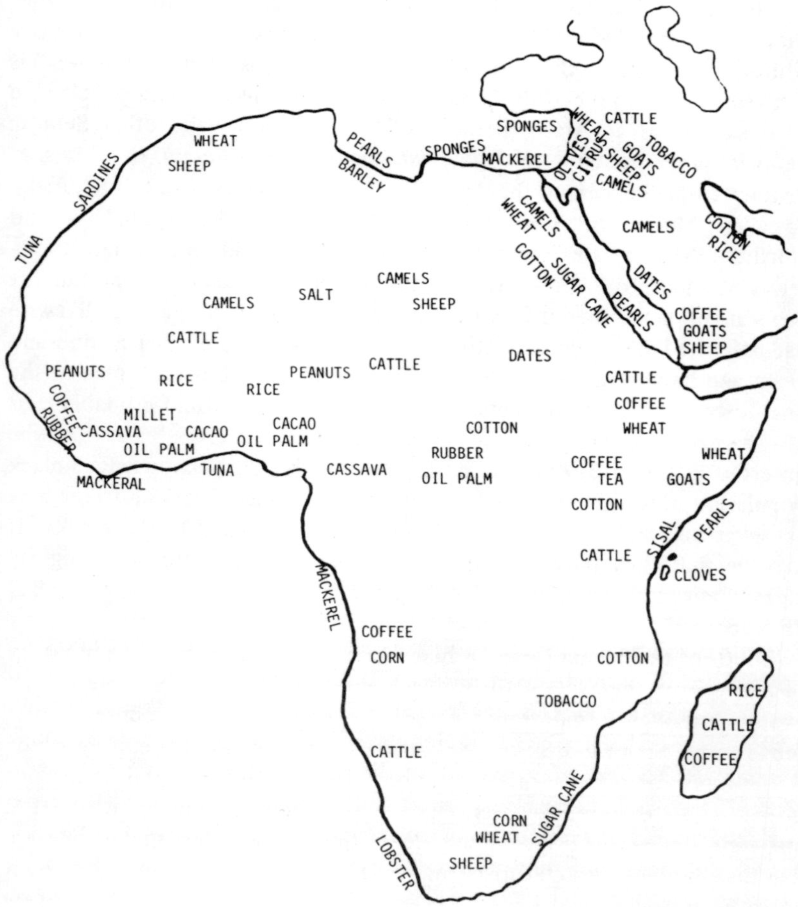

agricultural activities in which many are engaged do not result in impressive benefits, since the influence of colonial marketing patterns continues to be exploitive of the indigenous population. It is, therefore, useful to keep in focus the ecological patterns which evolved in Terramedia before the intervention of European vested interests, patterns which continue to influence living conditions and lifestyles. A survey of the human groups and languages of the area clarifies the connection between ecology and human geography.

Human Groups in Terramedia

The people of the Middle East and North Africa are Semitic Caucasoids, that is to say, "white" people—even though few of them are actually white-skinned. As is the case with most Europeans, their "whiteness" is not real but symbolic. Culture has, in turn, distinguished these people into such subgroups as Arabs, Berbers, and Jews.[6] Moors and other Semitic peoples, however, tend to distinguish themselves as *bidani,* or whites, as distinct from the *sudani,* the "blacks" of subSaharan Africa. In fact, many so-called "Moors" and even "Arabs" (such as the *Shu'ah* Arabs in Niger and Northern Nigeria) are Negroid rather than Caucasoid, yet refer to themselves as Moors or Arabs. Why is this so? In most instances one inherits one's name and other marks of identity from one's father, who likewise had inherited his from his father. However, one's forefather a thousand years ago happened to have been a Caucasoid Arab, but each man in the line down to the present married black women; one would probably thus be Negroid according to the usual biological criteria.[7] This can be observed in the Mediterranean basin with hardly any acknowledged black population, despite the forced migration that brought blacks into the area as slaves hundreds of years ago. What, then, happened to the blacks? It may be that they have remained in southern Europe with black, tightly curled hair and other modified Negroid features, while being labelled "Europeans."

South of the Sahara Desert is black Africa, even though only a minority of the people there are actually black skinned. Most Africans are in fact brown, although a wide range of color exists; skin color, consequently, tends to be a poor indication of a person's race. Indeed, it is culture which is the basis for realistic differentiation.[8] Because geographical conditions in part affect culture, however, cultures and their accompanying societies are very similar over vast areas, depending on whether the people are livestock herders, agriculturists, or traders—in desert, savanna or riverain environments.

Religious affiliation or belief is another means of cultural categorization in Terramedia. Out of the Middle East developed three of the great religions: Judaism, Christianity, and Islam. Islam was spread across North Africa and southward into the Eastern and Western Sudan, as well as southward along the East African coast into present-day Mozambique. Christianity is the most important religion in Ethiopia, although there are some Judaized Ethiopians, the *Falasha*; elsewhere, Christianity is the religion of some Lebanese and Syrians, but was carried into sub-Saharan Africa chiefly by European and African missionaries. The third important religion, because it is widespread in Terramedia, is not precisely a religion; it is, rather, many beliefs similar to one another. These are the traditional religions of African peoples, sometimes called *Animism* to indicate that they consist of the "animation" by possession of souls and spirits of natural man-made objects. This term is not very satisfactory simply because many traditional religions do not "animate" nature any more than do Judaism or Christianity. Other terms that still appear in some readings, unsatisfactory because they are derogatory, are *fetishism, juju,* and *superstition.* The most suitable term one might use would be the name of the tribal group plus *traditional religion,* such as "Gikuyu traditional religion."[9]

The significance of categorizing people according to religious belief or affiliation goes beyond the mere assigning of a place in an artificial schema: People's religious beliefs bear importantly upon their behavior, their livelihood, and their rights to territory. The practitioner of traditional religion, for example, who believes that an intentional spiritual cause underlies illness, is very unlikely to take himself to a mission hospital for treatment lest he further offend the god or other who had already beset him with the illness. The Europeanized Christian, on the other hand, may have more faith in the hospital and in European medicine, and if he is cured of an ailment he is that much more likely to accept European changes of other sorts.

An important means of grouping the peoples of Terramedia is by languages, which must be considered according to two broad classes: vernacular and vehicular languages. A *vernacular language* is the indigenous or "native" language. For example, English is the native language of the vast majority of Americans, Arabic the vernacular of the Arabs, and ki-Swahili the vernacular of the Swahili people of East Africa. By means of the vernacular language the people of a culture communicate with one another *within the culture.* In general, those who speak only the vernacular cannot communicate with people of another culture, unless, as with America and England, the language happens to be the same—which is rarely the case. All peoples the world over have a vernacular language expressing their ideas, feelings, and values; and in Terramedia there are approximately 1,000 separate vernacular languages. Some vernaculars, however, are related to others sufficiently that they compose language families. In Europe, for example, such language families are the Germanic and Romance languages. The existence of language families does not mean, though, that individual languages making up the family are mere dialects; the language families consist of distinct languages which, despite their (usual) mutual unintelligibility, can be shown to have a common source or other relation.

In Terramedia, the language families are the *Afro-Asiatic* in the Middle East, North Africa, the Sudan, and the Horn of Africa; the *Central Saharan* of Chad and Libya; the *Macro-Sudanic* of East central Africa; the *Niger-Congo* of the Guinea Coast and all of middle and eastern Africa south to the Cape; the *Click* of Botswana and parts of South West Africa and South Africa; and the very small *Songhai* of the upper Niger River (Figure 3.5). These large families of indigenous languages can be subdivided into somewhat smaller groups of vernaculars. For example, Afro-Asiatic includes such linguistic groups as Semitic, Egyptian, Cushitic, Berber and others; and the Niger-Congo family includes, most importantly, the two broad divisions of Bantu and Kwa families.

Sub-Saharan languages are particularly remarkable, among other things, because of their tonality, which poses difficult learning problems for Europeans and some other outsiders; Most of the Niger-Congo languages are tonal, which means that a switch in tone in a syllable of a word changes the word. For example, in the Igbo language of Eastern Nigeria, the word *ugwu* printed in this manner means nothing because it has no tones marked. But if we mark the tones of the syllables, the word takes on meaning and, indeed, becomes three words:

úgwú (High & High): “mountain”
úgwù (High & Low): “circumcision”
ùgwù (Low & Low): “prestige”

A *vehicular language* is one that acts as a means of communication across cultural linguistic barriers. Thus, English might be a vernacular language for Englishmen and some other peoples, but if the British conquer and colonize an area (which they did in Terramedia) and require all official and many trade transactions to be carried on in English, the subject peoples—or at least some of them—will soon have to use that alien language. The African, for example, had a vernacular language which tended to prevent him from communicating with Africans of other tribal groups; when all were forced to use English, this European language

Figure 3.5 Language Families of Terramedia (after J. Greenberg)

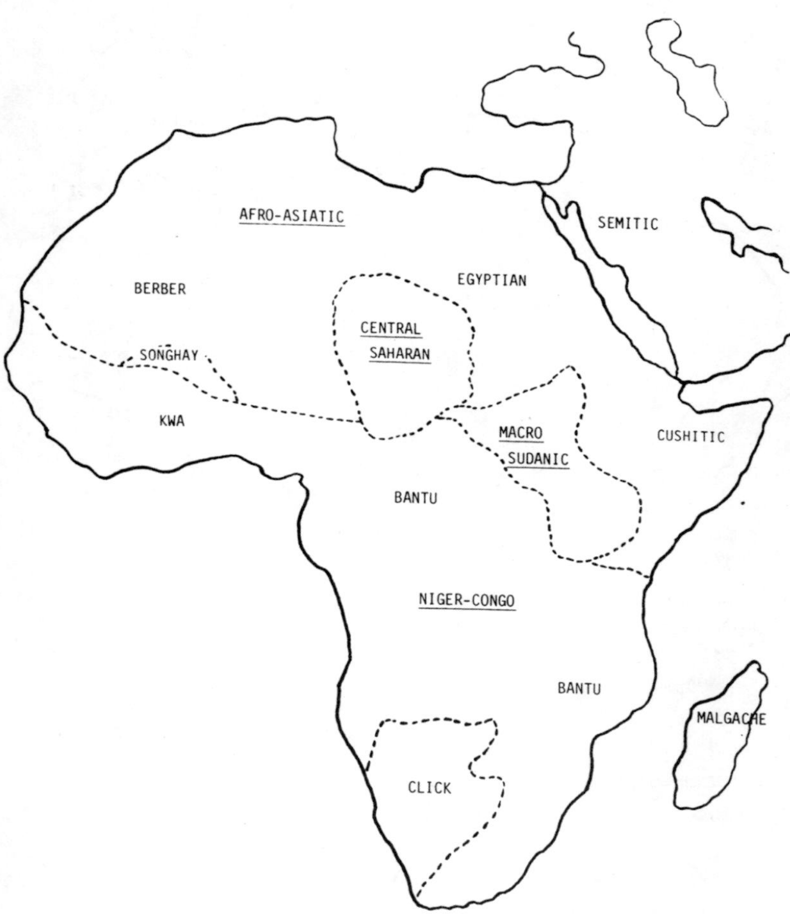

suddenly became–for them–a tool of communication quite different from what it was to native English speakers who knew no other language. It became a vehicle whereby *African A* could communicate his ideas (many of which concerned means of getting rid of the conquerors) to *African B*, who was of a hitherto unreachable group. As Figure 3.6 indicates, there are several classes or types of vehicular languages: Arabic, constituting a category of its own, spread by the Arabs and Berbers through the Middle East and across northern Africa; African languages which have become vehicular, usually through the spread of African empires–Hausa, for

Figure 3.6 Vehicular Languages of Terramedia

example, or Manding; amalgamated languages resulting from profound and widespread assimilation of an immigrated language, such as Ki-Swahili of East Africa and Hova of Madagascar; trade languages, usually amalgamated but quite often highly simplified, such as pidgin, krio, *petit negre,* and fanagalo or kitchen kaffir; and European languages resulting from colonial conquests or actual colonization by Europeans.[10] The European vehiculars are Afrikaans, English, French, Portuguese, and to a lesser extent, Spanish.

Human Ecology in Terramedia

The people of Terramedia have developed five general and overlapping patterns of adjustment to their environment. Although it is customary in ecological literature to talk about rural and urban societies, or of village, town, or nomadic societies, one derives a clearer picture of human ecology in Terramedia by examining the adaptations in relation to the five major environments of desert, mountain, savanna, forest, and riverain areas.[11]

THE DESERT

In desert country—although much of it is erg, or sand dunes—there is sparse vegetation due to extremely low rainfall. Agriculture on most of the land thusly is impossible except where irrigation can be practised and, of course, along the banks of watercourses. Virtually all of Egypt's farms, for example, lie either in the Nile Delta or along a very narrow strip of land on either side of the lower Nile; the rest of the nation is desert—arid, bleak, inhospitable. Inhabitants of the desert country usually own grazing animals (camels and goats, rather than cattle) able to survive on very coarse food. Such pastoralists are nomadic, wandering with their flocks from one place to another in "horizontal nomadism," the movement from site to site at approximately the same level above sea level being chiefly to seek out fresh pastures.

Nomadism is common in Saudi Arabia and Jordan, the Somali Republic, Botswana, Mauretania, and other desert areas in Terramedia. Although the particular nomads might differ as members of ethnic stocks, they tend to share some behavior and values simply as human beings confronting desert conditions. Nomads sometimes raise a few cash and food crops near waterholes and oases, and sometimes are hunters and food gatherers. Furthermore, they often trade—particularly Arabs, Bedouins, and Berbers—because they are so accustomed to wandering from place to place; and because they are wanderers, they seldom develop elaborate technology, for this development or achievement requires stability of location. Bedouins of Arabia, Jordan, and North Africa, like other nomads, consider hunting and raiding to be the pursuits worthy of a true man.[12] Furthermore, they are individualistic, or highly in-group oriented as nomads or seminomads, maintaining a keen distrust of strangers and are often endogamous. Such independence is reflected also in the relatively loose governments found in desert societies, a good example of which is Bushman society in the Kalahari Desert of Botswana.[13] Here social organization consists of a simple band with the eldest male acting as a sort of chief, although there is no institution of chieftaincy.

MOUNTAIN COUNTRY

In mountain country, unless the mountains are desert, there are occasional springs and small watercourses, and often fairly regular rainfall, even if it is sometimes seasonal. In such country the people practise valley and slope agriculture, and graze and herd goats, sheep, and cattle, where the vegetation permits. "Vertical nomadism," which can also be observed in mountain country, is the movement up and down mountainsides in search of fresh pasture lands or to plant different crops following changes in the seasons at different elevations. There is relatively little evidence of culture borrowing or acculturation among mountain people, chiefly because of the difficulty of getting around. Depending on the degree of isolation of the groups in mountain communities, there is relative autonomy which sometimes leads to group strength because of the development of extreme tribalism. Such is certainly the case, for example, with the Kurds of the Middle East, and perhaps to a lesser extent among the Sotho of Lesotho in southern Africa. The usual stability of locale of many mountain-dwelling peoples leads often to the formation of relatively elaborate systems of government, such as the centralized kingdom of the Swazi in southern Africa. Interestingly, among the Swazi, the queen mother is responsible for the all-important rains; droughts or floods are taken by the people to indicate royal displeasure. Ceremonialism, likewise, tends to be rather elaborate among settled mountain dwellers, and there is often well-developed historical or genealogical recording (usually oral) and detailed division of labor and specialization in occupations.

An outstanding example of the foregoing is the case of the Ethiopians who, through long centuries of settlement on their extensive mountain massif (mean height of 7500 feet), developed a number of the arts—including writing—to a high degree of sophistication, although their relative isolation, which effectively deterred much alien conquest, is considered by some to be a drawback. Perhaps most outstanding among their architectural accomplishments are the eleven churches at the ancient city of Roha, which was named Lalibela after the twelfth century king and architect. These churches at Lalibela, in the Province of Lasta, were hewn out of solid granite, the largest of them, Mahhane Alem, measuring 110 x 77 x 36 feet high.[14]

SAVANNA

Savanna is grassland, an environment conducive to grain agriculture. It is true, of course, that cereal cultivation occurs in mountain environments, as in Ethiopia where such high country grains as tef and barley are commonly grown; but never on such a scale as in savanna country, the more natural terrain for grasses. Most of the arable land of Terramedia is savanna steppe, and the kinds of grains raised include barley, rye, wheat, maize, millet, and sorghum. An important crop in the area of the Western Sudan and upper Gambia is the groundnut (peanut), which is raised as an export commodity; along the upper Niger River and in Zaire rice is a very important crop, although it tends to be associated with riverain rather than with savanna peoples.[15] Because of the widespread opportunity for agriculture, there is a tendency for some cultures and societies to stabilize in certain favorable locations and thus become influential because of the increase of population resulting from a steady and quite ample supply of good food. This was certainly the case in the growth of such savanna empires as Ghana, Mali, and Songhay in the Western Sudan, Kush in the Eastern Sudan, Zimbabwe in Rhodesia, and the old Persian empire of Iraq.

Savanna country is naturally inhabited by grass-eating animals, so men early developed pastoralism, particularly raising cattle, in grassland area. The whole of the Sudan, from the nation of Sudan west to Mauretania, and most of East and southern Africa are cattleraising savanna country; and one can safely say that, despite the widespread use of the camel in North Africa and parts of the Middle East as a beast of burden and source of food animal, cattle are probably the most important domesticated animals in all of Terramedia. There are many more cattle and they are much more intricately involved in the way of life of savanna peoples than is the camel. The degree of involvement of cattle and humans is indicated in numberless ways, including the use of cattle as a criterion for human handsomeness, as in this early nineteenth century praise-poem for the Tswana chief, Senwelo (of present-day Botswana):

> Radiant son of Molefe, sleek in body,
> Child of the one who resembles a cow;
> Compared to a cow, he surpassed it [in beauty]:
> He surpassed the cow, Nyetsane's brother.

Livestock among pastoral peoples becomes the basis for wealth and status, and religion and often family relationships are linked with the animals. Livestock are equated with women (for example, in marriage arrangements), with bridewealth being paid in the form of cattle. Division of labor often follows the needs of pastoralism, too. For instance, the Fulani of the Western Sudan characteristically associate men with cattle and women with the household, largely because women are incapable of handling the great, humped Fulani cattle, let along helping to defend them. Yet women milk the cows and make butter—activities considered to be socially proper and requiring less strenuous effort.

Savanna herders are often seminomadic, such as the Fulani, the Herero of South West Africa, and the Hova of Malagasy Republic. In moving about to seek fresh pastures, such nomads (very much like desert nomads, and some peoples are both), generally develop only what might be called "lightweight" technology, with few artifacts and with little material representation in their religion. It is not surprising that the seminomadic savanna peoples, the Fulani, were among the most important carriers of Islam in the Western Sudan, having received it in their turn from Arabs and Berbers to the north and east.[16] It is equally not unsurprising that the much more settled "Town Fulani," who were not pastoralists and not nomadic, developed elaborate written histories and religious works, and instituted a *jihad* during the nineteenth century to reconvert the peoples in a broad area extending from Guinea to northern Nigeria.

THE FOREST

Forest dwellers typically engage in a type of agriculture that cultivates root and tree crops rather than grain. Across West and much of equatorial Africa, these root crops are cocoyam, cassava, and yam. On the northerly edges of the forest belt and among the savanna peoples, groundnuts and groundpea are grown. In equatorial Africa, the major subsistence crops are plantains, which resemble bananas but must usually be cooked to be edible. Other tree crops are bananas, coconuts, kola, and oil palm. The most common agricultural method in Terramedia is "bush fallowing": The farmer burns a section of bush or forest and uses the ashes as partial fertilizer; he prepares the ground, plants his crop, and uses the ashes as partial fertilizer. The land is used for perhaps two or three seasons until it is virtually depleted; then the farmer clears and burns a new section of bush, allowing the older field to revert to bush again. The method is, to say the least, not very productive. Accordingly, much forest agriculture is *subsistence* agriculture, which means that the people consume almost everything they raise on their farms and thus have very little surplus for sale.

Agricultural existence normally leads to relative stability of community location. This circumstance is particularly true of forest-dwelling people whose "shifting" agriculture or bush fallowing does not entail mass movement of the community and clashes with neighboring groups.[17] Therefore, social and religious ties between the land and the family, and from one family to another, steadily proliferate, along with a numerical increase of spiritual forces which can be represented in statuary by skilled artisans.

The elaborate bronze casting of the Yoruba and Bini peoples in Western Nigeria, for example, could occur only among a settled people, for nomads would find it virtually impossible to transport the heavy equipment from place to place. Similarly, whereas masks among savanna dwellers tend usually to be of cloth, which can be carried easily, forest dwellers developed remarkable variety of carved wooden masks; for wood is plentiful and the communities, being agricultural, were fixed in their location.[18]

Among forest people, land is the basis of wealth, but one must understand that typically African (and, more generally, Terramedian) attitudes about land can differ in several respects from European and American attitudes. Among most Africans, the land itself is usually deified or spiritualized, or it is believed to have a special tutelary spirit protecting it; so its ownership is in the hands of a social group—a family, a clan, or a village. The earth, the land itself, is the sacred source of the people's livelihood, and needs to be treated with proper respect to ensure that the magical power of sustenance continues.[19] Thus the land or its spirit is regularly propitiated with ritual and ceremonial sacrifices, and it is ritually accorded respect. Even morality at times is linked with it. For example, the Igbo of Eastern Nigeria say of a person who has offended a god, *o mèrùrù àlà,* "he polluted the earth." Accordingly, the land where the people live, where their dead are buried, and where their shrines are located, is not sold, nor is it saleable. The farmland, along with residential land and village-owned bush, is defined not according to arbitrary physical measurement of boundaries, but to a social criterion: *The land of a social group is that which they by tradition consider theirs, which they control and, which they use, actually or potentially.* Igbo will say of the village of their birth: *Anye nwe àlà,* "we own the land," with emphasis on "we."[20]

These matters are important, because traditionally the use of land was not completely stabilized within a tribal area. Thus, communities or lineages could shift from using one section of farmland and clear some unused bush or forest, which would then become "owned" insofar as it was occupied and used. The *use* farmland and grazing land could be rented or sold; Europeans, however, could not comprehend such definitions of land and land tenure, or they deliberately ignored them. The fact is, nonetheless, that Europeans traditionally considered land and almost everything else saleable—a commodity; so misunderstandings and deceptions occurred, resulting in the alienation of African lands to Europeans, especially in Central and East Africa.

As noted above, forest-dwelling agriculturalists often develop elaborate systems of government, with divine kingship (in this instance the king being considered the "owner" of the land, which he shares with his people), enfeoffment, and a highly specialized division of labor. Apart from "strangers" who may "beg" land, there are craftsmen and artisans who enter into a client relationship with the chief or family elders. The former usually reward the latter with their labor or produce in exchange for protection or guardianship.

RIVERAIN AREAS

Rivers and river valleys are important because flood-caused refertilization of the soil and the possibility of irrigation vastly increase the yield of crops. In such localities, people usually establish permanent societies based on agriculture. Because they are stable and in contact with other cultures (insofar as the watercourse is a convenient means of communication and transportation), these societies can develop extremely elaborate technologies and social structures. Perhaps the most outstanding example of technological development is in Egypt, with its huge stone pyramids and statuary, which certainly required stability of locale. Other great cultures developed along river courses, among them the cultures of the Tigris and Euphrates valley in the Middle East, the kingdoms of the Congo, the Sudanic empires of the upper Niger River, and the empires of the Ashanti, the Yoruba, and the Bini along the Guinea Coast.

In riverain agricultural societies, as distinct from savanna and forest societies, people orient their lives toward the river rather than the land. They develop various social, political, and religious structures from their source of livelihood, the river. For example, among the Nembe-Brass people of the Niger Delta, society is organized around the War Canoe or War Canoe House, a group consisting of a notable man and the offspring of three branches of his people: his own children, his relatives, and his servants and "slaves"—the latter branch arising from trade, a natural practice of riverain peoples. Religious belief and behavior, similarly, is affected by the environment: Whereas forest and savanna agriculturalists make sacrificial offerings to the earth and the sky as sources of spiritual and material well-being, and develop rain-making as an important skill, riverain people tend to worship river spirits. One important aspect of ancient Egyptian religion, for example, was the sacrifice to gods responsible for the annual rise and fall of the Nile, the Egyptian source of livelihood. The ceremonies of the Ijaw of the Niger delta make use of masks, costumes, and statuary of fish or fish-like personages. The important gods of the Kalabari people are the *owu,* the Water People, who control the water level and waves in the creeks and the movement and depths of shoals of fish.

Some riverain people have a symbiotic relation with agricultural forest or savanna dwellers. For example, the savanna peoples in the great armies of the ancient Mali hero, Sondjata, depended on the fishing tribe of the Somono for any crossing of the Niger River. More to the point, the Ijaw of southern Nigeria are fishermen who, like Somono, trade part of their catch for vegetables from such forest agriculturalists as the Igbo and Ibibio.

Impact of Ecology on Societal Maintenance

People make various adjustments because of their geographical environment. Broadly speaking, there are two sorts of subsistence economies in *rural* Terramedia: those of the savanna and, to a lesser extent, of the desert, which are livestock-raising economies; and those of the forest, savanna, and mountains which are predominantly gathering and agricultural economies. Riverain communities tend to be specialized gathering economies. Agriculture falls into two large general classes and one smaller class (i.e., agriculture practised along watercourse where there is sufficient rich soil and water). The two large classes of agriculture are savanna and forest. In the latter, root crops are by far the most important, and among the most widespread is cassava or manioc, which is made into meal (*gari*) or flour. The sliced and dried roots of the cassava are eaten in Zaire and other French-speaking areas where they are known as *cosettes*; in Ghana they are called *kokonte.* In most forest zones, however, the staple root crops (cassava, cocoyam, and yam) are boiled and pounded into *fufu,* which is eaten with highly peppered palm-oil soup. In the savanna country of Africa and the Middle East, grain crops tend to be most important in the diet of the people. Among these the most widespread are maize and millet, which are usually pounded into meal or flour, mixed with water, and baked as unleavened bread, or boiled as porridge or "mealie-mash." Distinctly related to these diets, which are notably short of animal protein, are problems of life expectancy and fertility. Until Terramedia can more successfully cope with its environment, both life expectancy and fertility will remain far below the levels of people in Europe and America.

Throughout most of Terramedia there is a steady population increase, in most instances (as will be explained later) traceable directly to the rise in the number of monogynous rather than polygynous marriages. This increase is not matched at all by increased food production, for by and large the older traditional methods of agriculture and livestock-raising are practised. A result of this situation is the fairly steady maintenance of quite low life expectancies. Lebanon (excluding Beirut) has an estimated annual population growth of 2.2%, but the land can support only 300,000 people, or about one-tenth the present population. Syria, on the other hand, has twice as much arable land as it needs, yet it is used so inefficiently under the present agricultural methods that it does not properly maintain even the present population of about 7 million. The average Egyptian's life expectancy is about 33 years, less than one-half that of the average American. One-fourth of all Egyptians die before they are one year old, whereas only about one-fourth of Americans die before the age of 52. In Mali, which is chiefly savanna country, the life expectancy is roughly 20 years; in the Central African Republic, which is forest and savanna country, about 32; and in Zanzibar, which is forest and plantation, it is 43. What helps in part to account for these differences are the variations in the percentages of persons who are urban and rural; rural populations invariably have a far lower life expectancy. Zanzibar, for example, is heavily urbanized, and many of the people are engaged in trade or plantation agriculture which brings in high profits; Mali, however, has a population which is largely rural, including many nomadic peoples. In Guinea, rural populations have an average life expectancy of 30 years, whereas urbanized people can expect on the average to live to be 35. When one discovers that much of Terramedia's population is rural (95% of the people in Uganda, for example, and 85% of Zambians), the low life expectancy figures can be understood more clearly.

Illustrating such differences among groups of people in the Republic of South Africa, for example, are the following statistics. If the person lives until the age of 5, he can expect to live until the age of 66 if he is European, to the age of 50 if he is Asian, to the age of 43 if he is Cape Colored, and to the age of 36 if he is Black African. Why do more urbanized people have greater life expectancy (for such is the case even in South Africa)? There are several answers. Urban dwellers are likely to eat better foods more often than rural people because the urbanized earn wages and are exposed to products from more than one agricultural locality. Eating better foods more often and having a better balanced diet can help to build one's resistance to disease. Urban dwellers are also more inclined to have a constant supply of water which in most instances is potable and free of disease-bearing substances. Thus they can maintain a relatively high degree of personal cleanliness and sanitation, especially during dry seasons when rural populations suffer adversely. Urban dwellers are also more likely to use preventive drugs and techniques, such as the daily or weekly prophylaxis against malaria, regular inoculations and vaccinations, and the like. Finally, the urbanized, separated from traditional religion and magic, are more likely to seek help from medical clinics and hospitals for illness in general, and for prenatal and postnatal care of mothers and infants.

It has long been known that polygyny—along with the typically lengthy lactation and nursing period (quite often the village African mother nurses a child for two and sometimes three years), and the generally poor diet, sanitary conditions, and medical methods—is a very inefficient means of producing large numbers of children per wife. Even under ideal health, sanitary, and dietary conditions, polygyny is inefficient because, as the number of wives increases, the man will be able to have sexual intercourse with each one less often; so the chances of his copulating with any given wife during the peak of her fertility period necessarily lessen.

Let us consider a monogynous case in which the man and wife have coitus every day except during her menstrual period. If both persons are in quite good health and enjoy optimum fertility, the chances are that in one month the wife will become pregnant or, because of the vagaries of ova and sperm even among the healthy, pregnancy will occur almost certainly within a two-month period. If a man has two wives, on the other hand, he will ordinarily follow some pattern of coitus with them—usually determined by custom and certainly to avoid jealousies, quarrels, and fighting. Because of the variation in women's cycles, with exceptional luck both his wives could become pregnant during the first month;[21] it is much more likely however, that one of the wives would become pregnant during the second month. Yet the pattern of coitus would be maintained until the woman conceives; one might, therefore, presume that by the third month she would become pregnant—bringing the husband during the fourth month into a monogynous relationship with the other wife until she, too, became pregnant. Hence for both wives to become pregnant would probably take five or six months. Finally, if a man has ten wives and follows the same coital pattern, and each wife has a four-day fertility period (which is rather high even for American women), he would have no more than 40% probable fertilizing contact, and in the case of each of those four women, during only one-fourth of her fertility period.

Conditions in Terramedia, however, are such that, instead of perfect health, diet, sanitation, and medical practices, one encounters all too often quite the opposite. Diet is sadly deficient in body-building proteins and often deficient in vitamins; sanitation is usually poor, and medical practices are inefficient. So, health in general and fertility in particular suffer greatly. Most African and Middle Eastern women suffer varying periods of infertility, sometimes lasting for months; and it is balanced by impotency in men. This pathology might explain why over 75% of the visitors to traditional religious shrines and healers are men and women suffering from one or another form of infertility.

The following facts further illustrate some of the differences among groups of people in the Republic of South Africa, relative to the pregnancies resulting in live births: Over 90% of white women deliver living babies, over 75% of Asian and Cape Colored women, and only 6% of Bantu-speaking or African women. The rate of population increase, accordingly, in the Republic is as follows:

Asians: (2.12%) Asians are usually monogynous in South Africa, and have a fairly good urban living standard.
Cape Colored: (2.03%) Colored are monogynous and have a generally good living standard.
Whites: (1.54%) Whites practise pregnancy-control and birth-control; they have the highest living standards and the highest rate of pregnancy per woman not deliberately preventing conception.
Black Africans: (1.45%) Africans have the lowest living standards, are often polygynous, and are the least educated.

In spite of the restrictions of traditions and the disruptive events of colonial rule, Terramedia has become part of a world community obsessed with controlling the forces of geography. It may be that the rank and file continue to accept physical phenomena as a supernatural ordination to which they must adapt, including the willingness to endure unanticipated consequences. Their leaders, however, are compelled (in keeping with their pride as modernists) to engage in scientism and modernism which result in wilfull alteration of the schemes of geography. Such activities, although as yet incapable of controlling precipitation and temperature, for example, have the ability to relieve environments of the consequences of unmanageable physical forces. Existing technology is capable of influencing resource reclamation and utilization, environmental reconstruction, and human mobility and fertility. Hence, even as culture continues to influence the capability of Terramedians to see, to comprehend, or to desire new challenges to the determining influences of geography, scientism and modernism are bound to gain in significance. Subject to variations in the speed and extent of such influence, lifestyles will alter and escape the constraints which geography has so far been able to impose.

NOTES

1. L. Dudley Stamp, *Africa, A Study in Tropical Development* (New York: John Wiley, 1953), pp. 41-43.
2. William R. Polk, *The United States and the Arab World* (Cambridge, MA: Harvard University Press, 1969), pp. 130-34.

3. See Don Peretz, *The Middle East Today* (New York: Holt, Rinehart and Winston, 1964), p. 5; and George H. T. Kimble, *Tropical Africa,* vol. 1. (New York: The Twentieth Century Fund, 1960), pp. 225-51.

4. See A. T. Grover, *Africa South of the Sahara* (London: Oxford University Press, 1967), pp. 257-59, and Polk, *Arab World,* pp. 4-15.

5. Harm J. de Blij, *A Geography of Subsaharan Africa* (Chicago: Rand McNally, 1964), pp. 36-38.

6. See Jacob M. Landau, *Man, State, and Society in the Contemporary Middle East* (New York: Praeger Publishers, 1972), pp. 245-311.

7. See Ajayi and Espie, *West African History,* pp. 113-30, and Maurice Gaudefroy-Demonbynes, *Muslim Institutions* (London: Allen and Unwin, 1950), pp. 13-46.

8. See Polk, *Arab World,* pp. 4-25; and Robert A. Lystad, *The African World* (New York: Praeger Publishers, 1965), pp. 113-30.

9. See John S. Mbiti, *African Religions and Philosophy* (New York: Praeger Publishers, 1969), pp. 6-57.

10. See Robin Hallett, *Africa Since 1875* (Ann Arbor: University of Michigan Press, 1974), pp. 42-68; and Daniel Lerner, *The Passing of Traditional Society* (Glencoe, IL: the Free Press, 1958), pp. 47-65.

11. See Colin Turnbull, *Man in Africa* (Garden City, NJ: Doubleday, Anchor Press, 1977), pp. 18-188.

12. See Philip K. Hitti, *The Arabs* (Chicago: Henry Regnery Company, 1956), pp. 9-20.

13. See H. A. R. Gibb and Harold Bowen, *Islamic Society and the West* (London: Oxford University Press, 1957); and Leonard Thompson, *African Societies in Southern Africa* (New York: Praeger Publishers, 1969).

14. See Richard Greenfield, *Ethiopia, a New Political History* (New York: Praeger Publishers, 1965), pp. 33-36.

15. Cf. Kenneth L. Little, *The Mende of Sierra Leone* (London: Routledge & Kegan Paul, 1951).

16. See Paul Riesman, "The Art of Life in a West African Community," *Journal of African Studies* (1975): 39-63.

17. Cf. Kenneth L. Little, *African Women in Towns* (London: Cambridge University Press, 1973), pp. 29-48; and Fatima Mernissi, *Beyond the Veil: Male-Female Dynamics in a Modern Muslim State* (Cambridge: Schenkman Publishing Company, 1975), pp. 81-97.

18. See William Bascom, *African Art in Cultural Perspective* (New York: W. W. North, 1973); and Franco Monti, *African Masks* (London: Paul Hamlyn, 1969).

19. Cf. Robert P. Armstrong, *The Affecting Presence* (Urbana: University of Illinois Press, 1971).

20. See Austin J. Shelton, *The Igbo-Ibala Borderland* (Albany: State University of New York Press, 1971); and Manfred Halpern, The *Politics of Social Change in the Middle East and North Africa* (Princeton: Princeton University Press, 1963), pp. 79-104.

21. While frequent pregnancies, if not child-bearing, would satisfy a cultural basis for personal esteem, one must wonder if such occurrences must not be discouraged in the light of declining infant mortality and food supply. Here is an example of culturally-motivated practice that runs counter to rationality, given changes in health and farming practices.

Chapter Four

A CHRONICLE OF DISSIPATED INDEPENDENCE

Terramedian Historiography

It ordinarily requires no deep insight for one to accept the existence of some kind of history—a chonology, analysis, and interpretation of significant events and personalities—for any society. After all, if a society exists, it must have had a past which could easily be recorded. What is left to argue about, then, is the authenticity of the historical data and the degree of objectivity guiding their analysis and interpretation.

An examination of Terramedian affairs indicates that one cannot in fact assume the acceptance of such views, for the contrary assumption prevailed in "respectable" quarters that the sub-Saharan area of Terramedia had no history—at least none worthy of serious assessment. In fact, the entire matter was usually dismissed simply by asserting that no history existed until the contact of sub-Saharan Africa with Europeans. Such an attitude was supported among Europeans by their ethnocentric argument that writing and literacy were importations into most of sub-Saharan Africa, and that there was no history before their introduction. Today, however, written records are no longer recognized as the *sin qua non* of a history. Furthermore, the subversion of evidence about African achievements as one means of rationalizing alien domination of Africa makes it vital not only to correct the various misconceptions and falsehoods about the true heritage of a people but to use all the tools available to the historian.

It should already be clear that the Middle East and North Africa, known always to have been in direct contact with the emergence of "civilization" and with the technique of writing, were never subjected to the abusive charge of being a "dark" continent without a history that was levelled at Africa below the Sahara. After all, although not often realized or asserted, the "Cradle of Civilization" with its elaborate cuneiforms and heiroglyphics included Egypt, which, in turn, had always been a part of Africa. One could also mention Ethiopic and Vai as further evidences of other writing techniques developed even farther away from the Fertile Crescent. Nevertheless, the fact remains that most of Black Africa has to be examined—so far as its ancient affairs were concerned—in terms of impressions recorded by outsiders or on the basis of other than written evidence. After all, writing ought not be the sole criterion for judging advancement and societal excellence.

Until relatively recently only written records received widespread acceptance among Westerners as the "proper" sources of historical data. It is true, of course, that some of the other sources had been recognized for their utility by certain groups of scientists, and that historiography dealing with any society prior to the advent of writing demanded their use. But written records have always enjoyed a preferred status among historians and others, even though for most of Terramedia such records project the impressions of outsiders in contrast to the in-group perspectives characteristic of oral tradition. The inevitable exaggerations and misinterpretations that result from such differences in orientation can be minimized by using both written and unwritten sources correlated with other sources of information such as archeology, linguistics, and serology.

Since the recent liberation of most Terramedian states from colonial rule, various researchers have argued that sub-Saharan Africa has always been a part of the general reaction of man to the challenge of living on earth. Roland Oliver and J.D. Fage, for example, have described succinctly the evolution of man in Africa and his development of various tools, artifacts, and modes of living—nomadic and sedentary—in response to environmental realities.[1] More and more, the charges that Africa is "backward" or a "dark continent" are irrelevant to the actual situation, for there is steadily more evidence that Africa was the original locale from which hand-using and thinking man dispersed and became biologically specialized in other parts of the world.[2] Indeed, the potential for distortion of testimony which is inherent in oral tradition, on the one hand, and the ethnocentric misrepresentation which has been all too common in written records, on the other hand, are being corrected, or at least modified, by the evidence of archeology and rational analysis of data. A review of the applicable sources follows.

ARCHEOLOGY

A relatively old discipline, archeology is a legitimate source of historical data. Some parts of Terramedia, especially the regions in the Shatt-al-Arab and Nile basins, have always received attention for their pyramids, highways, and food-producing techniques; but such recognition usually was intended to supplement claims of European achievements and to deny or to denigrate African contributions or achievements. For this reason, special attention must be given to the persistent work of Dr. Louis Leakey, which gradually won for the African sector of Terramedia the serious consideration it had never received from historians.[3]

Dr. Leakey and his wife labored for at least three decades before they were able to bring Africa back into the center of historical interest. Through patience, optimistic intuitiveness, and expert analysis of strata, their work in the Olduvai Gorge area of Lake Victoria (adjacent to both Kenya and Tanzania) resulted in the discovery of fossils and artifacts which were ultimately to indicate that Africa was the original habitat of the immediate ancestor of modern man, *Homo sapiens.* The discovery of *Zinjanthropus boisei* in 1959 aroused much speculation because of the age—close to two million years—and the manipulative ability of this hominid. Many people remained satisfied with the non-Negroid (Peking Man, Neanderthalensis, Cro-Magnon Man) and non-African evidence of man's original habitat, especially "man" who seemed to rely more on his brains and hands than on his teeth and his brawn. They argued that backward and stagnant Africa could certainly not have served as the evolutionary milieu of modern man. But the skeptics withdrew many of their arguments when, in 1964, Dr. Leakey made a still more impressive discovery, that of *Homo habilis.* No longer was Africa to be considered merely the habitat of a less-developed, "manlike" creature who moved out of Africa and became superior by developing a more efficient brain and relying less on his teeth; the evidence now pointed to man as such—*homo*—with an efficient brain and reliable hands with which to adapt and to develop as Homo sapiens both in Africa and outside of Africa. In contrast to the relatively young fossils of Europe and Asia, Africa's man appeared not fifty thousand years ago, but about two million years ago. Debates over man's origins and the authenticity and relevance of Leakey's discoveries continue; and as the examination of data continues, the added significance of the most recent contribution of Africa via Leakey must also be considered: the discovery in Olduvai Gorge (reported in January, 1967) of the most ancient of manlike fossils, *Kenyapithecus africanis,* reputed to be about twenty million years old. Equally significant are the Laetoli hominids of 3.6 million years discovered by Mary Leakey in 1978, and considered to be "in the direct line of man's ancestry."[4]

OTHER NONWRITTEN SOURCES

Archeology will continue to modify the contention that Africa's past was stagnant—a legacy of rationalizations for the transatlantic slave trade and colonialism. Important also are other sources of information about Africa's past. Rock paintings, for example, offer data for the historiographer, as does serology. In themselves such sources are of limited value; their importance lies in their contribution to clarifying of data derived from other sources. Ethnobotany, too, is an important source: It is an attempt to determine the origins and diffusion of cultivated plants to relate African endeavor—along with dated tools—to other agrarian and industrial civilizations. Still another sources is linguistics, which seeks to determine commonalities in the structure of languages despite the observable environmental separation of peoples. Similarities in linguistic structure may well suggest directions and trends in the historical migration of peoples and their artifacts and cultures. Further enlightenment can be provided by still another source—ethnology, the interpretation of varying cultural and societal organizations, whether proximate or distant from one another.

Although an aspect of both linguistics and ethnology, oral tradition deserves special consideration. This source seems unimportant to people who emphasize written records and who view memory as a relatively inferior tool for preserving historical data. But it is important to note that, among a people without writing, such a technique of preserving the group's heritage has always been treated quite seriously. Because of the potential for distortion and loss of data, most illiterate societies found it advantageous to institutionalize the role of the verbal historian, like the *griot* among the Malinke-speaking and related peoples of West Africa.[5] Many are the occasions, such as the coronation of a king, election campaigns, rituals marking *rites de passage,* funerals, and recreational and economic activities, when segments of the heritage are recounted—in song, in poetry, in dance, in mimicry, and in other forms of expression.

WRITTEN SOURCES

Although there are some that are not very reliable, the availability of written records has enhanced—along with the sources aforementioned—Terramedian historiography. The fact of early contact between the Middle

East and the eastern coast of Africa can be deduced from a navigational handbook, The Periplus of the Erythrean Sea, written probably around 100 A.D. There are many other records prepared by Greeks, Romans, Arabs and, subsequently, by Portuguese and other Europeans.[6] Much intensive and extensive analysis of the many types of written records still needs to be done, but it is satisfying to note that scholars from many parts of the world—including Terramedian scholars—are currently engaged in using all possible sources, including nonwritten ones, to develop as accurate a history of Terramedia as possible.

While there is still much reconstructing to do, it is now possible to trace—on the basis of presently available data derived from various sources—the history of Terramedia to provide background necessary for the proper understanding of subsequent and contemporary developments. Until the fifteenth century, Terramedia stood equal to, and in some respects superior to, other major political, economic, and cultural centers of the world. Until then, many outsiders recognized the quality of Terramedian social and religious systems, as well as Terramedian commerce and military efficiency. Historical records show a succession of dynasties, some emerging indigenously and others invading from outside Terramedia, each of them manifesting varying weaknesses and strengths in their efforts to assert their dominance over others. Responsibilities and privileges during the period prior to the fifteenth century were sometimes restricted on the basis of ethnic or religious lines—as they were also in Europe and in Asia—but never was there a suggestion of any inherent and permanent superiority of one race or religion over all others. Accordingly, the fact that the Arabian peninsula peoples possessed clan or tribal organization before the advent of Islam did not preclude their having the prestige of an imperial power later on; nor did the relative skin darkness of the Arab imperialists prevent others, who were lighter but less powerful, from recognizing Arab power and from subsequently accepting second-class citizenship and the preferential device of "capitulations" or monopolistic concessions. In like manner, it can be said that the powerful city-states and empires which existed throughout Africa before the fifteenth century did not prevent their rulers from winning the respect of outsiders; nor were these political units unwilling to accept rules designed to define and guide the relation among those with power and those with less power and influence.

Preconditions of the Transatlantic Slave Trade

Highly and efficiently organized political entities existed long before the European subjugation of Terramedia. The Mongols, Hebrews, Assyrians, Persians, Egyptians, Greeks, and Romans have been placed historically in Terramedia; but very seldom has it been pointed out that great empires strictly indigenous to Africa were equally real and historical. For example, records now indicate that it was not necessarily Egyptian, Greek, or Roman civilization which brought iron technology and other forms of metallurgy to Africa, but that these, as well as agriculture and pastoralism, could have been indigenous developments. It is no longer adequate, therefore, to talk merely about the greatness of the Egyptian pharaohs or of the military genius of Alexander the Great as if these developments were unique; a sounder evaluation of ancient history demands proper coverage of the power and achievements of the kingdoms of Kush and Axum located in the general vicinity of present-day Sudan and Ethiopia. Only then can one begin to recognize that Africans had proved their ability to govern and to create long before Europeans were able to assert a superiority in scientific technology and modernization. It is unimportant to determine how black or brown or white the Kushites and Axumites were, or whether in their subsequent dispersal they in fact brought better technology and government to the sub-Saharan African. What is significant is that, at least as early as 100 A.D. and long before the Dark Ages which characterized precivilized Western Europe, people native to Africa–Africans–ruled themselves, as well as others who indirectly or directly came under their influence.

But there were also other indigenous kingdoms and empires of great prominence during this ancient period. Ghana, Mali, and Songhai, successively from 300 A.D. to about 1500 A.D., were the most powerful regulators of the commerce connecting Western Africa with North Africa, Europe, and Arabia. Although the main items were gold from the south in exchange for salt from the north, there were other commercial items such as ivory, books, crops, horses, swords, slaves, textiles, trinkets, and other implements and artifacts. The effectiveness and duration of each of these empires were, of course, related to the degree of control over commerce (especially control over the sources of gold and of salt), the efficiency and loyalty of provincial governors and other officials, and the changing loyalty of subjects to a central government or to local or ethnic groups. The grandeur of these early African empires, and the basis of their success, can be seen in summaries by modern scholars of accounts by chroniclers of the period. Here, in J. D. Fage's paraphrase, are the observations of al-Masudi:

> The greatness of Ghana seems to have stemmed from the commercial advantages of its position on the borders of the desert in the extreme north of the habitable area of the western Sudan. North African merchants who settled at Ghana could control the Sudanese trade in gold

> and slaves and exchange these commodities for the goods brought to Ghana by the Caravans from Morocco. These goods—salt, copper, dried fruits, and cowries—were then distributed throughout the Sudan. The gold came mainly from Wangara, a district which was just outside the political control of Ghana, where it was mined by the Mandingo natives and exchanged by them for the salt and manufactures brought from Ghana. This trade was conducted by a process of dumb barter usually known as 'silent trade.' The merchants from Ghana would deposit their wares on the banks of a certain river and then retire out of sight. The gold-miners would then appear and, if they wanted the goods offered, would place by them what they considered to be a fair amount of gold-dust. They in their turn would then retire, whereupon the traders would reappear and, if satisfied by the amount of gold offered, would take it and go. If they were not satisfied, they would leave it and again withdraw, hoping that more gold would be forthcoming.[7]

Another chronicler, al-Bakri, described the court of Ghana in 1067 A.D., when the empire was at the height of its prosperity and extended from the Lake Debo area to central Senegal:

> The city of Ghana consists of two towns situated on a plain. One of these towns is inhabited by Muslims. It is large and possesses a dozen mosques, one being for the Friday prayer, and each having imams, muezzins and salaried reciters of the Koran. There are jurisconsuls and scholars. Around the town are sweet wells, which they use for drinking and for cultivating vegetables. The royal city . . . is six miles away, and the area between the two towns is covered with habitations. Their houses are constructed of stone and acacia wood. The king has a palace with conical huts [around], surrounded by a fence like a wall. In the king's town, not far from the royal court, is a mosque for the use of Muslims who visit the king on missions. . . . The interpreters of the king are Muslims, as are his treasurer and the majority of his ministers. . . . Around the royal town are domed dwellings, woods and copses where live their sorcerers, those in charge of their religious cults. There are also their idols and their kings' tombs. . . . When the king dies they construct a large dome of wood over the burial place. . . . They put [into the grave] the king's ornaments and arms, his eating and drinking vessels, food and drink, and bring in those people who used to serve his food and drink. Then the dome's entrance is locked.[8]

Ibn Battuta visited the Empire of Mali in the 14th Century during the reign of Mansa Sulaiman:

> On certain days the sultan holds audiences in the palace yard, where there is a platform under a tree. . . . It is carpeted with silk and has

> cushions placed on it. [Over it] is raised the umbrella, which is a sort of pavillion made of silk, surmounted by a bird in gold, about the size of a falcon. The sultan comes out of a door in a corner of the palace, carrying a bow in his hand and a quiver on his back. On his head he has a golden skull-cap, bound with a gold band which has narrow ends shaped like knives, more than a span in length. His usual dress is a velvety red tunic, made of . . . European fabrics. . . . The sultan is preceded by his musicians, who carry gold and silver [guitars] and behind him come three hundred armed slaves. He walks in a leisurely fashion, affecting a very slow movement, and even stops from time to time. . . . As he takes his seat the drums, trumpets, and bugles are sounded. Three slaves go out at a run to summon the sovereign's deputy and the military commanders, who enter and sit down. Two saddled and bridled horses are brought, along with two goats, which they hold to serve as a protection against the evil eye. [The interpreter] stands at the gate and the rest of the people remain in the street, under the trees.
>
> They are seldom unjust, and have a great abhorrence of injustice. . . . Their sultan shows no mercy to anyone who is guilty of the least act of it. There is complete security in their country. Neither traveller nor inhabitant in it has anything to fear from robbers or men of violence. They do not confiscate the property of any white man who dies in their country, even if it be uncounted wealth. On the contrary, they give it to the charge of some trustworthy person among the whites, until the rightful heir takes possession of it. They are careful to observe the hours of prayer, and assiduous in attending them in congregations, and in bringing up their children to them. On Fridays, if a man does not go early to mosque, he cannot find a corner to pray in, on account of the crowd.[9]

Although it is for the kingdoms of the Sudan and the early Arab dynasties that the most evidence exists to document their grandeur and efficiently centralized administrations, one can infer that other kingdoms—about which much evidence is lacking or which were in their decline when Arab or European observers appeared—were probably similarly structured and equally affluent and influential in their respective areas. Perhaps, in time, evidence will be discovered that will enable us to assess better the nature of the political and social organization among the ancient Luanda or the domain of the ManiKongo, where control was partially effected by the distribution of the main medium of economic exchange—cowrie shells. Conceivably, a correlation of ethnology and ethnobotany, as well as archeology, might in the future indicate more clearly both the relationships which existed among the kingdoms that controlled the area from the Congo to the East African coast and the true extent of the indigenous achievement that is merely suggested by the ruins of Great Zimbabawe in the region of the Monomotapa (in present-day Rhodesia). In short, while understanding that alien Arabs dominated Zanzibar, Kilwa, Sofala, and other communities along the Indian Ocean by 600 A.D., there is no reason to doubt that indigenous centers of power operated in the interior of Africa and that there was sufficient continuity of such power to link it with that of Chief Lobengula and the Ndebele, who were encountered by the Pioneer Column of Cecil Rhodes in the late nineteenth century.[10]

In all the kingdoms and empires, survival of the rulers and control over their subjects, as well as over those who threatened their power, were related substantially to the administrative machinery and ability to secure revenue for operating expenses and programs. Where resources were plentiful and commerce was profitable, an unjust monarch was not readily rebuffed. Furthermore, rulership was often given the sanction of spiritual representation which, in turn, was further protected by the common system of potential hostages in the central administration and by fiefdom. On the other hand, there is a limit to the oppression and greed which even docile subjects can endure, and there were provisions for removing an improper ruler, short of social revolution, by sanctioned ritual murder. Here, again, one must not lose sight of the historical and customary continuity which might justify the murder of a Temne ruler, for example: since the slain ruler's "time might have been accelerated," his head was preserved to sit constantly at the "right hand" of his successor to guide him in his deliberations affecting the welfare of his people and subjects. The complex manner in which necessary revenue was gathered is described as follows by Henri Labouret:

> Everywhere their subjects had to give up a portion of their crops and of their herds. Then, too, there was a tax on the exploitation of salt, gold, and copper mines, and a tariff on goods entering or leaving the country. In addition, the king had all the spoils of war and the various fines and confiscations that he ordered. . . . The most frequent source of revenue was tithes on agricultural produce and livestock; that on produce fell heavily on millet. A tenth of the revenue stayed with the collector; the sheikh kept a fifth; a third of the remainder went to the district chief, and another third to the upkeep of the soldiery; the last third was used for public relief. As to livestock, the king exacted one bull out of every thirty, one cow out of every forty, one sheep out of every forty, and one goat out of every hundred. After deducting the collector's share, this tax was used in principle solely to assist the poor, to ransom prisoners, and to indemnify the creditors of bankrupts.[11]

Extant records indicate many similarities among the various kingdoms and empires of the early period, whether they were located in Africa proper or in the Arabian penisula. Political and social organizations were similar, with a pronounced division of the population into a ruling elite, the learned and the military specialists, ordinary citizens, peasants, aliens and minority groups, and slaves. In all of them, power was derived from commerce and military might, and minimally related to an all-embracing cultural ethos or religion.[12] This similarity was to be modified significantly, however, after Muhammed successfully developed the expansive and tolerant theocracy of Islam–a religion which subsequently became a vehicle for Arab imperialism and a basis for the growth of closer ties between Africa and the Middle East. Because of Islam, the Arab and Levantine sectors of Terramedia were able to retain a prestigious position in world commerce and politics, long after sub-Saharan Africa had been deprived of its grandeur by the slave trade and by colonialism–activities in which, in fact, the Arabs were to become the accomplices of European exploiters. How the change in destiny occurred for areas which had hitherto been so similar, and which were to become similar victims of European colonialism, can perhaps be clarified by an overview of the history following the ascendancy of Islam, and the emergence of empires created by this religion.

It seems bewildering that an illiterate such as Muhammed could have left an imprint of such significance upon so many people for so long. He was, of course, highly intelligent and had learned much from the Jews at Medina. Yet the fact remains that, from the sometimes epileptic experiences of a man of no social prominence in his own society, a religion and a system of regulations for all forms of human relationship emerged. It can be postulated that the harshness of a desert environment, which subjected men to the whims of nature and intimated the need for blind allegiance to spiritual forces and their dictates, contributed to Muhammad's success–as had also been the case with the religious "messengers" of Judaism and of Christianity.

Ahmed has said that Islam brought about a social transformation by introducing a psychological foundation of religious belief in monotheism into a tribal society organized around the principle of kinship and tribal laws of pre-Islamic times: "Its immediate purpose was not to create merely a political organization. Islam came to condition the patterns of thinking and actions of the people in order to fashion them into a new social unity." Others, however, suggest that the success of Islam and its ultimate diffusion derived from its early interest–psychologically necessary for Muhammed, who had been born of lowly origins in a milieu that valued aristocratic origins–in promoting social levelling. Levy, for example, has pointed out that, in Muhammad's time, the factor of birth was of paramount importance to any claim of authority. The major test of nobility was noble birth, and persons without impeccable genealogy were relegated to the humbler social classes and were compelled to engage in occupations marking them as inferiors. Accordingly,

> When the Prophet Muhammed first proclaimed his new dispensation . . . his lowly origin, coupled with his humble occupation as a camel-driver, put a serious obstacle in the way of his success. His primary task was that of convincing his meager following—made up largely of humbler members of society—that the new faith was to make them the equals, if not the superiors, of the unbelievers who had hitherto been regarded with awe as the aristocracy.[13]

Despite this suggestion of democratic intent, the early state established at Medina by Muhammed revealed evidence of a stratified society, with rights and obligations paralleling such stratification. Possibly Muhammad himself became an unconscious victim of the force of his own socialization and of custom. On the other hand, the need to promote loyalty and to reward such loyalty possibly made the establishment of a societal hierarchy unnecessary—as distinct from the broad division of mankind into believers and nonbelievers. Thus the subsequent hierarchy of sultan or caliph downward to provincial governors, tax-collectors, viziers, feudal landowners, peasants, and slaves found its legitimacy and precursor in the *de facto* (if not initially *de jure*) existence of a rigid system of social stratification. During the first decade of Islam, for example, a distinction existed between the "believers of Arab origin" and the *mawali,* or "converts of non-Arab stock." Even within these two categories, there was a difference in prestige between Arabs who belonged to Muhammad's tribe, the *Quraysh,* and the *Muhajirun* or people of other tribes. As for the non-Arabs, scholars, theologians, and jurists were accorded higher status than ordinary merchants and Negroes, who were placed at the bottom of the social hierarchy. Furthermore, the factionalism and the emergence of numerous sects in Islam derived from the prior recognition of varying prestige accorded different types of believers. A clear distinction, for example, subsequently prevailed among the *alids* or *sayids,* the descendants of Muhammad's son-in-law, 'Ali; the *Hashimites,* the descendants of Muhammad's grandfather, Hashim; the *ansar,* or "helpers" who were related to the original converts at Medina; and the *Zaids,* those descended from the prophet's daughter.

This part of our historical survey begins with the era of Muhammad, which lasted from 622 to 632 A.D., during which time a man who had been forced to flee his native community (hence the significance of the *hijra*) succeeded in establishing himself as a politician and administrator in Medina, as well as a man to be reckoned with by the power structure of

Mecca which had initially rejected him. The regime which Muhammed established in Medina depended on banditry and warfare, common practices of the day among people whose loyalty was to their clan or tribe, to promote the community. It must be noted, however, that Muhammad had a flexible force for uniting tribes and clans, the *umma*; and with the added incentive of a comprehensive apostolic religion which transcended tribal boundaries, expansion was possible. This was, in fact, what happened as more previously autonomous communities came under the spell of Islam and the charisma of Muhammad.

Arab imperialism, which resulted in the subjugation of parts of Africa, Asia, and Europe by 900 A.D., started during this period of confederation, and was made possible by Islam and its related military fervor. While territorial gains were minimal (and were restricted to the commercial environment of Mecca and Medina), this period contributed to the diffusion of tolerance and the protection of women's rights. Credit must be given to the genius of Muhammad whereby the conservative tendency of custom was treated with care to promote reforms of justice and equality. The provision whereby marriage became a contract between consenting parties was an improvement over a situation in which the woman was free to exercise little or no opinion; so too was the modification of polygyny and the widespread practice of very short "temporary marriages" which resulted in the imposition of a limit of four free wives. Here again prudence seemed to dictate that outright hostility could be prevented by allowing a limitless number of concubines who lacked the status and rights of wives.

The Golden Age of Islam and an Arab empire were not realized, however, until after Muhammad's death. There was a period of dissension and divided loyalty, an inevitable occurrence in view of Muhammad's great charisma and the absence of clearly defined regulations. Muhammad could get away with slight inconsistencies in his conduct and utterances, such as having more than the stipulated number of wives and reporting contradictory revelations. The successors in leadership, especially during the period of the *Rashidun* or "rightly-guided ones" (Abu Bakr, 'Uthman, and 'Ali) from 632 to 661, had a more difficult time explaining contradictions in the *Qur'an* and *hadith*. Despite such difficulties, Islam continued to grow within Arabia until the Umayyad dynasty (661-750) extended it into Europe and Asia. After the administrative capital was transferred to Damascus, the question of a successor which had been handled by election during the era of the Rashidum, was given a hereditary flavor by Muawiyah, the first Umayyad caliph, who nominated his own son. Under the Umayyads, with Islam as a vehicle, the empire extended into central Asia, into Europe, and across North Africa. Other Umayyad caliphs, Abd-al-Malik and his son, al-Walid, had conquered Spain and penetrated into France by 715, gaining, as has been noted by Hitti, "a hundred years after Muhammad's death . . . an empire greater than the Roman at its height."

In *An Introduction to Islamic Law*, Schact has observed that, although the Umayyads developed several important features of Islamic worship, their main concern was with political administration, in which they represented bureaucracy and order as distinct from Bedouin individualism and anarchy.[14] The Umayyads concentrated on warring against Byzantium and other enemies, and on collecting tribute and taxes. They restricted legacies to one-third of the estate, the other two-thirds going into the public treasury. They also created *qadis,* or Islamic judges, whose function was suited to the increasing urbanization of the Arabs under Umayyad rule.

The impressive Umayyad record did not, however, save the dynasty from decay; indeed, rivalry and greed among relatives were never eliminated, but the time finally came when usurpation of power by outsiders—although members of the *umma*—became imminent. It has been suggested that because "the last of the thirteen successors of Muawiyah were more interested in women, wine and chase than in state affairs," a new dynasty, the Abbasid, replaced the Umayyads in 750, with an administrative capital installed in the city of Baghdad in Iraq. Hitti described the usurpation of power as follows:

> The Abbasid series started with al-Saffah . . . whose general desecrated the caliphal tombs in Damascus by exhuming their contents, invited eighty Umayyad princes to a banquet near Jaffa and in the course of the feast had them all cut down. But the real founder of the dynasty was his brother al-Mansur (c. 754-775), builder of Baghdad and ancestor of the thirty-six caliphs who succeeded him. This was the longest-lived caliphate (750-1258). . . . Unlike the Damascus caliphs, those of Baghdad were Persian oriented. Persian vizirs, wives and wines became conspicuous in court. They looked more eastward than westward. . . . Under al-Rashid (786-809) . . . and his son al-Mamun (813-833), the Abbasid state reached the plateau of its might and influence. . . . With more fiction than fact the *Arabian Nights* have immoralized the splendor, luxury and intellectual attainment of the period.[15]

Although the Abbasids had quite a long reign and accomplished much—especially in systematizing the *Shari'a* and in expanding the areas of human relationships to be regulated by the state—their emphasis on centralization and greater bureaucratization in administration contributed importantly to the ultimate decline of their empire. Partly because they incorporated into central administration more Persians and Turks and partly because of the unwieldy size of the Empire, the Abbasids lost authority and influence. During the Abbasid period, for example, there occurred a reassertion of Umayyad sentiment in Spain and that province's resultant autonomy and freedom from control by Baghdad soon became an example for other provinces. It was only a matter of time before a strong rival regime of the Fatimids operated out of Cairo, and soon the Baghdad caliphate itself became merely a puppet for promoting the vested interests of the Seljuk Turks, who had gradually worked their way into positions of absolute power in the central administration. In fact, Tughril Bey, a Seljuk Turk, became "sultan" in 1058, and the complete usurpation of Abbasid authority resulted from the successful overthrow of the puppet dynasty by the Mongol Turks in 1258, under the leadership of Hulagu, who had the courtiers massacred along with their last caliph, al-Mustasim. Continuing disintegration of the Empire followed until the emergence of Ottoman Turk domination, which shifted the center of influence farther north and out of Terramedia, to Constantinople, in 1453.

Several factors contributed to the rise and to the decline of the Arab Empire. Religious and military factors are certainly important, but so too are technology and administrative reform. A revolution of rising expectations resulted from increasing travel, urbanism, and heterogeneity, which had contributed to a sense of wider identity. While these factors—including the development of wider loyalties—made change easier to effect, they also resulted in certain negative tendencies, particularly in the modes of replacement of one regime by another. Among these negative tendencies contributing to the decline of the Arab Empire are the following: the weakening effect of warfare; factionalism in administration; religious schism; corruption in state operations (particularly); accelerated secularism; and the decline of the caliphate's authority.

During its existence the Arab Empire made a number of contributions to human civilization. It made a strong impact on the non-Arab world, particularly in the spread of Islam to such disparate parts of the earth as China, Southeast Asia, Africa, and Europe. It also promoted the significant diffusion of Arabic as a language denoting religious and cultural sophistication. Furthermore, the Empire provided a synthesis and diffusion of disparate knowledge ranging from medicine and mathematics to logic and philosophy, while encouraging religion to serve as a basis for the integration and assimilation of peoples and ideas. Through the toleration of pluralism and the recognition of achievement over ascription, successful multiethnic nationalism was established; through a system of capitulation a type of diplomacy and monopoly was created; a comprehensive system of taxation and a bureaucracy for the efficient administration of an empire were established; and an extensive and efficient national militia was created.

But while North Africa and Arabia were gaining in influence and affluence, the glorious heritage and splendor of sub-Saharan Africa were being corroded under the consequences of the Portuguese grand design which began in the middle of the fifteenth century. Strengthening the possibility of achieving its mercantile and imperial interests, Portugal—and subsequent European incursors—could count on such other factors as: the fragmentation of centralized kingdoms; acquisition of fire-arms by subordinate vassals; shift in the locus of taxing authority and power; widespread feeling of restlessness and communal insecurity; acquisition of prisoners of war by communities with limited food supply; conflict between the client and chattel notions of slavery; and the temptation of European manufactured goods and luxury items.

NOTES

1. Roland Oliver and J. D. Fage, *A Short History of Africa* (London: Collings, 1974).
2. Turnbull, *Man in Africa.*
3. See Hallett, *Africa to 1875* (Ann Arbor: University of Michigan Press, 1970), pp. 35-37, and L.S.B. Leakey, *Olduvai Gorge,* 3 vols. (London: Cambridge University Press, 1971).
4. Mary D. Leakey, "Footprints in the Ashes of Time," *National Geographic* (April, 1979):450-456.
5. See, for example, Alex Haley, *Roots* (New York: Dell Publishing Company, 1977), pp. 714-20.
6. See Hallett, *Africa to 1875,* p. 227.
7. J. D. Fage, *An Introduction to the History of West Africa* (London: Cambridge University Press, 1962), p. 20.
8. J. F. Ade Ajayi and Michael Crowder, *History of West Africa,* 2 vols. (London: Longman Group, 1971), 1:126-27.
9. Ibn Battuta, *Travels in Asia and Africa.* (London: Routledge & Kegan Paul, 1929), pp. 326-30.
10. See Frank Clements, *Rhodesia* (New York: Praeger Publishers, 1969), and H.A.C. Cairns, *The Clash of Cultures* (New York: Walker & Company, 1962), pp. 27-29.
11. Henri Labouret, *Africa Before the White Man* (New York: Walker & Company, 1962), pp. 27-29.
12. See Basil Davidson, *The African Genius* (Boston: Little, Brown, 1969), pp. 67-203.
13. Reuben Levy, *The Social Structure of Islam* (London: Cambridge University Press, 1962), p. 54.
14. Joseph Schacht, *An Introduction to Islamic Law* (London: Oxford University Press, 1964), pp. 24-27.
15. Philip K. Hitti, *Islam and the West* (Princeton: Van Nostrand, 1962), p. 30.

Chapter Five

FROM ENSLAVEMENT TO COLONIALISM

The Influence of Portugal's Grand Design

We have seen that the peoples of Terramedia before the coming of the Europeans were quite capable of managing their own affairs through their own institutions. Naturally, as in all human societies, there were cultural borrowings, including the use of foreigners in administration and the incorporation of some alien ideas and values into the body of traditional beliefs and practices. Ultimately, the Terramedian posture of equality with—in some instances, a notion of superiority to—other national groups was destroyed, partly because of internal friction and partly because of the undermining influence of Europeans. In the Arab sector, there occurred a usurpation of power by the Ottoman Turks who (despite such appearances of indigenous identity as their adoption of Islam) were, in fact, outsiders and imperialists. By the middle of the 15th Century, a solid foundation had been established that would lead to the rise of Western Europe and the Ottoman Empire as world powers, and, subsequently to the total subjugation of the entire Terramedian area.

Outstanding in its impact on sub-Saharan Africa especially, but also on Terramedia in general, was the Portuguese "Grand Design" to bypass the Middle Eastern caravan trade routes and thereby gain for Portugal a lion's share of the commerce of the period. Until this design was implemented around the middle of the 15th Century, Portugal—along with other European countries—had been forced to pay tributes and tolls to operate caravans passing through lands controlled by African, Arab, and Turkish sovereigns. Even the European desire for gold, ivory, and other commodities was satisfied primarily along the lines defined by these sovereigns or their agents. By relying on ships and relatively sophisticated navigational techniques, however, Portugal succeeded (as would other European nations in turn) in circumventing the important land routes to and from Asia, and, in the course of such circumvention, discovered new trade possibilities on the Atlantic coast of Africa. By the end of the fifteenth century, Portugal had established itself as the first colonial power in Angola, and had developed trade so effectively along the African coast, particularly the Guinea Coast, that it drew revenues away from the various centralized African governments (for example, those of the Western Sudan). These, of course, were revenues, including taxes, from which the African governments had derived their power and influence.

It could be argued that the change in Terramedian destiny was an accident of history, that only a fascination for the unknown led to the navigational adventure of Prince Henry and his supporters. It could also be argued that religious zeal, strengthened by such legends as that of Prester John—a supposedly rich Christian King in the African hinterland—encouraged the Portuguese activity, or that a traditional social provision for the existence of a slave class which (from the European point of view) could be buttressed by racial visibility, made Portuguese involvement in the slave trade inevitable. Whatever the motives and reasons, and there were probably many of them, the fact remains that the early 16th Century saw most of coastal Terramedia, with few exceptions and in spite of sporadic resistance, subject to manipulation and domination, no longer by its indigenous rulers as heretofore but by foreigners. Furthermore, the highly centralized kingdoms and empires had almost given way to numerous smaller and less powerful city-states, such as the Hausa kingdoms, the city-states of the Niger Delta, and the city-states of coastal East Africa such as Patê.

Integrally linked with the ability of aliens to control developments was the promotion of activities which were in the interest of those aliens. The promise of wealth in the newly discovered Americas, the exploitation of which it was felt could be better advanced by cheap, "biologically-equipped" Negroes, led to the extension of the limited purchase of available African slaves for domestic and menial labor in Europe to a volume which could satisfy the American demand for field hands. It is, of course, true that trade in slaves had been established in trans-Saharan commerce, and that it extended to India and China as well as to Europe and the Levant; but until the Portuguese, Nuno Tristão and Gonzales, took their first dozen slaves from Cape Blanc in 1441, the volume of the traffic and the participation of Europeans in it can be considered quite minimal.[1] By the early sixteenth century, however, there was a significant increase both in volume of slaves and in the extent of direct involvement by Europeans.[2]

Among the causes of such changes can be listed the following: a manifest desire by the Roman Catholic Church to "save the heathen soul"; the demand by Europeans to satisfy their agricultural and domestic needs; the plea in 1502 by Bishop Bartolome de las Casas that Africans would prove more efficient than the Indians, who could not stand the plantation work for which they had been forcefully recruited (and who, furthermore, being native to the American territories in which they were enslaved, found it somewhat easier to remain free if they could manage to escape); the legitimization of trade in human cargo through the granting of licenses by Spanish kings and, subsequently, through the chartering of companies for such profitable and "prestigious" undertakings by other European rulers; the highly lucrative nature of the trade, which served as an attraction for more investment and competition; the favorable winds and currents across the Atlantic Ocean which afforded speed and minimal difficulty even for sailing ships; and the availability of grain and other food crops which could provide sustenance on the long voyage. All of these factors encouraged, first, a monopoly by the Portuguese and Spaniards during the fifteenth and sixteenth centuries, and, subsequently, the increased participation during the seventeenth century by the British, Dutch, French, and the Swedes. In short, the slave trade was a significant dimension of the great Atlantic migration:

> Its demographic importance is sometimes obscured by the even more massive movement of Europeans in the nineteenth and twentieth centuries. Nevertheless, for 300 years more Africans than Europeans crossed the Atlantic each year. This migration was not merely important for its demographic results; it also lay at the heart of a wide net of commerce and production that touched every shore of the Atlantic basin. This economic complex, sometimes called the South Atlantic System, centred on the production of tropical staples in Brazil, the Caribbean, and southern North America. Even though it was divided into competing national spheres, each under the separate rule of a European power, the patterns of society and economy had much in common. The system's influence reached far beyond the tropical plantations themselves—to Africa for labour, to Europe for managerial staff and commercial direction, to northern North America for timber, food, and shipping, and to mainland South America for monetary silver.[3]

For the British, involvement in the slave trade—especially after securing the coveted Asiento in 1713 which granted a monopoly in the shipment of slaves to the domains of Spain—brought a mixture of economic, social, and legal consequences. Wealth and national prestige were enhanced, but at the expense of impugning the sense of justice and charity which had influenced British values since the Magna Carta of 1215. Through the stimulus and example of naval captains, plantation owners, financiers, esteemed jurists, artists, and royalty itself, Britain became a society in which owning a slave conferred prestige while enhancing wealth. "Upright" Britain became the scene of announcements and activities as unjust and uncharitable as would have been the case in slave-owning Baltimore, Charleston, Kingston, or Petersburg: "Mr. David Lisle . . . had for whatever reason beaten his slave Jonathan Strong . . . so savagely that his head had become swollen, a disorder had fallen on his eyes, he was becoming nearly blind, and was so weak and affected by lameness in both feet that he could hardly walk."[4] Despite such inhumanity, however, Mr. Lisle had no hesitation in pursuing his legal claim to Jonathan Strong several months later, since—with the assistance of others—the slave had "once more become sleek and strong."

The Slave Trade and Its Consequences

What, then, was the nature of this new kind of voluminous traffic in human beings? As developed by the Europeans, the slave trade was a brutal and degrading, culture-shattering business. As the antislaver William Baikie much later observed, one must wonder why the poor African should have been selected as the victim of the cupidity of his brother man. As we have seen, this was due to a combination of reasons, among which is the fact that slavery was not unknown to the Africans; it was perfectly natural for the first contacted Africans to have sold some slaves to the interested Europeans, and from this point onward the practice grew almost uncontrollably.

The process of enslavement itself was peculiarly structured (not necessarily consciously) to develop a profound state of shock in the mind of the slave, as Stanley Elkins has pointed out clearly in his study of slavery.[5] Most of the slaves were taken by Africans in wars and surprise raids upon enemy villages, hence rank, titles, and other status symbols were no guarantee of security; and as captives, all were reduced to the same level. There was, of course, a desire for quality, which was reflected in the price per individual slave, which ranged from about \$15 to \$60, with the possibility of about 60% or more profit on one's investment. At the wholesale markets the sorting began:

> Those which are approved as good are set on one side; and the lame or faulty are set by as Invalides, which are here called Mackrons. These are such as are above five and thirty years old, or are maimed in the Arms, Legs, Hands or Feet, have lost a Tooth, are grey-haired, or have Films over their Eyes; as well as all those which are affected with any Venereal Distemper, or with several other Diseases.
>
> The Invalides and the Maimed being thrown out, as I have told you, the remainder are numbred, and it is entred who delivered them. In the mean while a burning Iron, with the Arms or name of the Companies, lyes in the Fire; with which ours are marked on the Breast.
>
> This is done that we may distinguish them from the Slaves of the English, French or others; (which are also marked with their Mark) and to prevent the Negroes exchanging them for worse; at which they have a good Hand.
>
> I doubt not but this Trade seems very barbarous to you, but since it is followed by meer necessity it must go on; but we take all possible care that they are not burned too hard, especially the Women, who are more tender than the Men.[6]

That slavers could perceive no cruelty or wrong in their acts may perhaps have been due to their connection with priests and religious agencies engaged simultaneously in the saving of heathen souls, on the one hand, and to their connection with indigenous chiefs to whom the slaves were prisoners and enemies, on the other. Slaves, indeed, were usually baptized in batches by a priest prior to embarkation, so that if the ships were lost they might die Christians.

Thomas Phillips' account provides further insight into the process of selection of slaves:

> Each brought out his slaves according to his degree and quality . . . and our surgeon examined them well in all kinds, to see that they were of sound wind and limb, making them jump, stretch out their arms swiftly, looking in their mouths to judge of their age; for the overseers are so cunning, that they shave them all close before we see them, so that let them be ever so old we can see no grey hairs in their heads or beards; and then having liquor'd them well and sleek with palm oil, 'tis no easy matter to know an old one from a middle-age one. . . . but our greatest care of all is to buy none that are pox'd, lest they should infect the rest aboard.[7]

Although chiefs were involved in the trade along with some indigenous middlemen who received cloth and iron and brassware, as well as rum and firearms, in exchange, the need to accumulate a sufficient supply of slaves to meet scheduled transatlantic shipping necessitated the establishment of *barracoons* or warehouses. Joao de Barros provides the following account:

> As this kingdom of Benin was near the Castle of Sao Jorge da Mina, and as the Negroes who brought gold to the market place were ready to buy slaves to carry their merchandize, the King ordered the building of a factory in a port of Benin, called Gwato, whither there were brought for sale a great number of those slaves who were bartered very profitably at the Mina, for the merchants of gold gave twice the value obtainable for them in the Kingdom.[8]

Kidnapping, too, was a method used for obtaining slaves. Bryan Edwards reports about a slave who

> came from a vast distance inland, was waylaid and stole, in the path about three miles from his own village, by one of his countrymen. It was early in the morning, and the man hid him all day in the woods, and marched him in the night. He was conducted in this manner for a month, and then sold to another Black man for a gun, some powder and shot, and a quantity of salt. He was sold a second time for a keg of brandy. His last mentioned purchaser bought several other boys in the same manner, and when he had collected twenty, sent them down to the sea-coast, where they were sold to a captain of a ship.[9]

Most of the slave-getting, however, was carried on by militaristic empires, kingdoms, or other social groups functioning primarily for this purpose. The Kingdom of Abomey, in present-day Benin, is a typical example. Slaves, obtained chiefly by raiding among the various tribes, numbered as many as 10,000 in the single year of 1776.

Despite the concern for getting the best human specimens, the essentially economic motive underlying participation in the slave trade led to overcrowded accommodation on the ships and some degree of torture to maintain order on board, and thereby to prevent loss of slaves. The slaves were demoralized to begin with, many of them certain that they were to become the victims of a terrible cannibalistic feast of the Europeans; and they were, as a rule, shackled and forced to lie in a prone position during the long voyage across the Atlantic. Any rebellion was crushed swiftly, as indicated in an eye-witness account by Alexander Falconbridge:

> Upon the negroes refusing to take sustenance I have seen coals of fire, glowing hot, put on a shovel, and placed so near their lips as to scorch and burn them. And this has been accompanied with threats,

of forcing them to swallow the coals if they any longer persisted in refusing to eat. . . . The place allotted for the sick negroes is under the half deck, where they lie on the bare planks. By this means those who are emaciated frequently have their skin, and even their flesh, entirely rubbed off, by the motion of the ship, from the prominent parts of the shoulders, elbows, and hips, so as to render the bones in those parts quite bare. And some of them, by constantly lying in the blood and mucus that had flowed from the afflicted with the flux, and which, as before observed, is generally so violent as to prevent their being kept clean, have their flesh much sooner rubbed off than those who have only to contend with the mere friction of the ship.[10]

RESULTS

Apart from the obvious inhumanity that forced many slaves to commit suicide enroute, there were other significant consequences of the slave trade. These include the forced emigration of millions (estimates range from 25 to 100 million) of Africans, resulting in the stagnation or decay of numerous societies; for Africa was deprived of its young and healthy, and of its creatively productive. Much natural cultural evolution was accordingly frozen in time by the slave trade; tribal and clan groups in some cases were almost decimated, and whole areas of land which at one time were cleared and under cultivation reverted to bush. Throughout the years of the trade, many Africans were adapting to some of the ways of the European traders with whom they had contact; but among those white men were necessarily many of the most brutal and commercially minded individuals of Europe and the New World, so the African tended to adopt much of such inhumane behavior, if only because it was financially expedient.

Further consequences of the slave trade include the following: the development of pronounced racial prejudice and notions of cultural supremacy among Europeans, as a means of rationalizing the traffic in human beings in relation to both religious and secular conceptions of brotherhood; accelerated economic and social development of the Americas because of the cheap labor force; the evolution of a caste-like society in the Americas, becoming most pronounced in what later was to become the United States; the emergence of a human hybrid in the Americas, resulting from the interblending of Caucasoids, Mongoloids, and Negroids; great capital formation, particularly by entrepreneurs in Europe, which hastened the Industrial Revolution; and, ironically, a steadily windening intent to assert basic human dignity and to diffuse or make real the ideals of humanitarianism and of Christianity.

ABOLITIONISM

The desire to promote humanitarianism, which subsequently led to a series of provisions for the termination of the slave trade and of slavery, was not widespread; rather, such desire was most pronounced among a few of the "radicals" of the day who finally won the support—albeit qualified and variously motivated—of industrialists and politicians. For example, Thomas Powell Buxton, who had succeeded William Wilberforce as the leader of the British antislavery movement, argued that the slave trade could best be ended by missionary activity and the development of natural resources, and held that Africa could be regenerated by means of the Bible and the plow:

> If, instead of our expensive and fruitless negotiations with Portugal, we had been, during the last twenty years, engaged in extending our intercourse with the nations of Africa, unfolding to them the capabilities of her soil, and the inexhaustible store of wealth which human labour might derive from its cultivation, and convinced them that the Slave Trade alone debars them from enjoying a vastly more affluent supply of our valuable commodities, and if we had leagued ourselves with them to suppress that baneful traffic, which is their enemy even more than it is ours, there is reason to believe that Africa would not have been what Africa is, in spite of all our exertions,—one universal den of desolation, misery, and crime.
>
> But why do I entertain a confident persuasion that we may obtain the cordial concurrence of the African powers? Because the Slave Trade is not their gain but their loss. It is their ruin, because it is capable of demonstration, that, but for the Slave Trade, the other trade of Africa would be increased fifty or a hundred-fold.[11]

But how difficult abolitionism was to become can be gauged by the xenophobic attitudes expressed even in the 18th Century. In the *Gentleman's Magazine* of 1764, it was opined that:

> The practice of importing Negroe servants into these kingdoms is said to be already a grievance that requires a remedy, and yet it is every day encouraged, insomuch that the number in this metropolis only i.e., London, is supposed to be near 20,000; the main objection to their importation is, that they cease to consider themselves as slaves in this free country, nor will they put up with an inequality of treatment, nor more willingly perform the laborious offices of servitude than our own people, and if put to do it, are generally sullen spiteful, treacherous and revengeful.[12]

While some in London were concerned about the insolence of slaves in a "free" country, there were others—notably Granville Sharp, Thomas Clarkson, William Wilberforce, and Thomas Buxton, as well as the African, Olaudah Equiano—who sought actively to put an end to slavery and the slave trade, and thereby restore to the African the right to exercise his humanity. Granville Sharp, for example, a mere government clerk, had been instrumental in winning the freedom of six slaves between 1765 and 1771, although his legal arguments failed to bring about the absolute condemnation of slavery which he and his sympathizers sought. In 1772, however, the persistent abolitionists won a significant breakthrough when, in the case of James Somerset, a slave, Lord Mansfield ruled that slavery was illegal in England:

> The only question then is, Is the cause returned sufficient for remanding him? If not, he must be discharged. The cause returned is, the slave absented himself and departed from the master's service, and refused to return and serve him during his stay in England; whereupon, by his master's orders, he was put on board ship by force, and there detained in secure custody, to be carried out of the kingdom and sold. So high an act of domination must derive its authority, if any such it has, from the law of the kingdom where executed. A foreigner cannot be imprisoned here on the authority of any law existing in his own country. The power of a master over his servant is different in all countries, more or less limited or extensive, the exercise of it therefore must always be regulated by the laws of the place where exercised. The state of slavery is of such a nature, that it is incapable of being now introduced by courts of justice upon mere reasoning, or inferences from any principles natural or political; it must take its rise from positive law; the origin of it can in no country or age be tracked back to any other source. Immemorial usage preserves the memory of positive law long after all traces of the occasion, reason, authority and time of its introduction, are lost, and in a case so odious as the condition of slaves must be taken strictly. Tracing the subject to natural principles, the claim of slavery can never be supported. The power claimed by this return was never in use here; or acknowledged by the law. No master ever was allowed here to take a slave by force to be sold abroad because he deserted from his service, or for any other reason whatever; we cannot say, the cause set forth by this return is allowed or approved of by the laws of this kingdom, and therefore the man must be discharged.[13]

An immediate consequence of such a far-reaching decision, in view of the several thousands of slaves already in England as a result of the partial emigration of slaves loyal to England during the American Revolution, was the liberation of about 20,000 persons. The Mansfield decision derived further significance from the fact that, until its rendering, law-abiding Britain had had to live with false assumptions by humanitarians and slave-owners alike, as well as with the contradictory decisions of jurists. Mansfield, indeed, must have been agonized by an existing opinion of 1729 by both Attorney-General Yorke and Solicitor-General Talbot whose authoritative and categorical opinion was that

> a Slave by coming from the West Indies to Great Britain, doth not become free, and that his Master's Property or Right in him is not thereby determined or varied: And that Baptism doth not bestow freedom on him, nor make any Alteration in his Temporal Condition in these kingdoms. We are also of the Opinion, that his Master may legally compel him to return again to the Plantations.[14]

The poverty of the slaves, their rejection by many whites, and their unemployment spurred those who had championed their liberation to further action.[15] For these "Black Poor," funds and food were collected, and medical care was secured, although such actions fell far short of relieving the grave situation. By 1786, therefore, it had been resolved that a better solution could be found in establishing a settlement for them in their "native" Africa. Based on a favorable report by Henry Smeathman, who had recently returned from West Africa, a decision was made to found a settlement along the shores of what was to become Sierra Leone.

That the British government agreed to give financial support to the founding of such a settlement had been criticized as a design to get rid of the "black vagrants," which might in part explain the disappointing turnout at embarkation time, despite all the previous enthusiasm. The trip, furthermore, was delayed for months while stores were being acquired, while petty bickering was being resolved, and while a fever epidemic was being quelled. When the three ships finally set sail on April 8, 1787, only 411 passengers were on board. At the Sierra Leone estuary, the settlers paid about 59 pounds sterling worth of goods to several Temne chiefs for a ten-mile strip of coastal land. Many of the settlers perished during the first year, only 130 remaining alive by early 1788. In 1790 the Temne destroyed the main settlement, Granville Town, and scattered the settlers.

This setback was not to end the dreams of Granville Sharp; indeed, his commitment won for him the help of Henry Thornton, a banker. Along with William Wilberforce and Thomas Clarkson, the settlement project was renewed energetically, with the sponsors becoming owners of a chartered company and rulers of a territory, rather than merely absentee benefactors. To secure new settlers, "Free Town," the new name of the community, beckoned to Canada, receiving 1,100 Negro "Nova Scotians" in 1792; later, in 1800, the settlement was enlarged by the arrival of 500 Negro "Maroons" from Jamaica. Sharp and his supporters could, no doubt, have secured replenishments in Britain which still "tolerated" slavery:

> Slavery was not deleted from the British Isles as a result of the Mansfield judgment. It was not even deleted by the Act of 1807 which prohibited slave-trading by British subjects . . . here and there, Englishmen emancipated their slaves. But it was not until 1834 that it can truly be said that black slaves in Britain were emancipated, as were their brothers and sisters in British Colonies in the West Indies. It is, therefore, going too far to suggest . . . that 'The Somerset Case marks the beginning of the end of Slavery throughout the British Empire. For behind the legal judgment lay the moral judgment. . . . Britain abolished the slave trade and slavery for economic reasons. . . . If, indeed, behind the legal judgment lay the moral judgment, it was in a coma until it was revived by economic necessity.[16]

Continuing their several legal and political efforts, and now aided by William Pitt, the abolitionists succeeded in having the slave trade declared illegal in 1807 (the same year it was so declared by the U.S. Congress). This development had a far-reaching effect on European and African history, and numerous problems arose from the involvement of Freetown (declared a Crown Colony in 1808) in the implementation of the changed law. An Order in Council of 1808 authorized the seizure and condemnation of slave ships by a British Preventive Squadron, which numbered more than twenty ships by the 1840s. Agreements were made between England and Holland, Portugal, and Spain for stopping and searching vessels sailing under their flags; later, similar agreements were made with Brazil and France. In all instances, captured slave ships were taken to Freetown, whose population by 1850 rose to 50,000 mainly because of the number of Africans liberated by the Preventive Squadron.[17]

The success of the Freetown settlement, apart from encouraging its sponsors to the extent of having the British Parliament declare slavery illegal in 1833, served as a stimulant to other abolitionists. The United States, for example, was to delay an official condemnation of slavery until 1861, although some of its citizens succeeded in founding a settlement for freed slaves in Africa as early as 1820. Interestingly, the first settlement of eighty persons sponsored by the American Colonization Society landed at Sherbro Island, a part of Sierra Leone. Problems of disease, hostility of the local Africans, and a shortage of land suitable for agriculture resulted in failure. It was not until 1821 that a third group, under the leadership of Dr. Eli Ayres, succeeded in establishing a settlement farther south, in what was to be Monrovia, Liberia. The settlers there contacted a Bassa chief, whom they intimidated until he "signed" a treaty which transferred the area of Cape Mesurado to the American Colonization Society for goods worth about $300.

Like the British experiment, the American effort was based on contradictory motives among those who believed in human dignity and its free exercise, and those who envisaged sponsored emigration as a neat device for the entrenchment of plantation slavery devoid of the liberating pressure of free Negroes. This contradiction continued even with later sponsored emigrations. By 1834, the parent group—the American Colonization Society—had lost control over the various auxiliaries, which now undertook independent courses of action. In that year two groups arrived in Liberia, not to join the original settlement at Monrovia, but to found independent settlements along other parts of the coast. The group from Maryland survived, but another group which had been jointly sponsored by abolitionists of New York and Pennsylvania was sacked by hostile natives and slavers.

Another attempt was made by the New York and Pennsylvania groups in 1838, and a settlement was established in that same year by a joint Louisiana and Mississippi group. All these groups, however, like the parent group in Monrovia, considered themselves not as Africans returned "home" (which indeed they were not, because "home" meant not simply somewhere on the continent of Africa but a specific geographical area and, more importantly, a specific localized social and linguistic area) but as Americans who were involved in colonialization. They maintained trade relationships with the United States, and used the U.S. dollar as the basis of their currency. Similar in their behavior as "black Europeans" who viewed themselves as superior to the indigenous peoples (acting as colonialists rather than as grateful liberated slaves), were the Creole settlers of Sierra Leone.

Lacking the strong support that Sierra Leone had received from its home government, Liberia nevertheless survived to declare itself an independent republic in 1847—amidst constant threats of annexation by the British and the French, and the equally consistent refusal of the United States to see Liberia as anything other than the concern of its private sponsor. Despite its declared independence, with a constitution closely patterned after that of the United States, Liberia did not receive diplomatic recognition from its "parent nation" until 1862. It is, furthermore, bewildering that this official blindness to Liberia's American "affinity" persisted until President Carter's visit of April, 1978. Of course, this long delay was consistent with the low visibility accorded all of independent Africa until pressing problems (inflation, petroleum supply, the Cuban involvement in liberation activities) necessitated a visit by President Carter to Nigeria during the same trip.

While West Africa was being used to provide settlements for freed slaves, East Africa was becoming the major center for the continuation of the slave trade. With their major control center in Zanzibar where slaves were employed to cultivate the extensive clove plantations which the Sultan earlier had introduced, the Arabs were indeed in the main slave-raiders and dealers. Tippu Tib became legendary for his ability to get to the best sources of supply as well as the markets, despite British efforts to contain him and to eliminate the trade itself. Nonetheless, Tippu Tib significantly was most instrumental in helping to put an end to the slave trade in Eastern and Central Africa after he agreed to become an employee of Henry Morton Stanley and the Congo Free State, during the last quarter of the 19th Century.

Other developments were ocurring, although still closely linked with the pursuit of European interests. The partial stability arising from the abolition of slavery and the slave trade—although not totally effective throughout Terramedia—encouraged some scientific expeditions and much more extensive missionary endeavors. Diverse interest groups, accordingly, soon pooled their efforts to venture into the heartland of Africa, to explore the "dark continent," to "discover" not only geographical sites and social groups of whose existence Africans had known all along but, perhaps more exciting to the nineteenth century European, vast forest and mineral deposits and the possibilities of vast markets for European manufactured goods.[18] Thanks to improved medicines and other achievements of the Industrial Revolution, as well as the curbing of intertribal wars which the slave trade had in part encouraged, some rivers were charted, a few mountains were scaled, numerous trade alliances were made, and men like David Livingstone, Henry Morton Stanley, and John Speke were to interest Europeans in the economic potential of Africa.

In the northern tier of Terramedian states, the Turks who had assumed control of the Arab land gradually lost colony after colony. Partly because of the strategic and economic interests of the major powers, Britain and France, the disloyalty of subordinates in the various provinces was encouraged; and sometimes direct military occupation made continued Ottoman control merely symbolic.[19] The invasion of Egypt by Napoleon in 1798 made a significant impact on the Ottoman Empire, revealing its peripheral weakness; and by the middle of the nineteenth century, events in most parts of the once vast empire were determined by European interests and pressures. France colonialized Algeria in 1830 and Morocco in 1911; the British and the French became the major stockholders of the vital and lucrative Suez Canal, which had been built in 1869; in 1882 the British colonialized Egypt; and Italy seized Libya in 1911 via an unprovoked declaration of war with Turkey.

By the last quarter of the nineteenth century, the various European powers had invaded and had asserted their presence in many areas of Terramedia. Sometimes this resulted from pleas by missionaries or from reports by explorers who urged European occupation of the area. At other times, such assertion derived essentially from the shrewdness of such treatymakers as Karl Peters or Henry Morton Stanley who in his *Autobiography* wrote:

> In Africa, the harassing, wearisome cares of the European are unknown. It is the fever which ages one. Such care as visits explorers is nothing to the trials of civilization. In Africa, it is only a healthful exercise of the mind, without some little portion of which, it were really not worth living.
>
> The other enjoyment is the freedom and independence of mind, which elevates one's thoughts to purer, higher atmospheres. It is not weighed down by sordid thoughts, or petty interests, but now preens itself, and soars free and unrestrained; which liberty, to a vivid mind, imperceptibly changes the whole man after a while. . . .
>
> I do not remember while here in Africa to have been possessed of many ignoble thoughts; but I do remember, very well, to have had, often and often, very lofty ideas concerning the regeneration, civilization, and redemption of Africa, and the benefitting of England through her trade and commerce, besides other possible and impossible objects.[20]

It was partly to avert a further extension of small skirmishes, sometimes among zealous individuals representing different national sentiments, at other times resulting from provocations deliberately instigated by governments, that the Berlin Conference was convened in 1884. Ending early in 1885, the Berlin Conference established ground rules to guide the "scramble for Africa," and might be said to have legitimized the colonialization of Africa and the more thoroughly impressed imperialism which all of Terramedia was to experience.

Colonies and Mandatory Enclaves

The meeting which the German Chancellor, Otto von Bismarck, convened at Berlin in late 1884 was intended to preclude the rise or continuation of political animosities among European states, especially with regard to conflicting desires for non-European colonies. The general belief was that there was quite enough of the exploitable tropical world to go around. This, in part, explains the representation of many countries who lacked the power to pose a threat to peace in Africa. Among those involved in the three months of deliberations from which emerged the Berlin Act of 1885 were Austria, Belgium, Denmark, France, Great Britain, Italy, Luxembourg, Netherlands, Prussia, Portugal, Russia, Spain, Sweden, and Turkey. The sovereigns and other leaders of these countries had been invited for several purposes: (1) to avoid future disputes over desired territory; (2) to guarantee free navigation on the Congo and the Niger Rivers; (3) to agree on conditions of trade and exploitation of Africa; and (4) to uplift the "natives" morally and materially.

It is questionable whether most of those invited had any significant influence on the outcomes of the conference at Berlin. Only a few of the European countries had important vested interests in Africa which required adjustment, if open military confrontation were to be prevented. Because of the fierce competition between Britain and France over control of the Sudan, the whole course of the Niger, and the Congo basin, Germany and Belgium could form alliances beneficial to themselves. Furthermore, few other European countries were directly concerned with the resistance posed to their economic interests by such indigenous leaders as Emperor Teodorus II of Ethiopia, Ahmad ibn 'Abdallah of the Sudan, Sultan Seyyid Barghash of Zanzibar, Muhammad 'Abdille Hasan of Somalia, Ovonramwen of Benin, Ja-Ja of Opobo, and Samori Ture of Guinea. Perhaps only a conference of this type could have checked the clash which might have resulted from the competition for territory and markets that engaged the energies of such men as Karl Peters, King Leopold, George Goldie Taubman, Trieich-Laplene, Colonel Charles Gordon, Pierre de Brazza, Joseph Thomson, and Adolp Woermann. Such squabbles occurred nevertheless, perhaps inevitably.

How deeply the destiny of Africa was planned by Europeans, without African advice or request, for that matter, can be seen from some of the decisions contained in the Act of Berlin of 1885:

(1) The trade of all nations shall enjoy complete freedom in the basin of the Congo, its mouths and circumjacent regions.
(2) Each of the powers binds itself to employ all means at its disposal for putting an end to the slave trade and for punishing those who engage in it.
(3) The navigation of the Niger, without excepting any of its branches and outlets, is and shall remain entirely free for the merchant ships

of all nations equally, whether with cargo or in ballast, for the transportation of goods and passengers.

(4) Any power which henceforth takes possession of a tract of land on the coasts of the African continent outside of its present possessions, or which, hitherto without such possessions, shall acquire them, as well as the power which assumes a Protectorate there, shall accompany the respective act with a notification thereof, addressed to the other Signatory Powers of the present Act, in order to enable them, if need be, to make good any claims of their own.

(5) The Signatory Powers of the present Act recognize the obligation to insure the establishment of authority in regions occupied by them on the coasts of the African continent sufficient to protect existing rights, and, as the case may be, freedom of trade and of transit under the conditions agreed upon.

(6) The Signatory Powers of the present General Act reserve to themselves to introduce into it subsequently, and by common accord, such modifications and improvements as experience may show to be expedient.[21]

Evidently all did not go smoothly as the Powers expected, because another conference had to be convened at Brussels in 1890, this time with the Sultan of Zanzibar invited, for the purpose of

> putting an end to the crimes and devastations engendered by the traffic in African slaves, of effectively protecting the aboriginal populations of Africa, and of assuring to that vast continent the benefits of peace and civilization; wishing to give a fresh sanction to the decisions already taken in the same sense at different periods by the Powers; to complete the results obtained by them; and to draw up a collection of measures guaranteeing the accomplishment of the work which is the object of their common solicitude.

The Brussels Act which resulted concerned itself primarily with suppression of the slave trade and the restriction of firearms and liquor. The following declaration of the Act illustrates this:

(1) The Powers declare that the most effective means for counteracting the slave Trade in the interior of Africa are the . . . progressive organization of the administrative, judicial, religious, and military services in the African territories placed under the sovereignty or protectorate of civilized nations. The gradual establishment in the interior of strongly occupied stations . . . as to make their protective or repressive action effectively felt. . . . The construction of roads, and in particular of railways. . . .

(2) Restriction of the importation of fire-arms, at least of modern pattern, and of ammunition, through the entire extent of the territories infected by the slave trade.
(3) To diminish intestine wars between tribes by means of arbitration. . . . To initiate them in agricultural works and in the industrial arts so as to increase their welfare. . . . To raise them to civilization and bring about the extinction of barbarous customs, such as cannibalism and human sacrifices. . . . To protect, without distinction of creed, the missions which are already or may hereafter be established. . . . To provide for the sanitary service, and to grant hospitality and help to explorers and to all who take part in Africa in the work of repressing the Slave Trade.
(4) Justly anxious respecting the moral and material consequences which the abuse of spiritous liquors entails on the native populations, the Signatory Powers have agreed . . . within a zone extending from the 20th degree north latitude to the 22nd degree south latitude, and bounded by the Atlantic Ocean on the west, and on the east by the Indian Ocean and its dependencies . . . to prohibit their importation. . . . The manufacture therein of distilled liquors shall equally be prohibited.

Many of the provisions in the Brussels Act, while violating certain indigenous customs, brought ultimate benefits in health and economic development. On the other hand, the many instances of atrocities, especially in the areas under Belgian and German control–not to discount those of settlers in South Africa–causes one to wonder about the sincerity of many of the signatories to the numerous provisions for promoting African "well-being." Africans indeed could have done without such "civilizing" influences![22]

Although most of the European countries had participated in both the Berlin and Brussels conferences, only a few subsequently gained territories which they could colonize in Terramedia. Apart from the European settlers in South Africa, and the Ottoman Turks and their "provincial" governors in the Middle East and North Africa, the new colonial powers secured their holdings only after 1885. Surely there had been various spheres of influence or scattered colonies, but these lacked the relatively permanent control which the legitimization of the Berlin Conference made possible. Only in the twentieth century, indeed, could Belgium, Britain, France, Germany, Italy, Portugal, and Spain operate their colonies without the fear of losing them to stronger powers.

TERMINOLOGY AND THE LANGUAGE OF COLONIALISM

A number of terms, sometimes slightly confusing, arise in any discussion of colonialism; furthermore, colonializing powers often use language strangely when expressing their motives or describing their actions. It might be useful, therefore, to pause in this chronology to examine some of the more important of these. Three basic terms of relevance are *colonialism, colonism,* and *imperialism.* Colonialism is the result of *colonializing* or *colonialization,* indicating securing control over a weaker nation by a stronger one, which might or might not be involved in imperial outthrusting and growth. The focus of this term is on the colony, and in colonialism the culture of the conquering power is impressed on the indigenous peoples who are colonized. Colonialism involves the contact of people who are culturally different, the colonialist arguing that his culture is superior to the conquered culture. *Colonism* is the result of the act of colonizing or colonization, which means planting settlers in a land different from their native land. In colonization there is often the implicit suggestion that the land being colonized is "open" and thereby "invites" the colonists, who do not necessarily impress their culture on the indigenous peoples. Good examples of colonism are the planting of Europeans and Africans in the New World, and the planting of Europeans and Arabs in Africa.

Imperialism is a word first used in English in 1858, and refers to the outward expansion of powerful nations over less powerful ones. As used in connection with the study of Terramedia, it means the outthrust of white Europe and the resultant control of the tropical belt. The focus of this term is on the empire or the imperializing nation, as distinct from colonialism, which draws attention to the colonialized indigenous peoples.

Even more important than the foregoing are the meanings of several terms and expressions commonly used by colonialists and colonial powers. To the colonialist or imperialist, the act of colonialization suggests bravery and glory, carrying "British law" (or in the late twentieth century, "American democracy") to the "backward" areas of the tropical world. Those involved in this activity, accordingly, are heroes, and some of them are martyrs who devote their lives to such "unrewarding" work among "ungrateful natives." The colonializing nation wants to maintain the "free trade of all nations" (although *all nations,* for example, did not include the Yoruba nation of Nigeria or the Gikuyu nation of Kenya); to "ensure the establishment of authority" (although not the authority of the Tswana monarch unless the British overseer approves, and not the authority of the Bamileke chief unless the French Commandant supports that authority); to "end inter-tribal wars" and to "protect the native population" (which mean, in essence, to conquer everyone and to impose European law on them). Such "enlightened" actions will "asure the benefits of peace" (although those benefits will accrue rather to the European than to the Arab or African). Should the native peoples misbehave, "punitive" expeditions will be sent against them, for it takes quite a long while for a "pacification" program to be completed. The main purpose of the colonialist, of course, is positive: he wishes to "raise the natives to civilization," by which he means to make them obey the alien laws and not do anything to offend their conquerors, who include not only the colonial officers but also the Christian missionaries and any white settlers in the area. Should they offend, of course, "punitive" expeditions will necessarily be sent to correct their behavior. In the course of "civilizing" the colonialized peoples, the European was interested in initiating "agriculture and wholesome commerce" (which meant making the Colony an efficient supplier of cheap raw materials for the European industries) and "bringing an end to the slave trade" (which did not apply to European-style slavery such as forced labor or *corvee,* nor to the payment of tribute as "taxes" to the colonial government). These are but a few of the expressions common to colonialism and missionary activity, and a base for understanding of the basic contradictions inherent in colonialism—the situation of "democratic" nations of Western Europe involving themselves in the essentially undemocratic acts of aggressive imperialism, racism, and cultural supremacy.

RESULTS OF COLONIALISM

The net effect of European paternalism and the pursuit of vested interests resulted in the relatively complete colonialization of Africa by 1914. Even in the Middle East, Ottoman authority was curtailed by an increased infiltration by Europeans. Some, such as the Germans, contented themselves with the opportunity to influence educational and economic developments; others, particularly the British and French, asserted greater domination by using their military superiority to colonialize such areas as Egypt, Morocco, and Tunisia, as well as territories along the Gulf of Aden and the Persian Gulf. Terramedia thus became the helpless victim of European imperialism which, to Rupert Emerson,

> appears to be far less the product of conscious human intent than of the working of forces of which men were only dimly aware. In sum, it may be said that the imperial peoples had both a dynamic drive and the power to make it effective, while the non-European peoples lacked the power to put up any sustained resistance.[23]

As we saw earlier, relatively few European nations gained control over most of Terramedia, and several of their stated intentions were not fully realized. For example, the intent to internationalize the major river basins did not succeed. Instead, there developed autocratic colonial policies which left each power free (subject to occasional modification, of course, because of "gunboat diplomacy" and changes in vested interests) to enforce in territories it controlled. From such freedom emerged certain distinctive colonial policies. The British, for example, developed a policy of pragmatism which made it possible for them to tolerate indigenous rulers (or where they did not exist, to create them as "warrant chiefs.") and the nonalienation of land in some of their territories, and white settlement and "direct rule" in others. The French, on the other hand, pursued a fairly consistent policy of "direct rule" which idealized *assimilation* while being tolerant of association, feeling that peoples could become black Frenchmen. All the other powers combined direct rule with a policy of paternalism, which often produced extremely harsh and cruel treatment of the indigenous subjects. The Belgians, Germans, and Portuguese were especially guilty.

Although the chapter on social change, which follows, treats the results of colonialism in greater detail, at this stage one might mention one or two other points. There was certainly an ameliorating influence on disease and malnutrition, as there was a check on tribal conflict and societal insecurity. There was also an exposure to the scientific and other developments from which Terramedia had received only indirect benefits. In time, with better local facilities for formal education and expanded opportunities for studying abroad, Terramedian peoples came more and more into the mainstream of twentieth-century civilization. Nonetheless, a negative result of colonialism was the feeling of inferiority which was constantly reinforced as Europeans failed to properly recognize accomplishment even along the lines of their own standards. Furthermore, there was disruption of family and societal organization caused by introducing a money economy and encouraging migration to industrial centers. The most pronounced result, however, was the emergence of modern nationalism among the peoples of Terramedia.

FURTHER PARTITION AND MANDATES

Considering the damage which the slave trade had visited on Africa, and the effective manner in which resistance to colonial rule by indigenous peoples was contained (Britain in Nigeria, and Germany in Tanganyika, for example, burned "rebellious" villages and crops, and Belgium in the Congo used floggings and imprisonment to promote strict obedience to their rule), it is doubtful that Africa and the Middle East could have severed the imperial umbilical cord after only about seventy years of foreign domination. But an accident of history, of which World War I was a part, set in motion a chain of events which was to result in the termination of colonial rule in most of Terramedia. This accident of history was the felt need for resolving the contradiction between United States idealism about the right to self-determination, and the attitudes of cultural superiority deriving from the British and French experience of being colonialists. Such a resolution, and the subsequent compromise which created the concept of the "mandate system," became most necessary during the deliberations at the Paris Peace Conference of 1919. Because the League of Nations soon became aware of the secret arrangements (and their contradictions) into which Britain had entered with various parties during the war, it was considered necessary to settle these, as well as to apportion the spoils of war composed of territories which belonged to the Ottoman Empire and to its ally, Germany.

The nature of the secret arrangements help to explain the dilemma which brought about the mandate system, just as similar "deals" had supplanted effective colonial rule in place of Ottoman imperialism.[24] In 1915-1916, a series of letters were exchanged between Sherif Huseyn, the Keeper of the Holy Places in Mecca, and Sir Henry McMahon, the British High Commissioner in Egypt. The Huseyn-McMahon Correspondences resulted in an agreement that Britain would promote the desire of the Arabs in Arabia for an independent state, in exchange for their aid in harassing Ottoman forces which were siding with Germany during the war. Another set of secret negotiations was carried on between Russia, Britain, and France at the same time (1915-1916), culminating in the Sykes-Picot Agreement between Britain and France in May, 1916. By this it was agreed that Ottoman booty would be divided into British, French, and Russian spheres of influence, without particular allowance for the British promises made to Sherif Huseyn. Finally, in 1917, a declaration made by Lord Balfour placed Britain in the position of supporting the aspirations of Zionism to establish a homeland for the Jews in Palestine—a promise which would, if fulfilled, conflict with the other agreements. Western Europe, then, and Britain in particular, was thereby placed in a position where it could not fulfill all its promises. A mandate system seemed necessary to ease much of the burden of such contradictions.

The Mandate System, which was a compromise growing partly out of President Wilson's Fourteen Points (8 January 1918), made possible a modification in colonial practices and expectations. Particularly germane among the fourteen Points were the following:

Point 5. An absolutely impartial adjustment of all colonial claims, based on the principle that the interests of the colonialized population must have equal weight as the equitable claims of the colonial government

Point 12. The Ottoman Empire, or more particularly its subject colonies, to be given free opportunity for autonomous development

Point 14. The formation of a general association of nations i.e., the League of Nations under specific convenants to afford mutual guarantee of political independence and territorial integrity to great and small states alike

A commission of the League of Nations acted as overseer of territories given over to Britain or France to rule as mandates, which were divided into three classes:

Class A. States provisionally recognized as independent but requiring an indefinite periof of assistance and advice. These were Middle Eastern nations; none of these were in Africa.

Class B. Territories to be administered by a power able to guarantee freedom and public order with equal opportunities for trade under specially devised governments. All African mandates except South West Africa were in this Class.

Class C. Sparsely settled areas to be administered according to the laws of the mandatory power as integral parts of their territories. South West Africa fell into this category.[25]

Although the League of Nations had promised independence for most of the newly acquired territories (such as Lebanon, Syria, and Iraq), only the nomadic Bedouins actually escaped the domination of Britain and France as these colonializing powers persisted in promoting their economic and strategic interests at the expense of the indigenous populations. Even Turkey, once the major colonial power in the Middle East, escaped being colonialized only because of the strong and almost reckless nationalism stimulated by the charisma of Mustapha Kemal and his Young Turks. Ultimately, especially in the Middle East, indigenous rulers received some recognition and encouragement from the European colonial powers. Yet, their authority remained subject to European modifications—whether by persuasion, military force or its threat, or exile of recalcitrant agitators—whenever indigenous desires ran counter to European interest. This state of affairs was to be the lot of Terramedia, even as missionaries and commercial firms sought to promote on a private level their "humanistic" ideals, until the beginning of World War II.

In the meantime, through the whole period of contact with outsiders, through the period of the slave trade and especially during the colonial era, societies and cultures were undergoing vast changes in Terramedia. Of particular significance, as a subsequent chapter will show, was the intensification of efforts by nationalists, to promulgate ideologies and movements which would remove the yoke of colonialism. Immediately, however, is the need to examine the values that have shaped the Terramedian heritage, and which have influenced the nature and direction of change.

NOTES

1. See Ajayi and Crowder, *West Africa,* pp. 240-48.
2. See Basil Davidson, *Black Mother* (Boston: Little, Brown, 1961).
3. Ajayi and Crowder, *West Africa,* pp. 240-41.
4. F. O. Shyllon, *Black Slaves in Britain* (London: Oxford University Press, 1974), pp. 18-19.
5. Stanley Elkins, *Slavery* (Chicago: University of Chicago Press, 1976), and Herbert Klein, *Slavery in the Americas* (Chicago: University of Chicago Press, 1967).
6. William Bosman, *A New and Accurate Description of the Coast of Guinea.* (London: Cass, 1967), p. 364.
7. Thomas Phillips, *A Journey of a Voyage Made in the Hannibal* (London: Lintot & Osborn, 1746).
8. See G. R. Crone, *The Voyages of Cadamosto* (London: Hakluyt Society, 1937), p. 120.
9. See Bryan Edwards *The History, Civil and Commercial, of the British West Indies,* 5 vols. (1793-94; reprinted., New York: AMS Press, 1966), vol. 2.
10. Alexander Falconbridge, *An Account of the Slave Trade on the Coast of Africa.* (London: J. Phillips, 1788).
11. Thomas F. Buxton, *The African Slave Trade and its Remedy* (London: Dawsons of Pall Mall, 1968), pp. 302-03.
12. See Michael Banton, *White and Coloured* (New Brunswick: Rutgers University Press, 1960), p. 214.
13. Shyllon, *Black Slaves,* pp. 109-10. See also, Prince Hoare, *Memoirs of Granville Sharp* (London: H. Colburn, 1828).
14. Shyllon, *Black Slaves,* p. 26.
15. Granville Sharp, *Tracts on Slavery and Liberty* (1776; reprinted., Westport, CN: Negro Universities Press, 1969).
16. Shyllon, *Black Slaves,* pp. 230-31. Cf. C.L.R. James, *The Black Jacobins* (New York: Vintage Books, 1963), pp. 53-54.
17. See Arthur Porter, *Creoledom* (London: Oxford University Press, 1963), pp. 35-40; John Peterson, *Province of Freedom* (Evanston: Northwestern University Press, 1969), pp. 17-80; and James Walker, *The Black Loyalists* (New York: Africana Publishing Company, 1976), pp. 360-75.
18. See C. Howard and J. H. Plumb, *West African Explorers* (London: Oxford University Press, 1951), pp. 74ff.
19. See William Yale, *The Near East* (Ann Arbor: University of Michigan Press, 1968), pp. 82-157.
20. Henry M. Stanley, *Autobiography* (Boston: Houghton Mifflin, 1909), p. 533.
21. See Leslie Buell, *The Native Problem in Africa,* vol. 2 (New York: MacMillan, 1928), pp. 891-907.
22. Cf. Imanuel Geiss, *The Pan-African Movement* (New York: Africana Publishing Company, 1974), pp. 176-98.
23. Rupert Emerson, *From Empire to Nation* (Boston: Beacon Press, 1962), p. 10.
24. See Yale, *Near East,* pp. 175-78.
25. See Buell, *Native Problem,* vol. 1, pp. 545-46.

Chapter Six

TERRAMEDIAN VALUE SYSTEMS AND THEIR SIGNIFICANCE

Introduction

Value systems are universal phenomena which are prominent features of all societies and cultures. They may be limited or comprehensive, essentially rational or mainly emotional; nevertheless, value systems—in relation to their specific cultures and societies—define the goals that are worth pursuing and, in turn, the behavioral patterns and attitudes which ought to be encouraged and safeguarded.[1] Value systems also provide continuity in that they relate past achievements and practices to present situations and aspirations, and to future goals.[2] Although subject inevitably to change, value systems generally assume an aura of sanctity which results in attempts to preserve them from the "destructive" tendencies of change.

Several important distinctions must be made before one can properly understand the values of a given culture. First, one must determine what the values of a people are by examining what the people themselves pronounce them to be—their stated ideals and beliefs; and second, what

AUTHOR'S NOTE: This chapter, now slightly revised, appeared in *Handbook of Intercultural Communication*, edited by Molefi Asante and others (Beverly Hills: Sage Publications, 1979), pp. 203-28.

people do—the values implied by their behavior. Furthermore, one must make a distinction between the traditional values of long standing and those whose recent adoption might have replaced or integrated themselves into the old, traditional package of values. Finally, one must understand that the values of one culture which are not shared by another culture are not necessarily superior or inferior. In short, one cannot use the values of one culture to make judgements about the "goodness" or "badness" of the values or behavior of people of a different culture.[3] Such cultural relativism, of course, applies primarily to values, not necessarily to technology.[4] For whether the most beautiful woman is fat or slender, or whether one's traditional God is the true God or not, are relative matters and cannot be determined outside the culture. But whether a particular medical technique of one culture works better to end or reduce infant mortality than another method is something quite different, and is not subject to culture relativism.

Terramedian Values

Despite the invasion of modernization, Terramedia has managed to retain—for better or worse—many values which date far into its past, and which continue to be influential in the thought patterns and lifestyles of the majority of its inhabitants.[5] It is particularly important, consequently, to analyze the nature of the principal traditional values so as to understand the extent of their influence; to weigh their significance to people who wish to hold on to cherished values, even as they simultaneously endeavor to modernize and reap some of the benefits available in less traditional societies. For the purposes of this analysis, a traditional society might be defined as one in which the social organization and the culture (the behavior and heritage of the people of the society) are determined by custom and tradition, and are, accordingly, resistant to innovation and other changes. Values, therefore, are important clues to the degree of traditionalism in any society.

Throughout Terramedia, values coincide in certain areas; at the same time, there are values that, because of peculiar responses to the challenge of living in different environments, are unique to certain regions. A meaningful analysis must take these historical and ecological differences into account, including the necessity of distinguishing the Northern Muslim sector from the Southern sub-Saharan sector of Terramedia.

As in most, if not all, societies, Terramedian groups have always recognized the importance of the family as the basic unit of socialization—the process whereby a person is made into an effective participant in inevitable human interactions. Unlike westernized societies, however, Terramedia has always made certain unique emphases in family living. Marriage, for example, continues in most cases to be a contract between families rather than between consenting individuals (which does not mean, of course, that the marrying couple have no say in the matter). This attitude results in a high value being placed on the extended, consanguine family, rather than on the nuclear, conjugal family. To illustrate the similarities of extended families in the Northern (Middle East) and Southern (sub-Sahara) sectors of Terramedia, we might briefly examine the structure of the Arabic Bedouin family and that of the Nsukka Igbo family of Eastern Nigeria. The Bedouin family is designated by the word *ahl,* meaning "kin," which is reckoned strictly (see Figure 6.1. In the ahl, EGO

Figure 6.1 Arabic Extended Family

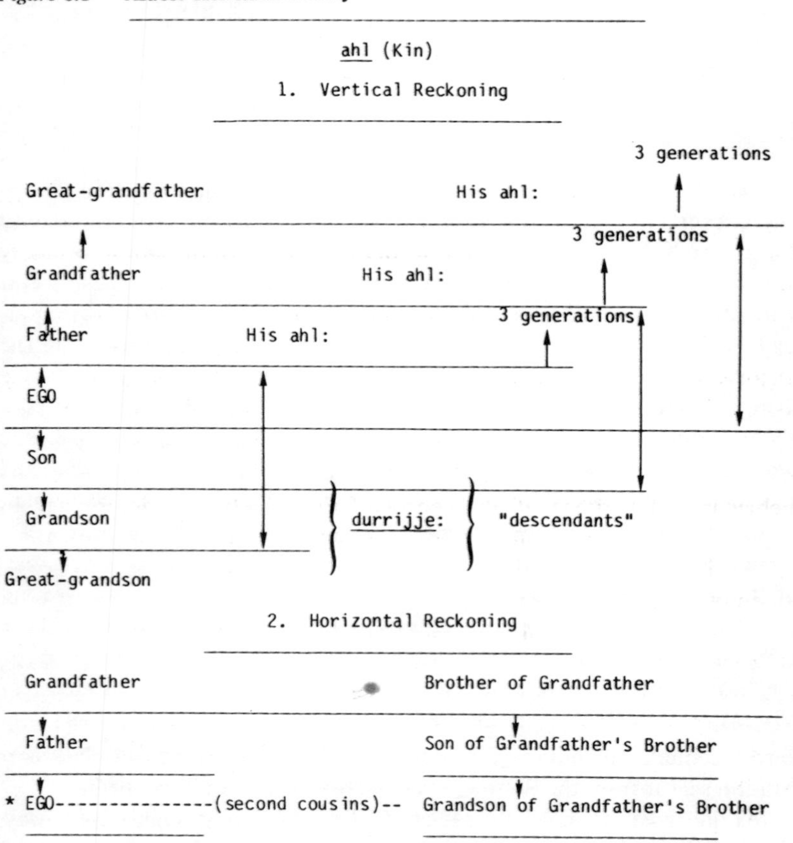

*This is the most distant relationship within the *ahl,* generally, although among some peoples it is extended by one generation.

(a Latin word meaning "self" used in kinship charts to enable the reader to place himself in the chart structure to better understand the relationships), reckons his kin according to the following criteria:

(1) *Blood:* his kin are "blood" relatives.
(2) *Patrilinealism:* his kin are male relatives in the line of his father, not in the line of his mother.
(3) *Three Generations Vertically:* he counts his kin for only three generations in the past and three in the future; therefore his father's ahl differs from his own ahl, and his son's ahl differs from his own ahl, and, accordingly, he, his father, and his son have rights and obligations to slightly varying groups of people. The "family," more extensively considered, includes the clan, or *qawm,* and comprises all those who possess blood relationship because of descent from the same forefather. Bedouin were, and are, largely endogamous in their marriage system, which means that they practised "inside-marriage" or marriage within a clan or kin-group—a practice varying from the exogamy of most of sub-Saharan Africa

The Nsukka Igbo family, similarly, is an extended family (see Figure 2), and is centered particularly on *umunna,* or patrilineage. Differing slightly from Igbo family structures in general, the northern Nsukka Igbo family also has a large unit which might be called "clan" in English, and *ukwu arua* in Igbo.[6] Unlike the Ahl of the Bedouin, the Igbo kin-group is reckoned broadly, although blood relationship and patrilineality are the major determinants. Belonging to the extended family or umunna are the living members, the ancestors, the unborn, and all descendants of the sons or brothers of the clan founder. Each lineage has an eldest man (the *okpube*) who is responsible for conducting worship directed toward the specific lineage forefathers, usually represented by small wooden statues, small mud pillars, or sacred stones.[7] Each lineage, in turn, consists of a number of compound families or households (made up of the eldest man of that family, his wives and children, his grown sons and their wives and children, and his unmarried daughters). The government of these northern Igbo family-societies consists of the gathered heads of compound families, the heads of the lineages, and the *onyisi* (the "head person" or eldest of the entire group). This results in gerontocracy, or a rule by elders who debate and derive a consensus in regard to problems of the extended family. These societies practice exogamy as their form of marriage.

There are other aspects of family organization which, while relevant at one time in most societies, remain prominent only in Terramedia and some other Third World societies. There is, for example, an emphasis on patriarchy (the vesting of authority in the male), and on partrilineality (tracing

Figure 6.2 Northern Igbo Extended Family

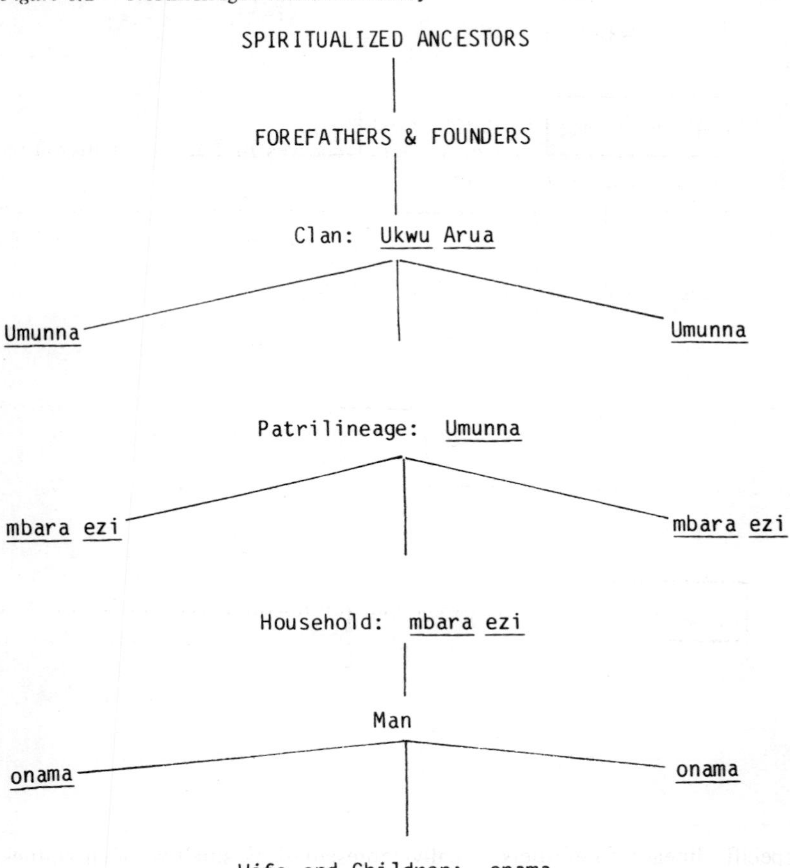

descent and determining inheritance through male ancestors). A consequence of such emphasis has been a preference for patrilocality, whereby the residence of married persons tends to be established in the compound or proximity of the father of the husband (see Figure 3). There is, furthermore, an acceptance of polygyny as the ideal type of marriage, in contrast to the emphasis on monogamy in westernized societies. It should be noted that, even though Islam permits a man to have four wives, the permissiveness entailed in adding a limitless number of "slave wives or concubines" parallels the nonrestrictive polygyny which prevails in non-Muslin societies.

With the high value placed on procreation, along with the stress on patriarchy, offspring are considered to be the property of the male line.[8]

Figure 6.3 Patrilocality

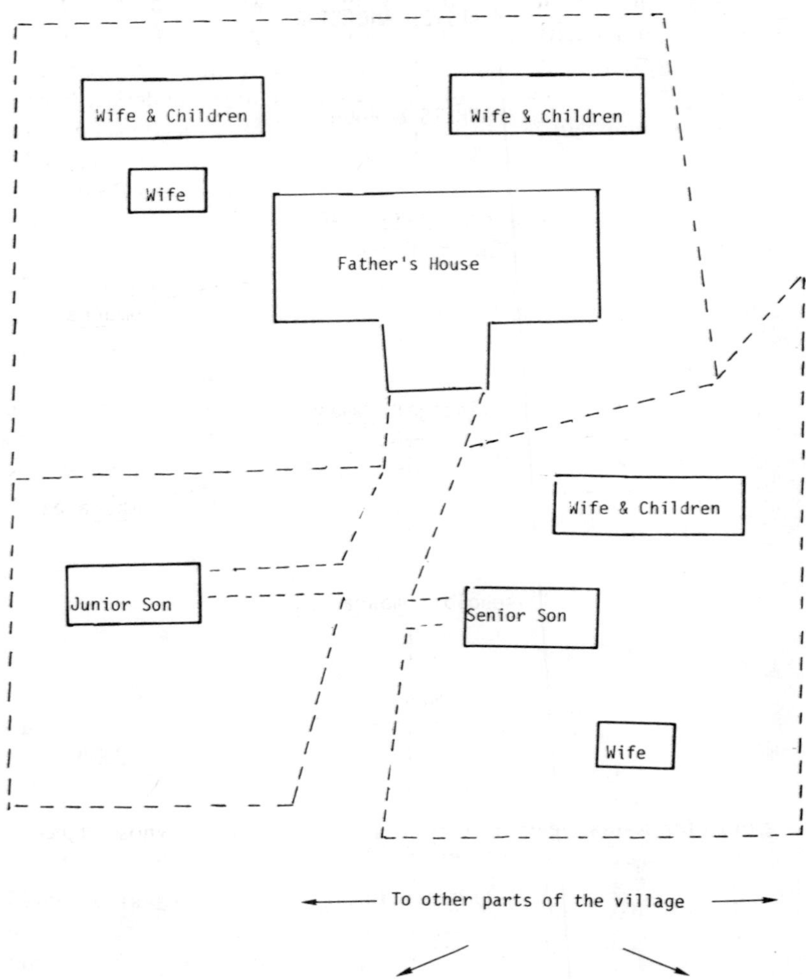

Accordingly, if a divorce should occur–relatively easy to obtain by the male but usually much more complicated and difficult for a female–the child becomes the responsibility of the husband's family. There is a modification of this provided by the *Shari'a* (the comprehensive code of proper conduct for Muslims), whereby the child of divorced parents can be cared for by the mother until the age of nine–with the financial support of the father–after which the child becomes the sole concern of the father.[9] Because marriage is arranged by families who give and accept bridewealth to sanction good faith, divorce is usually resisted to avoid having to return the wealth or gifts. The husband, who cannot then claim a return of his bridewealth, could get a divorce simply by evicting the wife, or by complying with the Shari'a stipulation and saying "I divorce thee" three times in the presence of two witnesses. Even under such easy circumstances he might be pressured by his family to forego his intention of divorce, because they want to protect their investment (the bridewealth) in the marriage. For a wife, on the other hand, divorce is difficult because her family would disuade her from beginning divorce proceedings so that they would not have to return the bridewealth. Nevertheless, an insistent wife can succeed in getting a divorce by proving that her husband is impotent, or is chronically ill, or is guilty of prolonged absence or desertion. A final general observation is that abstinence from sexual intercourse is expected of mothers until the child is weaned.[10]

Value is also placed on group solidarity and loyalty, although not at the expense of the recognized worth of the individual. An emphasis, therefore, is placed on those patterns of thought and behavior which promote the welfare of the entire group--such emphasis being more pronounced at the level of the family and clan, than at the level of the tribe or nation. This traditional value has aroused the charge of "communism" by those who lack understanding of the indigenous notion of "communalism" focusing on in-group loyalty rather than an ideology. Among the Mende, for example, the passage to adulthood via the *Poro* and *Sande* societies ensures individual competence for communal well-being. These socializing agencies, as William Bascom has observed,

> included nearly all adults and provided members with a general education. Boys and girls were isolated from society in separate groups for several years in secret initiation schools . . . whose objective was to turn them into men and women able to assume full status in the adult community.
>
> The initiates lived in a miniature world of their own that approximated life in the large community, and were given practical training for their future roles as adult men and women . . . girls were instructed in homecraft, child care, sexual matters, and correct attitudes toward husband, other men, and co-wives. Boys were instructed in the duties of a grown man, including clearing roads, clearing a farm, and other agricultural operations. . . . Boys were taught crafts, including the making of bridges, traps, nets, basketry, and raffia clothes.
>
> Poro . . . controlled periods of fishing and harvest, regulated trading, and judged disputes in secret tribunals. . . . The Poro and Sande schools imparted a sense of comradship for males and females that transcend all barriers of family, clan, ethnic group, and religion.

> There were also smaller associations, which specialized in such activities as military training, agricultural fertility, curing mental conditions, and enforcing the prohibitions governing sexual relations, including those of incest. In effect, general education, political and economic affairs, sexual conduct, and medical and social services were the concern of specific associations.[11]

Because the family includes the dead as well as the unborn, there is widespread recognition of man's spiritual relationship with God or godlings, and a resultant integration of spiritual and temporal existence. This value is manifest in the acquiescence to a theocratic imprint on lifestyles, featuring Islam, Cyclism, and Animism in varying degrees of importance throughout Terramedia.

The Theocracy of Islam

The term "theocracy" refers to prescriptions and proscriptions which derive from religious or spiritual force, and are concerned not only with the immediately relevant matter of religious behavior, but with temporal and secular affairs as well.[12] Northern Terramedia has been shaped by these stipulations, deriving essentially from Islam, for quite a long time.

The center of Islamic influence is in the northern sector of Terramedia, especially in the proximity of the holy cities of Mecca and Medina in Saudi Arabia. It is to be noted, however, that prior to the emergence of Islam in 622 A.D., other religions–particularly Judaism and Christianity–had begun in the same general area, and people there had also supported a variety of religious beliefs which included animism.[13] Some of these religions have remained fairly prominent, such as Christianity in Ethiopia and Lebanon, and Judaism in Israel. Nonetheless, it is Islam, and the resulting comprehensive Shari'a, which is the most influential determinant of values and human thought and conduct today. This influence, noticeable as far back as the seventh century in northern Terramedia, has even spread southward into West, Central, and East Africa.

Islam means "submission" or "act of submitting" (i.e., to God), and is related to the verb *aslama,* "to submit."[14] A *Muslim* is one who submits (to God), a believer and practitioner of the faith of Islam. As a religion, Islam consists of a set of beliefs and a number of expected behaviors. In the holy book, the *Qur'an,* this is made clear: "In the name of Allah, the Compassionate, the Merciful . . . Allah has promised those who have faith and do good works forgiveness and a rich reward. As for those who disbelieve and deny Our revelations, they shall become the heirs of hell."

THE BELIEF SYSTEM OF ISLAM

Among the very important religious beliefs in Islam are the following: 1. *The Oneness of God. Sura* IV, Verse 48, of the Qur'an reads: "Truly God forgiveth not the giving of partners to Him; other than this will He forgive to whom He pleases, but whosoever gives a partner to God has conceived a monstrous sin." 2. *The Omnipotence of God.* While an Arabic proverb makes clear that "the beginning of wisdom is the fear of God," the following declaration is made in Sura II, Verse 255 of the Qur'an: "There is no God but He, the Living, the Self-subsistent. Neither slumber nor sleep seize Him. To Him belongs whatsoever is in the Heavens and in the Earth. . . . He knows what is present with men what shall befall them, and they comprehend nothing of His knowledge save what He wills them to understand." 3. *Human Existence after death,* implicit in the notion of the *Last Judgement.* Sura XXVIII, verse 88 reads: "Call not on any other God but Allah; there is no other God but He. Everything shall perish except His being. To Him belongs the rule and to Him shall you be brought back for judgement." 4. *The Qur'an is the Word of God,* Who is merciful and Compassionate and furnished the revelations for man's salvation. Thus, as a prefix to every chapter of the Qur'an, but one, is the acknowledgement, *bismi'llah irrahman irrahim* ("In the Name of God, the Compassionate One, the Merciful"). 5. *Muhammad was the final Prophet.* It is believed that God's message was given to Abraham, but the people fell into idolatry; then it was given to Moses as the Pentateuch, but the Hebrews thought they were a chosen people, even after David had been given the Psalms; God's message was then given to Jesus as the Gospels, but the Christians deified Jesus; finally, God gave his message to Muhammad, as the Qur'an or Recitation. 6. Therefore, *Islam is a world religion,* not intended merely for the Arabs, but for all mankind.

EXPECTED BEHAVIOR IN ISLAM

Islamic belief and practice revolve around the 'Ibadat (acts of devotion) and the Shari's (the law). The acts of devotion are mandatory for membership in the umma (body of believers) who belong to a "world" distinct from that to which infidels and nonbelievers belong. An acceptance of Muhammad as the last and most accurate carrier of the intentions of the one God, Allah, forms the basic bond of unity among members of the umma. Of course, with room within the umma for all and sundry–subject to their compliance with the Shari'a–it is permissible to encourage the conversion of nonbelievers by force, to tolerate temporarily their "wrong beliefs," or even to impose such direct pressure as poll taxes or other forms of discrimination against nonbelievers. Indeed, the *jihad* (holy war) has been used at times as a means of extending the membership of the umma.

The 'Ibadat (acts of devotion) stipulates the following categories of actions, commonly referred to as the "pillars of Islam" because they are basic to being a Muslim (a believer of Islam):

(1) *Shahada,* or Creed, the fundamental profession of a Muslim's faith. This is a simple statement containing the core elements of the belief system: *la ilaha illa'llah muhammadun rasulu'llah* ("there is but one God; Muhammad is the Apostle of God").
(2) *Salat,* or ritual prayers to be spoken five times daily—at sunrise, noon, mid-afternoon, sunset, and at night before retiring. They must be recited with pure intention and cleansed body while facing the holy city of Mecca, Saudi Arabia.
(3) Giving of Alms (*zakat*) in support of the poor and needy, in the amount of one-fortieth of one's income. *Sadaqat* (free-will offerings above the minimum) are laudable as extra good works.
(4) *Sawm* or fasting, consisting of complete abstinence from food and drink during the hours of daylight, is required during *Ramadan* (the ninth month of the lunar year).
(5) Pilgrimage (*hajj*), entailing a visit to, and participation in the rituals at the *Kaaba* (shrine in Mecca) must be made at least once in one's lifetime, if health and financial resources permit.

The Jihad or "holy war" is thought by some to be a sixth pillar. In support of this viewpoint, reference is made to *Sura* II, verses 190-193 of the Qur'an: "Fight in the way of God against those who fight against you, but do not commit aggression.... Slay them wheresoever you find them, and expel them from whence they expelled you. . . . Fight against them until sedition is no more and allegiance is rendered to God alone."

The Shari'a is Muslim law in general, and prescribes the practical dimensions of Islam. It is concerned not only with the nature of man's relation with God, but also with marriage and family life, contractual obligations, property and inheritance, penal law, judicial organization and procedure, and international relations. Through the centuries, Islam has diffused the theocracy of the Shari'a so effectively that one can easily agree with Anderson's observation that, "to the Muslim there is indeed an ethical quality in every action, characterized by *qubh* (ugliness, unsuitability) on the one hand, or *husn* (beauty, suitability) on the other. . . . Thus all human actions are subsumed under five categories": those which are required by God and are thus obligatory upon all believers; recommended actions; legally and morally indifferent actions; those which are disapproved but not forbidden; and actions prohibited by God.[15]

The Shari'a is quite comprehensive and complex, and its interpretation has been the task of scholars and jurists through the centuries. Because of inherent ambiguity in the basic sources, there emerged four prominent *madhahibi* or "schools of law"–*Hanafi, Maliki, Shafii,* and *Hanbali*–which have differed in their interpretations of specific prescriptions and proscriptions. While there are not fundamental differences among these schools of law, the prominence of each one tends to be specific to particular communities. The Hanbali, for example, is centered in Saudi Arabia, unlike the Hanafi in Turkey (although also with strong support in Syria and Iraq). The influence of the Shafii is much more diffused (in Lower Egypt and in parts of Israel, Syria, Iraq, Saudi Arabia and Yemen), as is the Maliki which has strong support in Upper Egypt, Sudan, Bahrain, Kuwait, and Libya. It suffices to note, however, that through the Shari'a all possible questions which might face man in his spiritual and temporal affairs are provided for, or answered.

The Shari'a is based on several sources, the primary one being the Qur'an. Other sources are the *hadith* or anecdotes about the personal behavior and utterances of Muhammad; the *sunna* or community customs; the *qiyas* or conclusions drawn from analogical reasoning; and the *ijma* or consensus derived from the discussions of Islamic scholars (the *'ulema*).

In conclusion, the major values in Muslin societies are contained in the following propositions:

(1) God is best, superior in all respects, and ultimately determines everything except man's sinfulness.
(2) The human soul is superior to the body, hence matters of the soul are superior to material or temporal affairs.
(3) Islam is the guide and criterion for judging behavior.
(4) The community in which individuals or groups hold membership is all-important in the temporal sphere of human activity. This can be divided into the religious community of believers (umma); the blood community of the extended family or clan; and the political community which modern nationalism has evoked, such as *ujamaa* (from ijma–consensus) villages in Tanzania.
(5) Tradition is an important criterion for judging the worth of behavior and things in general. This, too, can be subdivided into actual Islamic tradition of the faith, and tribal or ethnic traditions. The latter can be perceived from such Arabic proverbs as a) "Your grandfather's enemy will never be your friend." b) "A jinn you know is better than a person you don't know." c) "They took the camel to school, and now he wants fried eggs."
(6) Change can be good, especially if it is developed without violating the Shari'a, and if it can be justified by analogical reasoning, the hadith, and by consensus of the learned (ijma).

(7) A sense of guilt for wrong-doing, rather than shame alone, tends to guide individual human behavior. Accordingly, the individual feels a sense of righteousness if he is a good Muslim and is law-abiding in the total sense of the word "law."

Values of Non-Muslim Africans

Unlike northern Terramedia where the theocracy of Islam minimized the importance of nontheological values, southern Terramedia—especially Black Africa—has retained its evolving and additive value systems. These can be examined under the following major categories:

SPIRITUAL FORCE

By observing natural phenomena, one comes to understand early in life that there are many forces which one is powerless to control. One is relatively powerless against the hurricane, flood, lightning, earthquakes and other natural catastrophes. Even persistent and diligent research has yet to save man from his relative powerlessness in regard to aging, disease, and morbidity. The African, therefore, has always considered it rational to recognize the power invested in natural and social phenomena. Traditionally, he has maintained a profound appreciation of the immensity of the power of those spiritual forces which can *cause* or *end* hurricanes, which cast the lightning, *cause* people to be born and to die, and *strengthen* the spirits of warriors and soldiers in armies. Indeed, spiritual force, often personified as the High God or Gods, as godlings or tutelary spirits or other beings, ultimately is believed to determine all that happens. Causality is not accidental, particularly that causality which otherwise would not be readily explainable by simple inference or logical reasoning. Thus, no chance exists, for accidents can be explained—if one uses the proper explanatory methods—as results of intentions.[16]

The High God, the major possessor of spiritual force, is tremendous and powerful. If He wills it, a child will be born, a person will die, drought will parch the earth, the people will have an abundant harvest, and so forth. God (*Chukwu* among the Igbo, *Olodumare* among the Yoruba, and *Ngewoh* among the Mende) is so powerful that He can do what He pleases. If He wants to kill you, He will do it, and you cannot stop Him. But perhaps you can placate Him by making a sacrificial offering to Him, to demonstrate that you duly appreciate His power and omnipotence. If your offering is satisfactory and is received by Him, the illness or calamity will be lifted. Knowing that God becomes provoked and that He possesses such power, you will regularly propitiate Him, worship Him, offering Him food and blood sacrifices and libations of palm wine, praising Him publicly and in a loud, clear voice—if you are at all intelligent. In this manner you can have greater peace of mind and, perhaps, avoid His wrath. Group antagonism (traditionalist versus Muslim), as well as the supremacy of God, is expressed in the following Yoruba verse:

> The Musllims are still lying.
> They say: "We are fasting for God every year."
> One day *Eshu* [High God's Inspector-General] went to them and said:
> "Why do you fast for God?
> Do you believe that God is dead?
> Or do you believe that He is ill?
> Or perhaps sad?
> Oludumare [High God] is never ill,
> And He can never be sad.
> We shall never hear of His death,
> Unless the liars lie."[17]

Spiritual force is possessed not only by the High God, but is diffused, although it is never weakened by the process. Force is diffused to somewhat weaker spirits than the High God—to godlings who guard farmlands, dwellings, sources of water, sacred groves and hills; who are responsible for the fertility of women and livestock, and who are simply related to other lesser spirits. These godlings, like the High God, can bring devastation upon a group or an individual, and therefore must be "fed," praised, "housed" in a shrine, and in general kept in a nonaggressive attitude. Spritual force is diffused also to certain human beings, such as blacksmiths who make objects of iron, to shrine priests who direct the worship of the gods, to healers, sorcerers, rain-makers and rain-stoppers, to magicians, diviners, members of animal societies, and to witches. As Father Placide Tempels has said,

> Any simple skill . . . is shot through and through with this dynamic conception of beings. . . . Coppersmiths and blacksmiths think that they will not be able to smelt the ore, thereby changing the nature of the material treated, unless they dutifully appeal to a higher force which can dominate the vital force of the "earth" which they claim thus to change into metal.[18]

Spiritual force is diffused also to amulets and charms, which protect the wearer against persons and beings wishing to do him harm while he is away from his village protectors. In fact, almost anything can be invested with spiritual force. Perhaps more important is the fact that spiritual power is diffused directly to human beings in one peculiar manner: The human soul is of the same basic substance as the creative spirit (usually the High God), and this soul is said to "belong" to God. Consequently, when God wants a child to be born, He permits a man's sperm to fertilize a woman's ovum, to "bring the baby to life"; and when God wants His "soul" back, the person will die. God's creative role in the direct emergence of each new child is thus illustrated in this Yoruba verse:

> *Obatala* [God] who turns blood into children:
> I have only one cloth to dye with blue indigo;
> I have only one headtie to dye with red camwood,
> But I know that you keep twenty or thirty children for me,
> Whom I shall bear.[19]

Spiritual force is power, spiritual power; it is neither good nor bad in itself. Indeed, spiritual power is so great that it transcends ordinary human value judgements. It does not matter whether God is good or evil; what counts is whether He has enough power to have His own way and do as He pleases. It is man's task to avoid the negative exercise of such power, not to make judgements about its essential goodness or evil.[20]

ANCESTRALISM AND CYCLISM

Ancestralism refers to the set of beliefs and behavior characterized by the spiritualization of the dead ancestors and the worship of them by the living. It is normally accompanied by veneration of the elders and by gerontocracy (rule by elders) in democratic societies, or by a belief that the king or chief is the living representative of the ancestors in a monarchy (see Figure 6.4). The First Men, or the founding fathers of the clan or tribe, received spiritual force from God(s). Although dead, they are spiritualized and participate in Divine Force; they are even mythicized so that they sanction certain religious behavior of the living, or certain social practices currently in effect. Among the Malagasy, for example, "the dead are the sole and inexhaustible source of all good things: Life, happiness, peace and, above all, fertility. . . . The word for 'child' appears frequently in the names of Malagasy tribes, and ultimately it is only the dead who are to the Malagasy what adults are to European children."[21] There is a similar view in other parts of Africa where it is felt that one's ancestors have the ear of God.

Becoming an ancestor, as a rule, requires a bit more than merely dying. One must die in adulthood, must have had living offspring, and must have been buried "properly" in accordance with prescribed funeral rites. The Yoruba, for example, make this clear in a proverb: "Only the man whom

Figure 6.4 Gerotocracy

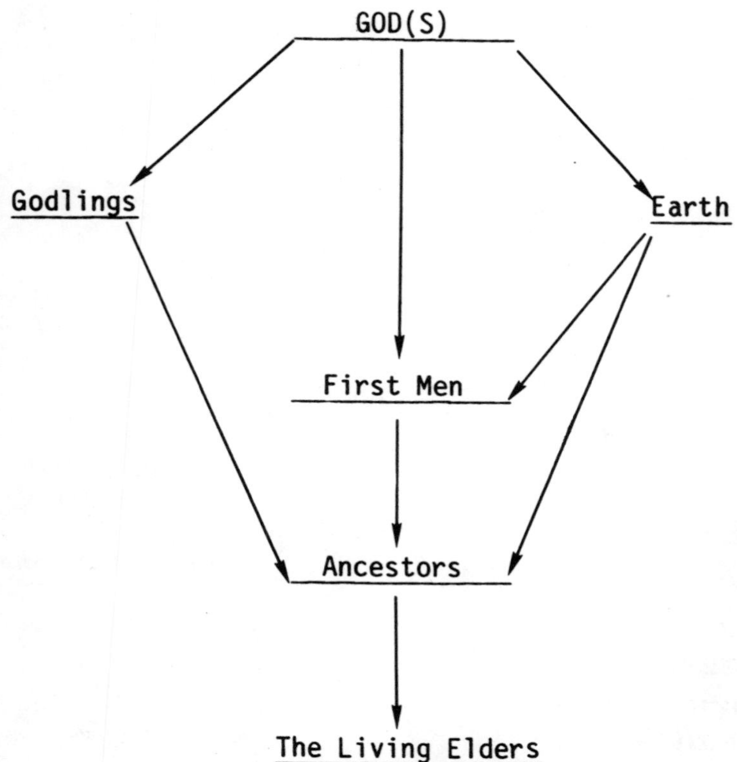

his child buries really has a child." Furthermore, although ancestors have spirit power, it is over their own offspring or blood kin; so it is their kin who must worship them. There is also a recognition of categories among ancestors—the collective dead, the named ancestors, and the titled ancestors.

Ancestralism and divine force play a dominant and widespread role in societal politics and government.[22] Traditional African temporal authority resided most commonly in the extended family and village group, or in the elected chieftaincy or monarchy (see Figure 5). In every instance, there was a close relationship between such temporal authority and divine sanction. In the system of divine kinship, for example, the king possessed

Figure 6.5 Monarchy

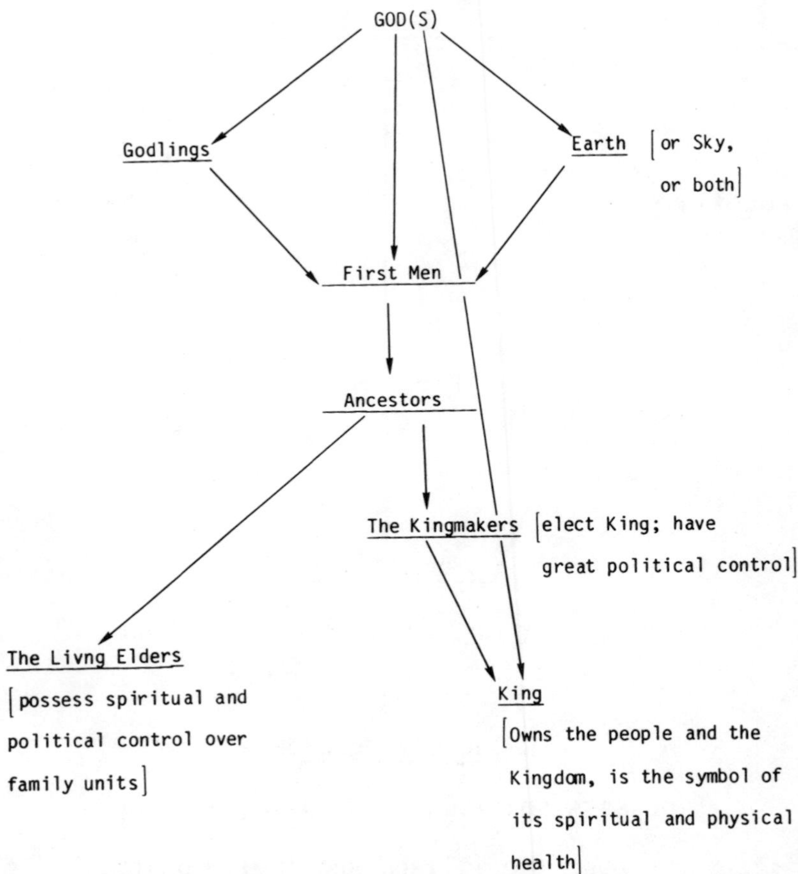

supernatural sanctions which were inherited or acquired by "medicine" or magic. If the king himself did not possess supernatural sanctions, the kingship was either supernaturally endowed, or rule as such was by divine sanction. The king or chief symbolized the kingdom or chiefdom, and his physical well-being was linked closely with the "health" of the domain. The king was believed to *own* the domain, including the people in it, and, like God, he diffused some of his power by delegating authority to others—legislative authority to chiefs and subchiefs, judicial authority to chiefs and village heads, military authority to chiefs and specialist warriors, and religious authority to shrine priests. When the king manifested signs of illness, impotency, or insanity, this would be construed as a weakening of his derived spiritual force, and he would normally be ritually executed by a group delegated to this task, so that a "fresh" king could be named and the health of the domain restored or maintained.[23]

The ancestors possess spiritual power and can be appealed to by the living children because they are "closer" to god and, as spiritualized beings, they possess greater powers than do any of the living. Among those "children" closest to the ancestors are the elders, or the king or chief, or both. The ancestors, furthermore, do not as a rule remain spiritualized in heaven or some dim never-never land of the dead; they are also reincarnated, as the notion of cyclism portrays (see Figure 6.6).

Cyclism, or the sharing of spiritual forces, refers to the belief that the pattern of human existence is cyclic, or cirular: one is born, dies, and is reborn. The inference is that a human being is an "incapsulated spirit, and not an animated body. . . . Living men too were essentially spirit, even if encased in flesh for a time."[24] Things which exist derive, in most instances, from the High God, Who shares His divine force with His creatures. Indeed, as has been argued by Mongamedi Mabona, the sacred character of all things seemingly increases with the degree of dynamism or

Figure 6.6 Cyclism

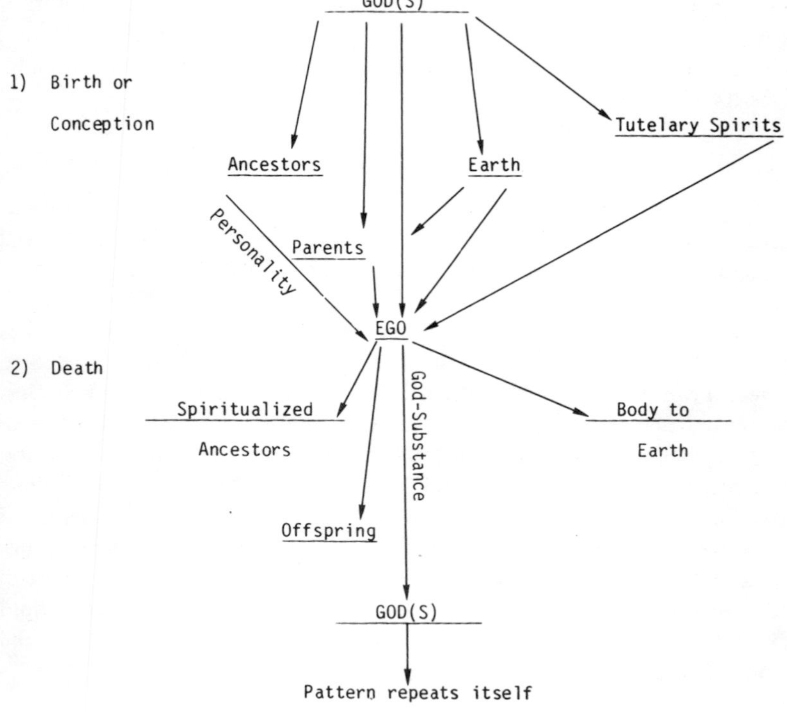

energy which a thing manifests in its own order—that is, with the degree of participation of the thing in vital or spiritual force.[25] The creatures involved in the cycle of human existence include the founders of one's clan or tribal group, or of the human race; the founders of one's social group, or those ancestors who migrated to the group's present location and established the existing lineage; the ancestors, in the order of time, down to the most recent dead of one's people; and one's elders and parents. From this line one derives his bodily features and personality, which are in part those of a reincarnated ancestor. It is not uncommon in many African villages to hear a small child being addressed as "grandmother" or "Father of my Father's Mother." The created beings also commonly include Earth, which is often spiritualized and personified as a god, from whom one derives his actual flesh, and who aided one's mother in conceiving—for it is in the actual earth that plants grow; earth sustains life, like a mother who feeds her children. Creatures also include godlings and tutelary spirits who sometimes transmit one's shadow or wraith (which among some peoples is believed to take the shape of a particular totemic animal), and who otherwise are responsible for one's general well-being. With death, the process is reversed and one's God-substance is taken back by God: His body is returned to the earth; unless the proper spiritual forces are asked for their help, one's shadow might roam about on earth as a ghost until it is properly sent—through appropriate rituals—to the spirit-world; and one's life is transmitted to one's children. The whole process, accordingly, consists of a vast cycle of birth and death and endless rebirth.

COMMUNALISM

The group is more important than the individual. So the community of residence or identity is valued. The community is made up of families and clans, and it is from these groups that the individual gains his rights in, as well as his responsibility to, the community of membership. Through family membership, and, by extension, membership in a community, the individual acquires a reliable "social security" that precludes the need to depend on outsiders. This "benefit" carries with it, however, a reciprocal responsibility as the community well-being demands. This spirit of communality has been formalized in Tanzania as *Ujamaa*—similar to the notion of "African socialism," "Arab socialism," and "Guided Democracy" being articulated in other parts of Terramedia.[26] There is ample evidence of westernized young people who, in choosing to scorn traditional attitudes and expectations of communalism and in behaving as "other-directed" individualists, tragically fall to their doom.[27] After all, the Krio would say, "Minister nor dey born baster pikin" (An ordained clergy is never the father of an illegitimate child.).

Several important values derive from the stress on the community. Dependence, for example, becomes a positive virtue because, in fact, one depends on the community and the Gods. The Malagasy, for instance, feel a sense of inferiority only when the bonds of their dependence on the dead ancestors are threatened; when their security is challenged they are not particularly concerned with technically solving the problem, but with avoiding any feeling that their ancestors might abandon them. The Malagasy want to belong to their family and social group and to their dead ancestor; they want to depend on them, because ancestors can solve all problems.[28] Similarly, as the Tswana proverb asserts, "one's parent is one's god." Arising from this dependence is respectful behavior toward elders as the only proper behavior for children and young people. The priority given to custom, furthermore, derives from this emphasis on communalism and ancestralism. The group, after all, has maintained the group wisdom and enculturated its members with it—just as it was transmitted by the elders, who remain the source of wisdom and truth. The elders are the ones with the knowledge to teach about the ancestors, the High God, and other sources of wisdom and power. Therefore, it is commonly held—and this is widely true of societies in general—that what was good enough for the forefathers has to be good enough for the descendants.

In traditional African societies there was a sharing of values. All the people of the community partook of the same value system, believed in the same things and beings, participated in the same destiny, and (by means of myths, stories, and proverbs) indicated their support of specific rituals and a common lifestyle. There tended to be relatively little privacy, and he who spent too much time alone was soon suspected of engaging in evil practices, such as sorcery or witchcraft, or simply plotting evil against others. There was, therefore, an emphasis upon conformity, and because of the rather public nature of one's life, *shame* rather than *guilt* tended to be the major stimulus to proper, approved behavior on the individual level.[29]

Let us take the example of a villager's failure to give daily offerings to the ancestors, especially where it is considered that person's duty to perform the ritual act. If he fails simply out of forgetfulness, he will feel little more than temporary fear that the ancestors will be insulted or angry at him, until he placates them with apologies and extra offerings; if he deliberately fails in his duty, he is in a state of defiance, and can become frightened, should sudden illness or an accident befall him or his loved ones; in which case he might repent—usually he would, or the society would sooner or later learn the cause of its new troubles and "solve" the problem caused by him. If he is publicly shown to be remiss in his duties, he will tend to feel ashamed of himself, because people will gossip unfavorably about him, indicating that he is "different," that he does not "belong," or even that he is accursed. In a public society, of course, shame works well as a deterrent to immorality and lawbreaking; but in societies which emphasize privacy and individualism, as in westernized societies, it is necessary for the individual to be inculcated with a sense of guilt over any actual or potential wrong he might commit.[30]

RATIONALITY

Arising from the foregoing, and related to all of the values in varying degrees, is the stress on rationality—the notion that a human being's reason is superior to his emotions, and that performance of human actions according to right reason is the best behavior.[31] Accordingly, it is reasonable for persons to share in spiritual force, for example, beyond what they possess as normal human quota. God can do whatever He pleases, because He possesses infinite power, so the human being's liberty of action is restricted accordingly; but a person can, nevertheless, increase his dynamism. Rational people want to be protected by the strongest spiritual forces so that they cannot, for example, be victimized by lesser spiritual forces. To acquire such protection, one must make payment in the form of sacrifices to the strongest spiritual forces, since one does not get a good thing for nothing. Once this powerful protection is acquired, it would be foolish to forsake or change it. Dependence, consequently, is rationally sanctioned, because it is intelligent to recognize limitations and to seek strength from God, the ancestors, and from the social group.

Similarly, whoever deviates from the behavioral norms of the society is irrational; unless the society possesses certain attitudes which provide flexibility in the normally rigid patterns of custom. Furthermore, it is always rational to do those things which have proved proper and practical. "My father told me that," or "Our forefathers did it this way," are sayings which commonly give the strongest support to custom, and illustrate one's reasonableness within society.

The widespread emphasis in sub-Saharan Africa (southern Terramedia) on gnomic literature, particularly proverbs, illustrates the high status accorded rationality in African scales of values. Proverbs themselves are intellectual forms, often structured with a high degree of skill at figurative language, and their content itself stresses the prudent, the reasonable, and the intelligent, while their tone ranges from the very serious to the ironic and satirical. A Fulla proverb asserts that "It is a wise father who does not acknowledge every misdeed of his child," whereas from the Mende comes the warning that "In a court of fowls a cockroach should expect no justice." "A man who brings home ant-infested wood," says the Igbo proverb, cautioning prudence, "should not be angry if he is visited by lizards." And, about reasonable limitations being put on sharing—despite the proverb, "He who gives is he who gets"—"It is good to send wine to the monkeys, but who will return the pot?"

In northern Terramedia (the Middle East), one observes a high degree of consistency in values because of the widespread effects of Islam—the submission of mankind to God—which furnished a predetermined belief system and a set of approved behavior patterns.[32] In southern Terramedia (Black Africa), on the other hand, there is a much wider range of values and value systems, reflective of the influence of localized and limited ancestralism. Nevertheless, one can draw some conclusions which are generally true for Terramedia as a whole. Spiritual force, throughout, like *baraka* or Grace in Islam, is valued highly because of its inherent power; men, accordingly, want to share in it, to increase their own dynamism. Along with ancestralism, divinity, as viewed by men, results in a widespread sense of dependence, which is considered to be good: dependence upon one's ancestors, subordination to one's living elders and to the community, and belief in the traditional wisdom of the group.

The community itself is a source of goodness, possessing power that it transmits to the individual, and acting as the safeguard of custom. Such values are good in themselves, or were good in themselves, so long as conditions remain the same as when such behaviors and attitudes developed. But, fortunately, or unfortunately, conditions have never remained the same, given the reality and inevitability of sociocultural change. Increasingly, the older traditional values have been challenged by systematic acculturation, whether planned or unanticipated. Only time will tell how well Terramedia can absorb these continuing incursions on its cherished values, and still keep intact its traditionalism.[33]

Terramedia has always been a crossroad of challenges, involving alien peoples and ideas. It was inevitable that its adaptation to the dominating influence of European imperialism would be challenged anew by ideas and experiences brought about by such domination. Reacting, as it were, to the needs of a new era, Terramedian values were thrust into a foray engendered by a vanguard in search of a proscribed loyalty: making Terramedia into a polity for Terramedians only, including the question of whose hand and brains should control and shape Terramedian affairs. Thus it was that nationalism became a rallying point, the analysis of which is attempted in the chapter that follows.

NOTES

1. Talcott Parsons, *Sociological Theory and Modern Society* (New York: The Free Press, 1967), pp. 8-9.

2. Robert P. Armstrong, *The Affecting Presence* (Urbana: University of Illinois Press, 1971).

3. Conrad M. Arensberg, and Solon T. Kimball, *Culture and Community* (New York: Harcourt, Brace & World, 1965); and Donald P. Warwick, *Comparative Research Methods* (Englewood Cliffs: Prentice-Hall, 1973).

4. Cf. George M. Foster, *Traditional Cultures* (New York: Harper & Brothers, 1962); Ronald H. Preston, *Technology and Social Justice* (Valley Forge: Judson Press, 1971); and George L. Beckford, *Persistent Poverty* (New York: Oxford University Press, 1972).

5. Cf. Kofi Awoonor, *The Breast of the Earth* (Garden City, NJ: Doubleday, Anchor Press, 1976), pp. 333-37.

6. See Shelton, *Igbo-Igala Borderland.*

7. See Awoonor, *Breast of the Earth,* pp. 54-61.

8. Cf. Daniel F. McCall, "Women in Gur Myth and Society," *Journal of African Studies* (1974):280-84.

9. See Schacht, *Islamic Law,* pp. 161-74.

10. See J. Spencer Trimingham, *Islam in West Africa* (London: Oxford University Press, 1959), pp. 163-78 and Majid Khadduri, *Islamic Jurisprudence* (Baltimore: Johns Hopkins University Press, 1961).

11. Bascom, *African Art* pp. 51-52.

12. Cf. Ali Mazrui, *Soldiers and Kinsmen in Uganda* (Beverly Hills: Sage Publications, 1975), pp. 265-71.

13. See J. Milton Yinger, *Religion, Society and the Individual* (New York: Macmillan, 1957), pp. 51-60.

14. See J.N.D. Anderson, *Islamic Law in the Modern World* (New York: New York University Press, 1959), and W. Montgomery Watt, *Islamic Philosphy and Theology* (Edinburgh: Edinburgh University Press, 1962).

15. Anderson, *Islamic Law,* p. 3.

16. Mbiti, *African Religions,* pp. 68-91.

17. Ulli Beier and B. Gbadamosi, *Yoruba Poetry* (Ibadan: Ministry of Education, 1959), p. 26.

18. Placide Tempels, *Bantu Philosophy* (Paris: Presence Africaine, 1959), p. 59.

19. Cf. explanation about *Eshu* and discussion of *Oludumare* by Awoonor, *Breast of the Earth,* pp. 72-73. Also, see Jean Laude, *The Arts of Black Africa* (Berkeley: University of California Press, 1971), pp. 101-36.

20. See Robert N. Bellah, *Emile Durkheim on Morality and Society* (Chicago: University of Chicago Press, 1973), and Eugene Bewkes et al., *The Western Heritage of Faith and Reason* (New York: Harper & Row, 1963).

21. O. Mannoni, *Prospero and Caliban* (New York: Praeger Publishers, 1964), pp. 50 and 60.

22. See J. F. Ade Ajayi and E. A. Ayandele, "Emerging Themes in Religious History," *Journal of African Studies* (Spring, 1974):34-35.

23. Cf. Kenneth C. Wylie, *The Political Kingdoms of the Temne* (New York: Africana Publishing Co., 1977), pp. 32-36.

24. W. E. Abraham, *The Mind of Africa* (Chicago: University of Chicago Press, 1959), p. 51.

25. Mongameli Mabona, "African Spirituality," *Presence Africaine* (Fourth Quarterly, 1964):158-162.

26. Cf. Ruth First, *Libya, the Elusive Revolution* (New York: Africana Publishing Company, 1975), pp. 19-23.

27. See Robert Chambers, *Settlement Schemes in Tropical Africa* (New York: Praeger Publisher, 1969); Melville J. Herskovits, *The Human Factor in Changing Africa* (New York: Random House, 1962); and D. A. Rustow, *Middle Eastern Political Systems* (Englewood Cliffs, NJ: Prentice-Hall, 1971).

28. See Mannoni, *Prospero and Caliban,* pp. 40-49.

29. Cf. Gerald Caplan, *Emotional Problems of Early Childhood* (New York: Basic Books, 1955), and Jack C. Ross and Raymond H. Wheeler, *Black Belonging* (Westport, CN: Greenwood Publishing Corporation, 1971).

30. See Anthony Giddens, *Emile Durkheim* (London: Cambridge University Press, 1972), pp. 39-140, and Robert Nisbet, *Emile Durkheim* (Englewood Cliffs, NJ: Prentice-Hall, 1965), pp. 137-52.

31. See Robert F. Davidson, *Philosophies Men Live By* (New York: Henry Holt, 1952), pp. 117-90.

32. See Alf A. Heggoy, "Arab Education in Colonial Algeria," *Journal of African Studies* (Summer, 1975):149-60.

33. See N. J. Coulson, *A History of Islamic Law* (Edinburgh: Edinburgh University Press, 1964), and Cynthia Nelson, *The Desert and the Sown* (Berkeley: University of California Press, 1973).

Chapter Seven

NATIONALISMS

The Nature and Evolution of Nationalism

The concepts of "nation" and "nationalism" are of limited concern to the rank and file of any society. People feel peripheral commitment to the loyalties that these concepts presuppose, and generally accept the symbols that the agencies which shape behavior patterns use to create their own ides of loyalty. This explains why several or fewer families and clans, limited or extensive territorial conglomerations, complementary or competing vested-interest groups can be prevailed upon, ultimately, to express a common feeling of belonging together. That is also why there can be nurtured—through a compelling and persistent vanguard of "nationalists"—a cooperative commitment to certain ideals and objectives among those who would otherwise remain restrictive regionalists or tribalists.

Most nations consist of pluralities. Even the land mass that constitutes the visible cement for national consciousness may be an imaginary one, like the "Zion" that preceded the founding of Israel in Palestine; and the "heritage" may generate varying, rather than uniform degrees of adherence or of awareness. When a society is relatively stable, these held-together pluralisms do not readily reveal their essential differences; during periods of drastic change, however, the seemingly harmonious ingredients

AUTHOR'S NOTE: This chapter, now slightly revised, appeared in *Journal of Black Studies* (June 1973):485-510.

of a nation (or the unharmonious units that some force is seeking to blend into a nation), reveal their disparities.[1] In nationalism, then, and among the persons who express the desire to promote its strength, liberty, and prosperity, one often finds "cloudy and undefined, competing or coexisting loyalties."[2]

The concrete limits of a nation or of nationalism can never really be known; limits can only be inferred, and are subject to modifications in the degree of support which they evoke among the component groups. This nebulous character of nation and nationalism makes precise definition impossible. Accordingly, the question of whether a nation exists for a group of people inhabiting a specific territory, or consists of distinct, adjacent communities, depends on definition–specifically the minimal characteristics expected. Only when such a definition is used to compare various potential or real nations, or nationalisms, does the occasion arise to suggest that these did not exist. It is this necessary caution to which Emerson calls attention: "Nationalism is so much with us, plays so large a role in shaping the setting of our daily lives, that it is often taken as a simple matter about which we know more or less as much as we need to know. . . . It is a far more complex and elusive matter than it is usually given credit for being."[3] And based on such an awareness, Emerson goes on to define a nation as "a community of people who feel that they belong together in the double sense that they share deeply significant elements of a common heritage and that they have a common destiny for the future."[4]

An examination of Terramedia reveals a tradition of national consciousness. It is true, on the other hand, that circumstances and personalities would manifest varying interpretations and recognition of what the significant elements regarding heritage and destiny should entail. Hence, at different times and among different groups, a feeling of belonging and of loyalty is manifested either to known or imagined, extensive or restricted, territories. The young Sierra Leonean, for example, who reverently sang "God Save the King" in 1935, was no less nationalistic than the follower of King Feisal in Iraq who advocated, during the same period, a policy of "Iraq outside of Britain."

Any assessment of nationalism, therefore, should carry with it the understanding that it is an ever-changing process that creates and modifies elements bringing people together into a nation. The ultimate goal of nations and of nationalisms–regardless of whether categorized by their promoters as juridical or symbolic concepts, as ideologies or social values–is to bring about "the acceptance of the state as the impersonal and ultimate arbiter or human affairs" among a people within a clearly prescribed and recognized territory.[5]

Our analysis deals with nationalism as it occurred in Terramedia, or in its behalf, from 1919 to 1960. We are concerned especially with those elements created or modified to develop different kinds of criteria for evoking new loyalties to heritages and destinies among varying groups of people. The beginning date of 1919 has been chosen because of the new policies which were introduced then, to modify the colonial relation which World War I had caused to come under scrutiny and challenge. The concluding date, 1960, has been chosen because it marked the widespread realization of self-government in Terramedia and the universal acceptance, with few exceptions, of the right of all the peoples of Terramedia to a government devoid of alien domination.

If it can be argued correctly that nationalism never died in Terramedia, then all that needs to be presented is evidence that only territorial loyalties have been subjected to modification.[6] It is a truism that no society or its components ever remains static, inasmuch as they are constantly exposed—in varying degrees—to internal or external stimulants for change or modification. An immediate concern, however, is to assess the peculiar nature of those stimulants to which the peoples of Terramedia became subjected once alien control and predetermination had become dominant. It would also be useful to show the types of reactions that were generated either against, or in keeping with, these stimulants, to achieve or reassert a preferred loyalty to a defined territory or set of social institutions. This endeavor, while evident during and after the period of the slave trade (as well as during the early nineteenth century with the greater incursion of alien powers into Terramedia), became intensified after World War I.

Much had happened in Terramedia prior to this intensity in national consciousness. People with different value systems continually met one another: Boers met Zulus, German missionaries met Bembas, French merchants and farmers met Berbers, and Russian Jews met Palestinian Arabs. Artifacts were exchanged, as were ideas, and in time whole institutional structures were transformed. Even the basis of legitimate authority changed; and by 1900, all of Terramedia had come under the control—whether as protectorates or absolute colonies—of European nations. Even countries such as Liberia, Yemen, Morocco, and Ethiopia—nominally independent—came under the spell of alien masters. It was inevitable that segments would emerge in various parts of Terramedia, and even outside of Terramedia, to implore or demand a return of control to the indigenous peoples.

By 1919, several distinct, often uncoordinated, voices had expressed a desire for indigenous self-government or self-determination. There were pleas based on religious compulsion, as well as on humanistic or political imperatives. Yet, the reaction to a DuBois or a Lobengula, a John Chilembwe or a Jamal al-Din, a Muhammad Abdu or a Samory Toure, was either indifference or rejection. Incipient Pan-Arabism or Pan-Africanism, tribal or chiliastic movements, were checked until after World War I. By that time, a combination of political, economic, and humanitarian factors had emerged to force an examination of the necessity for, and justice of, colonial rule. Besides, strictly indigenous efforts, devoid of the overt manipulations of European powers, had indicated a way to the successful attainment of nationalist goals—as indeed was exemplified by the establishment of sovereign states in Turkey and Saudi Arabia by 1924. Even then, however, such movements had to endure "changing patterns of new political and economic alignments," usually entailing "a complex pattern of apparent demise, resurgent assertion, consolidation, fusion, and faction."[7]

Greater inspiration was to come, however, from personalities and developments outside Terramedia. Not only would the revolution in Czarist Russia provide a cue for emergent reformers or revolutionaries, but the compromise necessitated because of conflicting promises made by Great Britain during World War I would guarantee ultimate self-determination. For, although presumably unintended at the time, the establishment of a "mandate" relation for some colonial territories would become the springboard for complete independence. Acculturation, resulting in greater exposure to a variety of ideas and things, would generate—if only among a few—the desire to rectify recognized anomalies in living standards, institutional structures, and decision-making processes. An attempt would be made to react differently to the common desire being expressed by peoples of different regions or ethnic background. Yet, at the core, the conditions which generated the common desire for self-determination, as well as the ultimate goals, would remain the same. This dilemma or anomaly has been noted by Hodgkin:

> The revolts of Greeks and Serbs against the Ottoman Empire in the 1820s, and the revolts of West and East Africans against the British and French Empires in the 1950s, belong to the same historical process. But . . . it was easier for our ancestors to regard the national movements in the Balkans with 'sympathetic objectivity' than it is for us to show the same attitude to the national movements in contemporary Africa. For the eventual aim of the former was the destruction of the Ottoman Empire; but the eventual aim of the latter is the destruction of our own Western European Empires.[8]

Perhaps it was this difference in reaction that explains why even the people in the Middle East felt, for a long time, that their lot and their fate were unlike those of the "colonialized" below the Sahara. The fact that the whole area would remain subject to the will of Europe, until the emergence of a more widespread wind of change, attests to the validity of such a view.

No doubt, there was differential treatment for "Northern" and "Southern" Terramedia. Where willingness to recognize nominal sovereignty was possible for sheikhs, undignified subservience was often the lot of their sub-Saharan counterparts. For example,

> the missionaries of Bena Makima, although they were living only two days from the government station, put the chiefs of the Bakuba in chains, because these chiefs refused to build for them; and . . . the Superior of Luluabourg caused women who had voluntarily left the mission station to be bound . . . because these women were not "free."[9]

Ultimately, the psychological scar would manifest itself strongly enough to evoke an attitude as inherently contradictory as that of one of Nicol's characters in "The Devil at Yolahun Bridge":

> I am beginning to feel particularly redundant in this damned country . . . especially when I meet educated natives like our mutual friend here this evening. They brought us up as children saying that Africa was a white man's country, and that for centuries to come we were to help and teach the black man slowly and certainly what it had taken us hundreds of years to gain. But here in my own lifetime I see these people trained to do all sorts of things, and the trouble is they sometimes do them well. Mind you, I don't say they are as good as we are. They can never be that.[10]

And because the feeling remained in powerful circles that "they can never be that," the struggle for self-determination had to be long and bitter. In time, the humanitarian niceties of a DuBois would give way to the fiery challenge of a David Diop:

> In those days
> When civilization kicked us in the mouth
> When holy water slapped our cringing brows
> The vultures built in the shadow of their talons
> The bloody monument to tutelage
> In those days
> There was laughter torn from the metallic hell of the roads
> And the dull drone of the Paternoster
> Drowned the screams that rose from the plantations
> O the bitter memory of extorted kisses

Of promises broken with the barrels of machine-guns
Strange men who were not men at all
You knew all the books you did not know love[11]

Elements of Nationalism

There can be no denying the fact that pluralistic enclaves, motivated as they often are by their own vested interests, are not easily molded into nations whose entities share an equal exuberance for profound nationalistic ideals. It is also true that wielders of power and controllers of individual and group conduct—especially when they are alien—do not readily yield to pressures seeking their expulsion. And while it required an overt commitment and a spirit of accommodation, if not genuine cooperation, by the major world powers (beginning in 1945), to promote indigenous self-determination, Terramedia all along had the elements needed for the emergence of nationalism. There was, first of all, a relatively *common territory* in almost every case—whether in the colonies or protectorates arbitrarily created by Europeans before and after the mandate of "legitimacy" granted by the Berlin Conference of 1885, or within those borders where the inhabitants were made to realize that, like it or not, they "shared" a common territory. In short, different tactics—military, administrative, economic, and religious—were used to effect a common territorial awareness by European colonial administrators and by indigenous nation-builders alike, in Saudi Arabia, in Liberia, in Ethiopia, and in Nyasaland.[12]

There was also a *common vehicular language* such as Arabic or Swahili, to serve as a bond, or likewise the language of the ruling colonialist power. Although the majority of people in the territories that would become nations did not speak or understand the European vehicular languages (English, French, German, and Portuguese), the few educated members of a budding "New elite" had knowledge of them. It was through the use of the vehicular language, for example, that John Chilembwe, though unsuccessfully, tried to remove the yoke of oppression in Nyasaland;[13] and it was through the same medium that nationalists like Nasser and Nkrumah and Nyerere, not to forget Lumumba, evoked an interest in self-determination among their people. Through the vehicular language, leaders could communicate with the European "masters"; and they could, as a result, point out many of the discrepancies between what the colonialists said, and what the colonialists actually did. Not only did the ability to understand the factors and tactics which had guided the process of self-determination in Europe and the Americas provide ideals for indigenous leaders, but their own failure at total acceptance by the "masters" (despite having met the stipulated criteria), and the "enlightenment" of their potential followers, intensified their commitment to nationalism. It was through a common language that the impact of the colonial presence was made more apparent, and it was through it that the contradictions and restrictiveness of the values and actions of the alien incursors were made a subject for indigenous revulsion. The cogent assessment by Rivlin and Szyliowicz of change in the Middle East applies to all of Terramedia:

> At first, only the elite imitated Western ways as they sought to increase their prestige, power, and material comfort. But it was not long before the rest of society was also affected. The introduction of cheap manufactured goods, for example, threatened the position of the traditional handicraft worker, upset the native economy, and led to the deformation of traditional society. Western ideas and values were communicated to the Middle East in a variety of ways: Conquest by European imperialist forces, governments copying Western techniques, educational and missionary activities of foreign nationals, and economic exploitation by foreign powers.[14]

The process of Western impact, along with indigenous emulation or revulsion, would escalate to observable tensions everywhere—"village versus town, land versus cash, illiteracy versus enlightenment, resignation versus ambition, piety versus excitement"—creating a fertile soil for nourishing the nationalism which evolved from the stimulus-response so aptly observed by Lerner: "Everywhere . . . increasing urbanization has tended to raise literacy; rising literacy has tended to increase media exposure; increasing media exposure has 'gone with' wider economic participation (per capita income) and political participation (voting)."[15]

The over-all modernization and its attendant tensions did not, however, produce overnight the desired objective of nationalists. Many suffered imprisonment or exile, or even rebuff from their own "constituencies." But the vehicular language sustained them, as they persisted in their quest for the way to justice in human relations. They combined ideologies, even as they experienced frustrations in their efforts to determine whether to seek a broader territorial base in religion or some other commonality.

Another element was a *common history,* at least of rule or domination by aliens who were, in almost every case, Europeans. Even in the Middle East which did not experience absolute "direct rule" by Europeans, it can be said that sovereignty maintained by Ottoman and successor overlords did not derive from indigenous will. The Europeans had assumed control through the show of force, or had negotiated commercial or religious "treaties" which granted them the capability to influence behavior, or the direction which changes in behavior patterns would take. The Germans, for example, invoked absolute control in their East African colonies, and in so doing influenced traditional authority and economics. While Germany's influence in the Middle East was channeled through indigenous rulers (as well as through educational and commercial activities), its impact, in combination with that of other European vested-interest groups, brought about subservience to Europe's will and values. Throughout Terramedia, European desires and ways of doing things resulted in exploitation for the sake of Europe.[16]

There was an economic aspect to this history of Terramedia being colonialized: Most Terramedians were poor, whereas the Europeans with whom they interacted were rich; most Terramedians showed a veneration for ancestralism, along with beliefs deriving from Islam or Animism, whereas Europeans were at least nominally Christian; most Terramedians were peasant farmers or herdsmen or traditional craftsmen (there were some, of course, who were engaged in commerce and industry, and who participated in sectors that had been introduced to satisfy European interests), whereas the Europeans were magistrates and judges, administrators and police officers, head teachers and supervising missionaries.

The usurpation of the right of indigenous peoples to shape their own destiny became more and more glaring with the passage of time; the effect of European subterfuge created a common history of alien control for all of Terramedia. Even before the arbitrary claim to Egypt by Great Britain in 1882, Europe influenced justice and access to rewards:

> Whereas in 1830 a British consul had been unable to enter the city of Damascus, in 1840 another British consul actually picked the man who was to be governor of Lebanon. British consuls intervened even in the most minute political affairs of remote areas. For example, in 1854 in the port of Beirut a native and a foreign ship collided. No court then constituted could try the case. It was the British consul not the Ottoman governor whose powers were adjudged most nearly able to meet the requirements of the situation, and he constituted a mixed commission to assess damages and responsibility. . . . By the middle of the nineteenth century all foreigners enjoyed more privileges than do modern diplomats. Foreigners on criminal charges could appeal their cases to courts in their native lands; even when their crimes involved natives, the local government was powerless to punish them. So flagrant were the abuses possible under this system that it was to be regarded as one of the great triumphs of Egyptian nationalism to get the great powers to recognize and participate in the creation and functioning of "mixed courts," in which Egyptian judges, though a permanent minority, could have a voice in the decision of cases involving their countrymen with Europeans.[17]

If diplomats did not have their way, alien pressure groups would persist until their vested interests were satisfied, even if this were to be (as was often the case), at the expense of the indigenous peoples. Europeans usurped inalienable tribal lands in Kenya and in Algeria, and at times made it criminal to speak against the government; so too were the following acts in some areas:

> delay in paying taxes; keeping stray animals more than twenty-four hours; giving shelter to any stranger without permission; leaving the commune without notice; neglecting to have a travel permit visaed wherever one stops for more than twenty-four hours; the gathering without permission of more than twenty persons on certain festive occasions; opening any educational or religious institution without permission.[18]

DuBois has given a succinct description of the situation which served as an impetus to nationalists throughout Terramedia:

> Determined effort was thus made . . . to cut the natives off from any union of forces or of interests with the educated. . . . "Protectorates" under autocratic white rule were attached to the colonies and the natives in the protectorates were threatened with loss of land, given almost no education and left to the mercy of a white colonial staff whose chief duty gradually came to be the encouragement of profitable industry for the great companies. These companies were represented in the governing councils, they influenced appointments at home and especially they spread . . . a carefully prepared propaganda which represented the educated "nigger" as a bumptious, unreasoning fool in a silk hat, while the untutored and unspoiled native under white control was nature's original nobleman.[19]

By the first decade of the twentieth century, Terramedia had been exposed to a pattern of power politics whereby aliens reorganized the Terramedian environment and peoples to achieve alien objectives. The reality of this common history did not become apparent until much later, but it already existed to help cement the frustrations of the "new elite" and the rising expectations of the masses into a useful force for nationalism. At the Berlin Conference of 1884, to which no African had been invited, the Europeans in their wisdom recorded humanitarian concerns for the indigenous peoples of Africa whose burdens they were determined to assume. Following World War I, a similar magnanimity was displayed when the Europeans agreed to a mandate system rather than to outright colonialism. Yet, these were meaningless distinctions, for Europeans persisted in denying Terramedians their claims to minimal dignity, as well as their rights to self-determination. Tom Mboya, a Kenyan nationalist, was thus able to observe that "colonialism has been the biggest hindrance to the development of the indigenous people. Under colonial rule, little attention has been paid to the need to invest in education, health, technical training, and general community development."[20] A more revealing observation for the Middle East, but equally applicable to the rest of Terramedia, has been made by Lewis:

> Between 1918 and 1945 Britain and France, in fitful association and rivalry, were the dominant powers in the Arab East. Aden, Palestine and the Sudan were ruled directly through regimes of a colonial type; elsewhere control–if that is the right word–was indirect. It was maintained through local governments, some of them under mandate, others nominally independent, with a variable and uncertain degree of responsibility for their own affairs. . . . Anglo-French pre-eminence in the Middle East . . . brought immense and irreversible changes, on every level of social existence. By no means all the changes were the work of Western rulers and overlords, most of whom tended to be cautiously conservative in their policies. Some of the most crucial changes were due to vigorous and ruthless Middle Eastern westernizers–rulers who sought to acquire and master the Western instrument of power, men of letters and of action fascinated by the potency of Western knowledge and ideas.[21]

Another common element in Terramedia was a general unity of *race* (of being nonwhite), insofar as the colonialists were "white" (Caucasoid Europeans, and the Terramedians were inferior "black" Negroid peoples or "uncivilized Arabs." While it is true that Arabs had once considered themselves different from, and superior to, the Negroes south of the Sahara (the Berbers had, in fact used the word *guinea* to refer to "black" or "Negro"; "dumb" or "unintelligent"), their subsequent treatment by Europeans erased physical differences to the point where all Terramedians–class and physical differences notwithstanding–found themselves in a common "race bag" by the end of World War I. Their reaction, in turn, even while remaining unaware of this common experience of denigration throughout all the colonialized territories, assumed the same mold–providing a basis for nationalist activity. The Arab anomaly, vis-à-vis the sub-Sahara Terramedians, is explained in the following assessment by Edward Shils:

> Conquest and maltreatment were not first brought to Asia and Africa by the European imperial powers. Long before, Asians had

> conquered other Asians; Arabs had exploited and enslaved black African rules. Still, it is the European conquest that is remembered. It is remembered most vividly because it is the most recent, extending well into the memory of all living adults and many young people. It is also remembered because it was experienced more painfully than previous imperial conquests. The greater painfulness stems, in part, from the vividness of freshly remembered events. Moreover, this more recent dominion—imperial and internal—inculcated moral, political, and intellectual standards for its own criticism, a practice previous imperial rulers had not employed. The acquisition of the standards implicit in the religious and political culture that the whites brought to Asia and Africa and that they preached and partly observed in their own countries made the discrepancy between those standards and their own action and presence in Asia and Africa and their conduct toward colored peoples in their own countries uncomfortable to bear.
>
> Tyranny is always painful, but tyranny exercised by the ethnically alien, whose ethnic alien-ness is underscored by the most easily distinguishable color difference, is especially repugnant.[22]

Tyranny took the form of economic exploitation and of military force or threat; it took the form of laws and "treaties" which projected "white" superiority; and it found its rationale in a comprehensive ethnocentrism with no tolerance for cultural relativism. Racism became manifest through Terramedia in residential, educational, commercial, and other forms of social separateness. Ultimately, the Terramedian repugnance of racial discrimination and prejudice, meted out to them by Europeans in their own homelands, came to be assessed eloquently by one of the nationalists, Patrice Lumumba:

> Our lot was eighty years of colonial rule; our wounds are still too fresh and painful to be driven from our memory.
>
> We have known tiring labor, exacted exchange for salary which did not allow us to satisfy our hunger, to clothe and lodge ourselves decently or to raise our children like loved beings.
>
> We have known ironies, insults, blows which we had to endure morning, noon, and night because we were "Negroes."
>
> We have known that the law was never the same depending on whether it concerned a white or a Negro: accommodating for one group, it was cruel and inhuman for the other.
>
> We have known the atrocious sufferings of those banished for political opinions or religious beliefs; exiled in their own countries, their end was truly worse than death itself.
>
> We have known that there were magnificent houses for the whites in the cities and tumble-down straw huts for the Negroes, that a

> Negro was not admitted in movie houses or restaurants or stores labeled "European," that a Negro traveled in the hulls of river boats at the feet of the white in his first class cabin.
>
> Who will forget, finally, the fusillades where so many of our brothers perished or the prisons where all those were brutally flung who no longer wished to submit to the regime of a law of oppression and exploitation which the colonists had made a tool of their domination?
>
> All that, my brothers, we have profoundly suffered.[23]

A final element evolved from nationalist actions: *Some sense of unity* among the more Westernized of the colonialized people was created by the consistently iron-handed way in which nationalist leaders were often treated by the Europeans. Wallace Johnson of Sierra Leone, for example, was detained for writing seditious material; France bombarded Beirut as a response to nationalist agitation; and Nnamdi Azikiwe of Nigeria was prosecuted in 1936 for having published an article titled "Has the African a God?" This article included, among many fiery passages, the following: "Personally, I believe the European has a god in whom he believes, and whom he is representing in his churches all over Africa. He believes in the god whose name is Deceit." As late as 1950, Felix Houphouet-Boigny was arrested when his political party, *Rassemblement Democratique Africain,* began demonstrations, boycotts, and strikes in opposition to French colonial mistreatment. Fifty-two Africans were killed, several hundred wounded, and 3,000 thrown into prison. Kwame Nkrumah of Ghana—then the Gold Coast—was imprisoned along with other nationalist leaders in 1948, when a demonstration and boycott to lower the price of imported goods led to a riot.

In the Ottoman-controlled areas of the Middle East, Turkish discrimination and upper-handedness promoted a sense of unity among nationalists who were being denied their "rights" by European and Europeanized overloads. But the Committee of Union and Progress which took over the Ottoman Empire in 1908, espousing an interest in progress and equality for all Arabs, failed to satisfy the aspirations of most nationalists. The Committee became Turko-centric, alienated non-Turks, and engaged in the persecution of their leaders and their ideas of semiautonomy or national pluralism. Don Peretz, has provided a picture of the situation which developed:

> At least ten groups opposed to the Turkification program sprang up among Arabs in Istanbul, Damascus, Bierut, Aleppo, Baghdad, and other Arab cities. Some were secret and others were public; all probably worked in some degree of harmony.

> The best organized and most widely known of the Arab groups was the Ottoman Decentralization Party established in Cairo during 1912. Its program called for a multinational, multiracial empire rallied about the Ottoman throne. Each Ottoman province would control its own internal affairs through locally elected representative bodies; Turkish and the language of each local population would be official, and education would be offered in the local tongue.
>
> In Beirut in 1913, the interfaith Committee of Reform roused sentiment for Arab autonomy. Public meetings cheered it in Damascus, Aleppo, Acre, Nablus, Baghdad, and Basra. Later in the year when the Young Turks began to suppress the committee and arrested several of its leaders for disloyalty, Beirut shops and offices closed and the press went on strike. Agitation became so great that the government released the leaders and announced the acceptance of the committee's proposals. . . . The stated objective was an Ottoman government that was neither wholly Turkish nor wholly Arab, one in which all citizens would have equal rights and obligations, whether they were Arab, Turk, Armenian, Kurd, Muslim, Christian, Jew, or Druse.[24]

This ideal of Pan-Arabism under Turkish tolerance had elements similar to that of Pan-Africanism which had been proposed around 1900, and might have become a reality—thus breaking the common bond of imperial control shared with sub-Sahara Africa. But the War of 1914 and events following its conclusion exposed the Middle East to the common fate of all Terramedia as territories and peoples to be held under European "tutelage" and dominion, with the pleas of nationalists falling on deaf or indifferent ears.

The Role of Ideologies

Out of the desire to check discrimination, to win some or greater participation in local and territorial government, or the wish to assume full control of their own affairs in their own homelands, nationalists clustered to various European capitals (chiefly Paris and London), and gained a more concrete awareness of a common sense of purpose. In addition, they became exposed to, and embraced, ideologies urging revolution. A people who had been content to manifest loyalty mainly on the basis of tribe or religious belief were now to have, as their spokesmen and leaders, persons whose disenchantment with tradition and their understanding of the duplicity of alien overlords compelled the use of instruments in the cause of partial or total liberation. They came to realize the necessity for "a reasonably coherent body of ideas concerning both the rationale and the means for changing or maintaining a social and political order."[25] Colonial rule, real or disguised, had contributed to the liberation and enlightenment of a "new elite," a group comprising professionals and unskilled workers, highly educated and illiterate Terramedians alike. From a greater awareness of domination by a racially distinguishable minority (which violated traditional norms in many parts of Terramedia), to a feeling of frustration from being denied the due rewards of Westernization, the self-exiled, emergent ideologists found an ally in the helpless protesters who had stayed at home, sometimes in resentful acquiescence to the reality of the alien will.[26]

Inasmuch as tradition throughout Terramedia had made the notion of allegiance to a nation-state irrelevant, it required a "de-traditionalized" intelligentsia—within and outside of Terramedia—to reflect upon, and to ultimately develop, concepts and symbols which would win support for nationalism. Among the Arabs, the masses had been satisfied with the policy and practice of gaining their identity through, and manifesting their loyalty to, family, tribe, and socio-religious community:

> Loyalties transcending religion were unknown. Thus Muslims, Christians, and Jews often lived side by side within a single town, each group under the jurisdiction of its own clerical hierarchy, each governed by its own religious law. Muslims owed allegiance to the sultan-caliph; Jews to the grand rabbi; and Christians to their respective patriarchs. . . . Since communal and religious loyalty were indivisible there was little concern about loyalty to the state. An Ottoman subject was regarded abroad and by his fellow Ottoman subjects as a Christian from the Levant, a Jew from Salonika, or a sunni from Tripoli, hardly ever as an Ottoman citizen.[27]

But the substitution of European "rule" for Ottoman imperialism could not change attitudes overnight!

In the overtly colonialized areas, of course, no effort was made to press the masses into manifesting loyalty to the common territory which had been carved to encompass them. Tribes and subcultural groups in Nigeria, or in Uganda, or in Algeria, were left to their traditional designs—so long as these did not detract from their individual recognition of the locus of political power and domination, the alien government. This was easily satisfied by paying taxes and complying with the master's direction and pace of institutional change. This pattern of "divide and rule" posed obstacles for Terramedian nationalists who sought strength in unity. When an attempt to promote change in West Africa by nationalists after World War I was undertaken, for example, the divide and rule principle contributed to its failure:

> The immediate cause of the failure of the Congress's deputation to London was the unwillingness of the British government and the several colonial governments to treat the Congress in pan-territorial terms. This response was largely justified, insofar as the Congress's general demand "firstly to effect a Union between the four colonies" was illusory. Such illusion stemmed directly from the emergent bourgeoisie's exalted sense of its calling—its natural right to lead the masses into modernity—as well as of the real potential of its own modern attributes. More particularly, the rising elites were victims of a false consciousness in regard to the political capacity of their class. Like many rising classes, they assumed that the process of self-discovery as a class generated enough momentum to realize both the aspirations and the objective needs of the class. . . . The colonial governments throughout British West Africa, possessing the power to shape the limits of political change, made it clear to the leaders of the Congress that whatever advances were to be made toward greater African participation in government would be made only within each individual colonial territory.[28]

This was the mood that justified the banning or suppression of various "agitation" groups during the decades preceding World War II, including the Muslim Brotherhood, the Syrian General Congress, the Kavirondo Taxpayers' Welfare Association of Kenya, and the Tanganyika African Association. It required the experience of World War II and the diffusion of a renewed feeling of humanism to give concrete results to the efforts of nationalists, who had, in the interim, found strength and optimism (if not courageous determination), in their exposure to, and review of, various ideologies. The feelings evoked among the Western powers following World War II, and their willingness, with few exceptions, to heed the pleas for self-determination, could be seen as their continued contribution, howbeit unconsciously, to modern nationalism in Terramedia. For, as Rivlin and Szyliowicz have observed, "the West not only supplied the ideology but ensured its acceptance, for by undermining the traditional social organization it broke down the existing system of loyalties, thus creating the conditions which allowed the concept of allegiance to a new unit, the nation, to develop."[29]

While it is true that religion was considered by some nationalists as a means of social mobilization and reform, the emphasis on territory, which permitted geographical demarcation along with social heterogeneity, made such a base ineffective. Prophetic and chiliastic movements, like Pan-Islam and Judaism, proved unsuccessful, except where they incorporated other than religious similarities into their politico-social assertions and aims. Ultimately nonreligious ideologies received greater attention among heads of states.

Throughout Terramedia, whether the advocates for self-determination were working in their homelands or in foreign lands, the commitment was to ideologies which required extensive support and a broad base of loyalty. It was inevitable that nationalists would focus on such ideologies as Pan-Arabism, Pan-Africanism, Garveyism, Judaism, Socialism, and Negritude. Under the impetus of such ideologies, nationalism and nation-states ultimately emerged from the combined efforts of pressure groups and voluntary associations, mass political parties, and charismatic leaders. Although independence would subsequently be attained under indigenous leadership, the ideas and programs which guided such leadership were formulated or inspired by outside forces and personalities, with very few exceptions. And where these "nuclear nationalists" claimed Terramedian identity (as might be said for Césaire, Garvey, Gökalp, and Afghani), this was at best tangential or sentimental. Sarte, DuBois, and Mustapha Kemal contributed as significantly to Terramedian nationalism as did Casely Hayford, Jomo Kenyatta, Kwame Nkrumah, and Abdel Nasser!

Pan-Arabism and Pan-Africanism provided the first set of integrated aims and assertions for removing the inequities imposed upon Terramedia by aliens. These ideologies, prominent in Terramedia even today, grew out of the efforts of intellectual reformers who could not lay claim to any specific homeland in Terramedia. Muhammad Jamal al-Din, for example, in founding the Blessed Socialist Party in 1908, influenced the emergence of nationalist movements which sought, during the period between the two World Wars, "to achieve economic democracy by replacing the feudal and capitalist system with a socialist system in which the interests of the community would have priority over individual claims."[30] Equally significant was the influence of Jamal Ud-Din Afghani, a native of Iran:

> For forty years, he was behind most patriotic movements, revolts and demonstrations in Egypt, Turkey and Iran. While he detested autocratic rulers, he was not opposed to benevolent despotism whenever the pressure of events proved too great a strain upon democracy. . . . Nationalists in the Middle East have been strongly influenced by Afghani's prescription of first eliminating the corrupt kings, their courtiers and the hand-picked assemblies packed with feudal lords, and then establishing a benevolent dictatorship until the prerequisites for the success of a multi-party representative government are met. Afghani, although he was unable to unite the Muslim world, succeeded in molding a generation of political thinkers and statesmen, including such men as Muhammad Abdoh, Saad Zagloul, Mustafa Kemal, Abdullah Al-Nadim, Benbahani, Tabatabai, Adib Ishag, Taliboff and Kawakebe.[31]

In pursuing the goal of unity among people sharing some basis for common identity, such as Arab-ness or African-ness, Terramedian nationalists, following the World War I, were also influenced by the ideas of Ziya Gökalp who, borrowing from the French sociologist Emile Durkheim, had emphasized the notion of solidarity in nation-building. According to Gökalp, "as Turks love freedom and independence, they cannot be communists. But as they love equality, they cannot be individualists. The system most suited to Turkish culture is solidarism. Individual ownership is legitimate only in so far as it serves social solidarity."[32] The successful secularization of Turkey by Kemal Ataturk, based on some of the ideas of Gökalp, encouraged other nationalists to seek unity along other than religious lines.

While ideas were being formulated by roving activists within Terramedia, there were persons whose concerns led them to propose programs for a region which, while physically and experientially removed from their existence, had evoked in them strong desires for identification with it. Thus it was that a Sylvester Williams of Trinidad felt compelled to petition Queen Victoria on behalf of Africa, and to convene the first Pan-African Congress in London in 1900; for the same reason, perhaps, W.E.B. DuBois became involved:

> As I face Africa I ask myself: What is it between us that constitutes a tie that I can feel better than I can explain? Africa is of course my fatherland. Yet neither my father nor father's father ever saw Africa or knew its meaning or cared overmuch for it. . . . But the physical bond is least and the badge of colour relatively unimportant save as a badge; the real essence of this kinship is its social heritage of slavery; the discrimination and insult; and this heritage binds together not simply the children of Africa but extends through yellow Asia and into the South Seas. It is this unity that draws me to Africa.[33]

DuBois organized several other Pan-African Congresses, inspiring the thinking and activities of Terramedian nationalists until they openly asserted their own urgency at the Manchester Conference of 1945—pleading not for the right to win participatory dignity, but immediate independence for those still under colonial rule. The objectives of the West African National Secretariat, formed by Nkrumah, Wallace-Johnson, and George Padmore in 1946, included the following:

> (1) the complete liquidation of the colonial system;
> (2) absolute independence of all West Africa;
> (3) the right of peoples everywhere to organise trade unions, coopera-

tive societies, farmers' organisations within the shackles of imperialist officialdom;
(4) the industrialisation of West Africa including technical and scientific knowledge.

Given the reality of neocolonialism and the disabling effect of ministatism under independence throughout Terramedia, one can appreciate the prescience suggested in the truly Pan-African aim of the West African National Secretariat:

> By a united West Africa we mean that strip of land with all its waterways, hills, mountains and habitations stretching from 30 degrees south of the Sahara and 10 degrees west of the Congos.
>
> West Africa comprises all the territories which have been invaded and are now temporarily occupied by foreign powers. "British" West Africa, "French" West Africa, "Portuguese" West Africa, the "Belgian" Congo, "Spanish" West Africa and the Republic of Liberia–all put together into one united country, is what we mean by West Africa.[34]

This fever of nationalism, stimulated by exposure to the conflict between liberal democracy and authoritarian colonialism, was similar to that which had given rise to Pan-Arabism earlier in the century. Inasmuch as the assertion by Nkrumah and his "radical" colleagues in 1945 derived from the seeds of transformation planted by the first Pan-African Association in 1900, the basis of a parallel movement among the Arabs would seem applicable to their African counterparts.[35] Just as nationalists in the Arab sector of Terramedia had given varying interpretations to the ideas of their mentors, so did Africans see different possibilities in the movement generated by DuBois and his articulate contemporaries, especially Marcus Garvey, Aime Césaire, and Langston Hughes.[36] Pan-Arabism and Pan-Africanism served as instruments, in part, to secure the independence of individual nation-states–not the large social enclaves which their proposition of unity had enunciated. Yet, both ideologies remain quite vital and may yet provide the cement for bringing into reality a United States of Terramedia. For as Crutcher has observed,

> The essence of what many of these leaders express in various ways is that before colonialism Africa was an integral being not yet perfected; under colonialism Africa suffered a kind of exile and passion in which it was divided, enslaved, and humiliated by alien peoples, but also steeled and introduced to modern ideas; and with the Pan-African national-independence movement Africa has its own exodus, regeneration, and salvation, by which the original independence and

> unity is regained at a higher level. . . . Some of the reasons given by African leaders for the need of African unity are these: It will secure Africa from the dangers of reimposition of colonialism and of economic and cultural dependence on nonAfrican powers, give Africa a strong and respected voice in world affairs, overcome tribalism and Balkan-like conflicts, spur economic development, facilitate the exchange and assimilation of new yet Africanized ideas, and restore to Africans the peace and happiness of being at one with their brethren.[37]

The dilemma of total or partial commitment to a unity of all Africans parallels the commitment to Pan-Arabism with which it overlaps, and which also has prompted varying enthusiasm:

> When unity of all Muslims appeared to be a practical impossibility, it was replaced in the minds of many by what seemed to be a more feasible scheme: Pan-Arabism, or the concept that all Arabs, sharing a more or less common racial and cultural as well as religious heritage, should fight for freedom from colonialism, with the eventual goal of uniting into one Arab state. These ideas, held by many Arab leaders at the turn of the nineteenth century, were publicized widely in North Africa by Chekib Arslan, a learned man of Syrian origin who operated from various points of exile, usually Geneva. His ideas influenced many . . . making them think in terms of eventually obtaining independence for Tunisia—but only as a first step towards the formation of a greater Arab state. Eventually, of course, these ideas . . . would conflict with the plans of others, who wanted to be just plain Tunisians.[38]

The quest for self-determination continued to find its stimulus in the history of political justice. In the United States, in France, and in Russia, that experience had been conferred on peoples who arose to remove the yoke of colonialism or of "taxation without representation." Even Woodrow Wilson after World War I strengthened the will of the oppressed, by objecting to the designs of Britain and France to perpetuate and extend colonial rule into parts of Terramedia which had been colonies of Turkey, Germany, and Italy. Even the potential independence manifested in the mandate system remained out of reach for at least a decade, amidst disappointment by pan-nationalists that the unity which theory and pragmatism dictated was not being realized. Ultimately, widespread awareness of the nature of white control evoked other ideologies for the consideration of nationalists, among them Garveyism, Baathism, and Negritude. All these ideologies, like Pan-Arabism and Pan-Africanism before them, were a reaction to European thought and practice, endeavoring to encourage their negation. In time, bolstered significantly by world events challenging the leaders of the "civilized" powers to show consistency in words and in deed, Terramedians saw their nationalist struggles translated into sovereignty. And by 1960 it became clear that—with few exceptions—Terramedian colonies could be recognized as nations, with the privileges and responsibilities appertaining thereto! Nationalism and its consequences, however, were but an aspect of change. New political processes and images were brought into focus, but in the context of certain enduring experiences and social structures that have continued to influence Terramedia.

NOTES

1. See George Simmel, "Conflict as Sociation," cited in Lewis Coser and Bernard Rosenberg, *Sociological Theory* (New York: Macmillan, 1976), pp. 175-77.
2. Hodgkin, *Nationalism,* p. 17.
3. Emerson, *Empire to Nation,* p. 89.
4. Ibid., p. 95. Cf. Wendell Bell and Walter Freeman, *Ethnicity and Nation Building* (Beverly Hills: Sage Publications, 1974), pp. 10-11.
5. K. H. Silvert, *Expectant Peoples, Nationalism and Development* (New York: Random House, 1963), pp. 18-19.
6. Cf. First, *Libya,* pp. 14-24.
7. Andre Du Toit, "Ideological Change," in *Change in Contemporary South Africa,* ed. Leonard Thompson and Jeffrey Butler (Berkeley: University of California Press, 1975), p. 27.
8. Hodgkin, *Nationalism,* p. 17.
9. Basil Davidson, *The African Past* (New York: Grossett & Dunlap, 1964), pp. 364-65.
10. Austin J. Shelton, *The African Assertion* (New York: Odyssey Press, 1968), p. 14.
11. Gerald Moore, *Seven African Writers* (London: Oxford University Press, 1962, p. 19.
12. See Peretz, *Middle East Today,* and Robert Rotberg and Ali Mazrui, *Protest and Power in Black Africa* (New York: Oxford University Press, 1970).
13. See Mekki Mtewa, "The Saga of John Chilembwe," *Journal of Black Studies* 8 (1977):227-48.
14. Benjamin Rivlin and Joseph Szyliowicz, *The Contemporary Middle East* (New York: Random House, 1965), pp. 107-08.
15. Lerner, *Traditional Society,* pp. 44, 46.
16. See Franklin W. Knight, *The Caribbean—the Genesis of a Fragmented Nationalism* (New York: Oxford University Press, 1978), pp. 146-88.
17. Polk, *Arab World,* p. 89.
18. Charles Gallagher, *The United States and North Africa* (Cambridge, MA: Harvard University Press, 1963), p. 68. Cf. Frederick S. Arkhurst, *U.S. Policy Toward Africa* (New York: Praeger Publisher, 1975), p. 13-25.
19. Philip Quigg, *Africa, a Foreign Affairs Reader* (New York: Praeger Publishers, 1964), p. 44.

20. J. Duffy and R. Manners, *Africa Speaks* (Princeton: Van Nostrand, 1961), p. 21.

21. Benard Lewis, *The Middle East and the West* (New York: Harper & Row, 1966), pp. 35-36.

22. See John Hope Franklin, *Color and Race* (Boston: Houghton Mifflin, 1968), pp. 2-3.

23. See Alan Merriam, *Congo, Background of Conflict* (Evanston: Northwestern University Press, 1961), pp. 352-53.

24. Peretz, *Middle East Today,* pp. 143-44.

25. C. J. Friedrich, *Man and His Government* (New York: McGraw-Hill, 1963), pp. 89-90.

26. Bell and Freeman, *Ethnicity,* pp. 50-53.

27. Peretz, *Middle East Today,* pp. 137-38.

28. Rotberg and Mazrui, *Protest and Power,* pp. 580-81.

29. Rivlin and Szyliowicz, *Contemporary Middle East,* p. 199.

30. Adbul Said, *The African Phenomenon* (Boston: Allan & Bacon, 1968), p. 101.

31. Rivlin and Szyliowicz, *Contemporary Middle East,* pp. 231-32.

32. Ibid., p. 223.

33. Colin Legum, *Pan-Africanism* (New York: Praeger Publishers, 1962), p. 24.

34. Geiss, *Pan-African Movement,* pp. 412-13.

35. See Yale, *Near East,* pp. 187-93.

36. See Thomas R. Frazier, *Afro-American History* (New York: Harcourt, Brace & World, 1970, and Okon E. Uya, *Black Brotherhood* (Lexington: D. C. Heath, 1971).

37. John Crutcher, "Pan-Africanism: African Odyssey," *Current History* 50 (1963):2-3.

38. Lorna Han, *North Africa: Nationalism in Nationhood* (Washington, DC: Public Affairs Press, 1960), p. 11.

Chapter Eight

THE RAMIFICATIONS OF SOCIAL CHANGE

The Nature of Sociocultural Change

It was inevitable that the increasing pace of European infiltration into Terramedian societies, and reactions to such incursion, would have a serious impact on the nature and direction of social and cultural change. These, in turn, would influence existing and evolving lifestyles. While accepting the universality and inevitably of change, one must, nevertheless, recognize that the final outcome would certainly have been different had not European control occurred so rapidly and so intensely. Not only were the normally expected changes in institutions and social structures modified, but, in changing, the institutions and structures had to cope with the introduction of what were essentially alien values.

In the Middle East, the long period of supremacy over thought and behavior which Islam had enjoyed, became subject to challenge as greater exposure to other systems of thought and belief became possible. The effect of Napoleon's invasion of Egypt, for example, resulted in an increased awareness of the benefits of modernization and rational planning. Even though technology, traditionally, had not occupied an extremely important place in Middle Eastern values, the products of modern European technology found relatively easy acceptance, leading to further sociocultural changes.[1] The Middle East, moreover, could not escape the consequences of its favorable geographical position:

> Connected with these geographic features, which contributed so greatly to the welfare and cultural progress of the Near East, were certain disadvantages. The caravan and sea routes became avenues of invasion accessible to the Indo-European nomads from the north and to the Turkish and Mongolian nomads from the east. The caravan routes crossed arid and semiarid lands suitable only for wandering tribes, who were ever a threat to the trade routes and the agrarian and urban population. The great wealth of the Near Eastern cities was a constant temptation to invasion by "barbarian" nomads, as well as by predatory civilized states.[2]

The changes that had occurred within sub-Saharan Africa, on the other hand, remained, for the most part, within the limits of the typical subsistence economies and kin-bound social structures. At certain stages in recent history, however, changes occurred which were not merely changes within these systems, but were to become changes of systems.[3] The factors underlying such changes included: trade contacts between Africans and outsiders; the establishment of colonial rule, and in some cases the actual colonization of the land by European settlers—as in Kenya, Rhodesia, and South Africa; the establishment of Christian missions, the development of schools, and the insistence on the use of a vehicular language; and the development of an exchange economy. The establishment of industrial activities, as well as the introduction of taxation based on the colonialist currency, forced many Africans (and Middle Easterners to some extent) to migrate to the available centers of employment, with resulting disruption in traditional patterns of social organization. Even people who remained secure within the confines of their rural villages felt the effect of their kinsmen's involvement in migratory labor contracts.[4] For other villagers, simply having a highway or railway running nearby affected their lives. Such experiences affected the norms which had always seemed adequate in the traditional way of life; but they confused the locus of authority.

Based on the foregoing, several generalizations about the characteristics of social change in Terramedia can be made: (1) Social change, especially as a result of the European presence, occurred with great speed, particularly since World War II; (2) It has been vast and widespread, affecting virtually all aspects of peoples' lives—beliefs, clothing, food, housing, marriage, recreation, and the like; (3) It has occurred rather unevenly, juxtaposing pockets of drastic change and enclaves of rigid traditionalism; (4) Some of the change has been quite superficial, affecting only a minority of people within a larger group, or has been diffuse and eclectic.[5]

Before examining the ramifications of social change in Terramedia, it might be useful to survey the basic topic of social and cultural change itself. Sociocultural change entails alterations of societies and, perhaps more importantly, of the cultures of people. *Society,* the base term, refers to a group of people living together more or less in the same environment. They regard themselves, and are regarded by others, as constituting a relatively homogeneous entity or community. A society has an identifiable membership and a patterned arrangement of relation among its members.[6] *Culture,* on the other hand, refers to the patterned and customary behavior of the people of a society, varying from person to person within a range openly or implicitly approved by the membership of the society; culture is learned by the individual.[7] Social change consists of alterations in the society, in the structure and relations of the people. Cultural change, on the other hand, refers to alterations in the actions, beliefs, and values of the people of the society. People can retain older social structures and assimilate new behavior, or they can change their society and its structures while retaining older values. Furthermore, they can change both their society and their culture—this is often the case—although they usually do not change both at the same time and to the same degree. The term "sociocultural change" is broad enough to include all types of modifications or alterations in interpersonal relationships and their supporting symbols and artifacts. It implies an alteration, over a period of time (which may be short or long), in the roles, institutions, and norms of a society.[8]

CULTURE LEARNING AND CULTURE CHANGE

It is important to understand that all people have a culture, and that culture is learned: We all learn our own culture within our respective societies. For example, when the baby notices that the dog puts its head down to eat, and decides that that method is worth imitating, mother corrects the child, saying: "We don't eat our food that way, but with a spoon," and mother shows the child how to use a spoon. So the child learns the approved behavior of his people based on the value system established by his own people. Learning of one's own people's culture, is called enculturation.[9] Three mechanisms are involved: (1) *imitation,* the child's mocking of others' roles, including adult roles, such as having a little water pot analogous to mother's large water pot, and accompanying mother to the river for water; (2) *instruction,* both direct and indirect, formal and informal; (3) *motivation,* consisting of the reward or punishment invoked in response to conforming or nonconforming behavior.

Related to the foregoing are several other matters which can be listed as postulates or general statements about culture and change:

1. Because culture is learned, it can be forgotten, and of course, it can be changed. In fact, no culture is unchanging or static; all cultures change. Modern experience reveals how dramatically customs can change—as with the development and consequences of nuclear fission and rockets being sent to outer space—and how superficially too, as in the rise and fall of women's hemlines. Such changes which occur within a society result usually from invention, which is the new combination of old elements.

2. Every society has a system of values by which the members of that society make judgments to determine what is to be approved and what is to be condemned, what is good and what is bad. Any value judgment made about the culture of a different society from one's own, therefore, may prove to be invalid, for cultural values are relative. For example, among some groups of Igbo people a fat woman is considered beautiful. A Fula judgment that an Igbo woman might not be beautiful, simply because she is fat, is a judgment which has validity only among other Fula. Values, therefore, are cultural and relative, not absolute. This is simply because different people have different cultures and different bases for their value judgments. On the other hand, one must remember that certain judgments might be made which are not completely determined by culture. One can make an assessment, for example, of the degree of success of two different methods of performing a practical operation, such as fertilizing crops or saving the lives of children who commonly die from epidemics of measles. Such a judgment—that Method X works more efficiently than Method Y—can indeed transcend the normal relativity of cultural value judgments.

3. The contact between peoples having different cultures often results in what is called culture shock to both groups, and the reaction to this shock is usually rejection of the other culture and the belief that one's own ways are superior. Culture contact has been extremely varied in Terramedia, and has included, among others, the following modes: colonialization; communication through newspapers, radio, and television; conquest and occupation; diplomacy; education; migrations of people; mission activity; tourism and trade. Important to remember is that contact between people having different cultures can result in borrowing by one person from another; and what is borrowed might be adopted. When this occurs, one is acculturating, for acculturation is the process of culture change resulting from adopting of elements borrowed from persons not of one's own society.

4. Change is usually selective rather than total. This means that when people borrow from other people, they do not as a rule adopt the whole culture of the other people, but adopt some elements and ignore other

elements of the contacted culture. For example, initiation into a divining cult ordinarily requires contributions by the initiate of foodstuffs, some sacrificial animals, strips of cloth and other items, and some money. Traditionally, the money consisted of cowries, so the use of modern currency for this traditional purpose reflects a certain bit of culture change—it is an innovation.

5. A great deal of change, particularly in Africa, is additive rather than substitutive. This means, simply, that people might adopt a new method of doing something, or a new value, yet retain the older method or the older value. This accommodating quality can be found among numerous human groups around the world, although some groups are resistant to almost all change, and accommodating societies themselves can be rigidly opposed to some change.[10]

The important process of acculturation depends on three key elements: exposure of beliefs and values related to new goals and ideals; access to the new goals provided by the new situation; adoption of the behavior related to the new situation. These elements certainly lay at the base of the relationship between Terramedian and European cultures, although, at different times and in varying situations, they were more or less intense. As Aidan Southall has observed, "norms must change before society changes." Such change in norms implies the approval of ideas and actions which were previously regarded as experimental or even disreputable; it does not necessarily imply the approval of new ideas or new actions. What was considered daring a generation ago might be considered commonplace or even dull today. The more formal the structure of a social situation, the more unequivocal and definite its norms might be, and the more the people involved in it are compelled to conform until there is a change in rules.[11] Consequently, not only must change normally fit the needs of the people before it will occur, but it will not occur until their system of values somehow accommodates it. It is, accordingly, important that people perceive and interpret the new artifacts, behaviors, or values of the alien culture which they have contacted. Reinterpretation occurs commonly in culture change, leading to syncretism, which is the amalgamation of conflicting or different parties, principles, values, ideologies, and even cultures. Victor Uchendu, a Nigerian anthropologist, has pointed out that the attitude of Africans toward magic, medical innovation, protective medicines, divination, and sacrifices indicates that the Christian religion has not satisfied the psycho-cultural needs which were provided by the traditional religions. But, on the other hand, sacredness of the traditional sanctions has been fairly well discredited, and no effective sanctions have replaced the traditional ones. In such a situation marked by conflicts in beliefs, the so-called "native" Christian churches have arisen. Such churches often do satisfy the psycho-cultural needs of the worshippers, and offer sanctions satisfactory to certain traditional attitudes: For example, most of them permit polygyny.[12]

An example of several aspects of culture change is the Anchau Scheme of the British Colonial Government in Northern Nigeria, described in "Culture Change Under Pressure: A Hausa Case."[13] About the year 1928, sleeping sickness reached the epidemic stage, and the colonial government decided to institute a plan to clear bush along the streams in a 700 square mile area inhabited by 50,000 Hausa people. This clearance of brush was intended to destroy the breeding places of the tsetse fly, which carries sleeping sickness.

The Hausa greatly feared sleeping sickness, and believed that it was caused by *iska* spirits which inhabited the brush along the streams. They also called the disease *kunturu,* designating a region under malign supernatural influences; but the role of the tsetse fly in relation to the disease was unknown to them. The colonial government persuaded the Emir to send a personal representative to remain at Anchau and to see that orders were obeyed. At first it was necessary to hire laborers to cut the brush, because the Hausa peasants refused to cooperate; shortly afterwards, the hired laborers stopped working because they had come to sacred bush. The government, therefore, had to import non-Hausa workers to cut this area. When the time for brush-cutting came up the following year, however, the local Hausa workers refused to appear. Hausa headmen were removed from office, and all the peasants were fined, so they reluctantly gave in and cut the brush. The result was that sleeping sickness was virtually eliminated from the district.

What were the Hausa interpretations of the entire affair? They felt that the brush-clearing was useful because: (1) It got rid of tsetse flies, which gave painful bites and were annoying insects; (2) It got rid of monkeys who destroyed crops; (3) It improved the pasturage for Fulani cattle. According to them, it had nothing whatsoever to do with sleeping sickness, which was caused by the *iska* or spirits. When they were asked if they would continue to clear brush if they were not forced to, every Hausa headman replied in the negative. The new cultural pattern of annual brush-clearing was adopted only because of governmental pressure, not because of any change in the norms and values of the people, and it illustrates the all-too-common temporary adoption of an innovation without its integration into the culture.

This abbreviated description of the Anchau scheme points more directly to several of the important factors in the change of societies and cultures. In the Anchau scheme, change was enforced, it was introduced by outsiders, the Hausa had imperfect knowledge of its intended purpose, and serious Hausa values were not positively involved in it except negatively—it was dangerous in that it entailed cutting bush inhabited by spirits. The negative results suggest that change might more successfully occur if, among other factors, the to-be-changed artifact of behavior is: (1) introduced by an agent who is well known, trusted, and accepted, rather than by a stranger; (2) if it is properly understood in terms of the beliefs of those who are to accept it; (3) if its value can be related positively to existing values of the society, and if it can somehow be conceived favorably; and (4) if it promises or guarantees increased prestige, status, or wealth for those who adopt it.[14]

What will generally change slowest in any society are those beliefs and behavior felt to be most crucial to the continued existence and order of the society—agricultural methods, sexual behavior and kinship association, health and medical practice, and some aspects of religion and ritual.[15] What will generally change fastest, on the other hand, is that behavior thought to be least crucial to the basic well-being of the society.[16]

Moreover, there are different kinds of change. A common sort of change is the addition of a behavior to already existing behavior, and a slight modification of the existing behavior to accommodate the borrowed element. But there is also change aroused by a new situation (or set of situations) which had not been encountered in the past, and for which the society has no means of accommodation. Such change as this is related mainly to acculturation, and most specifically to the relation between Terramedians and Europeans. For example, if youngsters go to school, they learn not merely more things than their elders know, but totally different things. So the old knowledge of the village is simply not applicable to the new situation in which the youngsters find themselves, and they in turn feel a kind of superiority of knowledge: They know what the elders know—or they are aware of the range of the elders' knowledge—but the elders do not know what the youngsters have learned.

Forces of Change in Terramedia

There have been three major forces of change seriously affecting Terramedia: trade and economic contacts, conquest and colonialism, and mission activities conducted primarily by Christians. These influences overlap and interlock with one another—the trader leading the way for the missionary and colonialist, or even sometimes being the conqueror and colonializer; the missionary being supported by colonialist military power; "Christianity" being used to support presumed European cultural and racial superiority, and thereby rationalizing the colonialization of the African or Middle Easterner, and so forth.

TRADE

Terramedian peoples have experienced trade and related economic contacts with outside cultures for many centuries. The Middle East, particularly, was for many hundreds of years the major trade junction of the world: All the trade between Europe and Asia of necessity had to pass through that area. With such trade contacts there was great opportunity for peoples of different cultures to exchange artifacts, ideas, and technology. There was a similar, although not quite so widespread, cultural exchange in several areas of East Africa and the Sudan because of sea trade, or the location of societies along caravan routes. But many areas of sub-Saharan Africa were more isolated, and people had contact with a far more limited number of outsiders and the behavior, ideas, or technology of quite different cultures.[17]

Under such circumstances, many African societies were thrown on their own resources, having to depend heavily on invention as the major mode of innovation of their cultures. But as societies become or remain relatively isolated, with limited contacts with other human groups and with a narrow range of differentness among those other groups, custom and conformity to past behavior and ideas tend to become more and more rigid. Furthermore, invention and innovation tend often to be frowned upon, unless they fall within the usually narrow range of acceptable innovative behavior. This does not mean that invention does not occur in relatively isolated communities, but, rather, that invention is usually less acceptable in such communities than it is in communities with wider contacts. In addition, human beings everywhere tend to invent far less than is supposed; rather, they modify and adopt ideas and things learned from others. Thus traditional sub-Saharan Africa manifests cultural "pockets" of highly developed specialized ideas and technology which often were guarded jealously by the tribe or nation possessing the developments, and not generally disseminated very widely to its neighbors. For example, the bronzes and brasses of Ife were passed on to Benin, and possibly carried by early Bini to Onitsha, but certainly not handed over to the Igbo, Ibibio, Itsekiri, or other groups of people in southern Nigeria.

The trade which existed tended to be village trade, sometimes intervillage trade, and more rarely intertribal trade.[18] The trade between such social groups, however, did not carry with it the exchange of such technology as that which was required to cast the bronze and brass statuary of Ife and Benin, but was trade usually limited to foodstuffs and, less commonly, items of medicine. During the fifteenth century, however, the patterns of trade, particularly in sub-Saharan Africa, changed drastically, with effects on all of Terramedia: The Portuguese developed a "Grand Design" to circumvent the Ottoman Empire which had virtually closed off the Middle East. And in so doing they made initial contacts along the West and Southern coasts of Africa, introducing trade items (such as firearms) which were substantially different from those common to the tropical African markets. The most important trade items which the Europeans soon sought in return for the goods which they introduced were slaves. Almost needless to say, by the value standards of most human cultures today, the effects of the slave trade were horrendous: the setting of tribe against tribe, clan against clan; the development of the notion that human beings can be considered as nothing more than commodities subject to the laws of supply and demand; the vast depopulation of large areas of Africa; the growth of extreme racism and the expansion of attitudes of cultural superiority which still plague many human groups today. My intention, however, is not to argue this point in detail, but rather to stress the fact that trade, particularly the slave trade, was one important force of social and cultural change in Terramedia.[19]

By engaging in trade with Europeans—whether in the early spice and ivory trade, the much vaster slave trade, or in the later palm oil trade—the African made much more extensive contact with peoples more greatly different from himself than were his African neighbors. It involved exposure, access, and adoption—the African becoming aware of the use and value of certain European items such as firearms, having economic access to these items by furnishing goods or slaves desired by the Europeans, and adopting the items. With such adoption, guns steadily replacing bows and spears as hunting or military weapons, for example, changes in behavior followed. Some coastal groups, acquiring superior arms, became ascendant over their fellows in the hinterland, and greatly changed their social structures and organization to meet the needs of empire. Whereas slave-raiding had not widely existed in the past, largely because human beings had not been considered particularly marketable commodities, it became common practice, developing almost into a way of life for some peoples, stimulated by the desire for the new and appealing goods of the Europeans.[20]

Africans were acculturating in other ways, too, because of trade contacts. Writing of his voyages from 1786 to 1800, John Adams said of the people of Old Calabar: "Many of the natives write English; an art first acquired by some of the traders' sons, who had visited England, and which they have had the sagazity to retain up to the present period. They have established schools and schoolmasters, for the purpose of instructing in this art the youths belonging to families of consequence." Such culture change indicates clearly that some Africans had learned that the Europeans possessed certain subtle powers which those Africans did not have—that is, that new behavior experienced by the African, and not at all part of that

African past, was given value and was adopted to the benefit of the African.

Although many such changes were occurring among Terramedians because of their own assessment of the values to themselves of European behavior and technology, the acculturation which was to develop with the movement of Europeans into the interior of Africa (and the Middle East in less direct fashion), was much more controlled, Terramedians having far less to say about what behavior they might think useful to adopt.[21]

CONQUEST AND COLONIALISM

Some of the impact of Europeans on Africans is suggested by Magnus Ade Opoola, writing on "Relics of Colonial Rule in Nigeria." "My grandfather used to tell me of the 'oyinbo alawofunfun' (the white man) who has helped in the intertribal wars, whose sense of justice and fair play was unsurpassed. He also stood as a pillar of trust; but in the interim, has constituted himself into the local almighty—the be-all and end-all in everything."[22]

In penetrating the interior parts of the African continent (whether for increase of profits in trade, for diplomatic reasons and the accumulation of colonies, to end the slave trade by striking it at its "source," because of apostolic zeal, or any of the myriad other reasons and rationalizations expressed by explorers and colonialists), the Europeans were often entering strange and sometimes dangerous areas. They, therefore, felt that they required protection and, to consolidate control of the areas, means of establishing order so that European-centered and European-focused desires could be fulfilled. A certain degree of what might be called controlled acculturation was accordingly necessary, at least to the extent that Africans had to be limited in their activities ("pacified" was a popular euphemism) and instructed in new activities. Such activities included paying taxes, obeying alien rather than family or traditional authorities; working in agricultural, industrial, or mining occupations, less for subsistence than to earn the European currency necessary for the payment of taxes, and the like. The subject peoples were given no choice but to agree with the Europeans, chiefly because the latter possessed superior military technology. As an aside, one might remark that Ethiopia atypically avoided being colonialized, primarily because it had acquired great quantities of modern arms and was able successfully to repel the Italians at Adowa in 1896. Africans otherwise, however, were "pacified" militarily or by treaty (behind which always crouched the spectre of armed might), to suit the colonial powers and their various socioeconomic needs and wishes.

The behavior, furthermore, which was insisted upon by colonial governments and personnel as being "proper" was that which the African (and to a lesser extent, the Middle Easterner) was urged, and in some cases forced, to emulate. Such change in behavior to suit the European was linked with possibilities of advancement for certain Terramedians, and was the chief means by which the latter might gain position and earn salaries. In the different territories, especially in Africa, the change in behavior was very similar; the French referred to their system as assimilation, whereas the British chose to let the process remain nameless. The apparent purpose in assimilation was to integrate "Overseas France" with Metropolitan France by the creation of *evolues*—Terramedians who had "evolved" into Frenchmen through education and the overt acceptance of French culture. Assimilation suggested that for the colonialized subject there was no culture higher than French culture, and that the colonialized person would be rewarded through being assimilated if he evolved sufficiently. It implied, however, that the colonialized individual was a carte blanche upon whom French culture could be purely impressed.

Whereas the French often preferred imitators of their own culture, the British wanted to "pacify" their colonial subjects, although they did not, as a rule, systematize the process. Subjects of the British Empire—particularly African subjects—were never given the impression that they might "evolve" into Englishmen or Scots, but, as in French colonialism, they too were promised rewards (prestige, jobs) if they altered their behavior to suit their masters. Although a colonial establishment was important in the acculturation process, what came to be more important was the stress placed by both British and French (and others, as well) on changes in individuals, necessitating personality alterations which Europeans felt might be easily enough managed. The most effective means to effect such changes, to create the elite and evolues who one day would use the changes to argue against these very forces of change, were missionary activity and education.

The missionary made the most revolutionary demands of Terramedians, intending to control their souls rather than their lands. This conquest of souls was not divorced from the colonialist conquest of bodies, however; indeed, the colonialist and missionary must be considered as only slightly varying aspects of the same European force. The missionary was perhaps more often accepted with some degree of friendliness, whereas the colonialist was invariably cast in the role of conqueror. Sixteenth century Benin, for example, received the Portuguese missionary, John Alfonso d'Aveiro, and his fellows with great cordiality. At that early period they were associated with Portugal itself and with Portuguese traders in ivory, pepper, and Benin cloth; and the Oba (King) of Benin conducted sovereign to sovereign relations with the King of Portugal. For quite a long time, mission priests lived at Benin or visited Benin at frequent intervals; but by

1695 the Bini had reverted to their traditional religion, and Christian mission influence diminished throughout the time of the slave trade until the end of the nineteenth century. In 1892, Oba Ovonramwen made a free trade treaty with the British Government; a political and trade mission, meant to influence the Oba to carry out the terms of this treaty, was attacked in 1897; a month later the British sent a "punitive" force which conquered Benin and established British colonial control over midwestern Nigeria. Almost immediately afterward, the colonial government began to send young Bini to the Church of Scotland Mission at Calabar, and Church of England missionaries worked extensively in Benin itself. Thus in Benin (in present-day Nigeria), which is something of a pattern for much of Africa relative to the relations between Africans and missionaries, there were two kinds of contact: The early contact in which the missionaries were welcomed, and the later contact in which the missionaries were part of the invading European force, linked almost inextricably with colonialism.[23]

What did Christian missionaries wish to do? In general it is fair to say that missionaries felt that they were propagating the "true faith" in what they considered to be apostolic work among the "heathens," and one must also agree that it required some dedication for a man or a small group of men, generally unarmed, to come out to lands where the "Devil" himself seemed to have delighted in creating a special hell for them—a hell of diseases unknown to Europe, which could strike a man dead in a matter of days—a hell of dangerous reptiles and insects, as well as larger beasts, and—to them—a hell of human cultures. If they could not fully stop disease (although medical missionaries later began to work seriously at this, too), or kill off the insects; if they could not change the inhospitable weather, they felt they could do something about the African. They could "civilize" him, teach him the "truth," develop in him "decency" and "honour," and they could shed the "light" of European knowledge over the "dark continent." J. Otumba Payne expressed several of the foregoing attitudes in a memorial of Dec. 7, 1892, addressed to the Archbishop of Canterbury. The reference is to Bishop Samuel Crowther of the Niger Diocese:

> The facts of his Mission—e.g., thousands of converts won from the most debasing kind of heathenism and idolatry, and many of them from cannibalism, infanticide, and other cruel practices also; Christian congregations, Churches and Schools here and there in what was before a moral and spiritual wilderness.

In short, missionaries wanted to bring about personality changes in their flocks and not have them adopt only superficially the Christian teachings.

They wanted to develop inner change, change in the covert behavior of the African, an automatic Christian response to any situation which the African convert might encounter.

The effect of missionaries was widespread. The report of the All Africa Churches Conference on Christian Education held at Salisbury, Rhodesia, early in 1963 points up the neglect and intolerance of traditional African culture as a basis of mission education. The report also condemned the creation of divisions in the community through sectarianism, the fostering of dependence rather than self-reliance, and the use of schools for proselytizing rather than for education. But the effects of mission work were more extensive than this. Central, and perhaps most important, was the spread of the use of a vehicular language, normally the language of the colonializing power. In their contacts with traders and in their quite early, peripheral contacts with missionaries, Africans developed trade languages and, in some instances, learned European languages which appeared useful for them to know.

Vehicular languages became more widespread with colonialist control of the continent because they were required for all official matters, and only those who could effectively communicate with the colonialist could hope to obtain positions of importance. But with mission activity, particularly education, the vehicular language was more accessible to greater numbers of colonialized peoples. By understanding this kind of a language they were able to communicate not only with colonialist and missionary, but with other colonialized peoples of the plural society or colony in which they lived. When such widespread communication is possible, it is more likely that social and cultural change will occur and increase, as was the case in Terramedia in the nineteenth and twentieth centuries.

Consequences of Change

As a result of several developments following the onset of colonialism, migration of peoples and numerous changes occurred in social structures and behavior. These developments included: (1) the pacification of the colony, resulting in greater safety in travelling, improved transportation, and generally an increase of population because of improved sanitation, nutrition, and medical care; (2) the spread of the vehicular language, usually that of the colonializing or "protecting" power, so that one could communicate with others of different language groups; (3) the desire to escape localized supernatural dangers, to escape the limitations of one's social or economic class, and to escape from tribal responsibilities and proscriptions; (4) the establishment of job centers in the cities, and the insistence by the colonialists on a money exchange economy, with the resulting lure of higher wages and access to manufactured goods and possibly increased status.

Increased urbanization naturally followed such increased migration. We might define urbanization as that process which encourages the concentration of a large, heterogeneous population into a limited land area where economic activities are essentially nonagricultural, and interpersonal relationships are highly formalized.[24] There are many who see urbanization as the most significant determinant of change, viewing the city as the focal point of sociocultural change. Accordingly, reference has often been made to some of its prominent concomitants, such as the following: industrialization; a complex and diversified system of communication; increased social mobility, both horizontal and vertical; increased reliance on social institutions and laws in place of folkways and mores; greater flexibility in systems of stratification, with emphasis on achieved rather than prescribed statuses and roles; more frequent incidence of social disorganization and of social problems; increased assumption of the responsibility for promoting social and personal well-being by the government; and the proliferation of voluntary associations and vested-interest groups.[25] But urbanization is not the norm in Terramedia, as it has become in the United States and Europe. Most countries, in fact, are no more than 40% urbanized, as the following percentages of urbanization show: United Arab Republic, 35%; South Africa, 35%; Israel, 30%; Morocco, 29%; Nigeria, 19%; Ghana, 17%; Ivory Coast, 8%; Guinea, 6%; Sierra Leone, 6%.[26]

Related to migration and urbanization is the process of detribalization, whereby the individual is removed from participation in his culture, with a subsequent loss of special loyalty to his culture and society. Judith Alves Martins, writing about Macua and Maconde peoples of Mozambique, argued that detribalization, especially among women, occurred because of the attraction of urban centers and the woman's removal from traditional village controls; missionary activity, which set itself against tribal customs; the attractiveness to women of modern medical practices; and the protection of women's individual rights under Portuguese colonial law.[27] Although detribalization does occur in a greater or lesser degree across the continent, one must always be cautious in assessing its degree.

As a rule, the Terramedian villager who goes to the city does not throw away everything of the village and take on everything of the city.[28] Indeed, he might adopt some of the city's culture while retaining his village culture, and in some behavior might syncretize the two-cultures. Saburi O. Biobaku illustrates this in his description of the effects of culture change on a Muslim Yoruba:

> As a Yoruba, Ade is bound to be hierarchical in his thinking about society; he naturally respects his elders and defers to authority

> without being subservient; when he visits his aged relatives they greet him with ancestral praise poems, and these inevitably strike a chord of response in his soul. He cannot ignore the yearnings of his poor relatives and however he may rationalize he must control his individualist tendencies for the good of the community, encompassed by his extended family.[29]

Such separation from village culture, the results of urbanization, often produces a special syncretistic structure known as the voluntary association. A voluntary association is a group freely organized to respond to new situations and needs which its members feel cannot be realized through other means. Voluntary associations arise partly from tribal associations. People finding themselves in a city far from their villages seize upon kinship and tribal bonds for mutual aid, and tribal associations are formed for general welfare purposes. But as people are removed from their home territory, they tend to form associations based on common interests and expressing similar status regardless of tribal lines. These are voluntary associations, which have served as important bases for the growth of national consciousness and nationalism, as well as for other changes in culture.[30]

Migration, urbanization, and the formation of voluntary associations furnish exposure to beliefs and values related to new goals and ideals; acculturation, however, depends not merely on exposure but also on economic access to the new goals and the change in norms which will result in adoption of the changed behavior. Sometimes, as we have seen, the Terramedian—although exposed to new beliefs and values—did not fully understand these as the European understood them. So, his adoption of the new behavior was partial, or the borrowed element was used differently. Moreover, quite often, Terramedian peoples might have been exposed to beliefs and values related to new goals and ideals, but were denied economic access to these new goals. Here is the problem of what is called "rising expectation." This is the awareness that poverty is not the inevitable lot of mankind, with the subsequent demand for improved standards of living and for accelerated transformation of the society and the economy, usually by the class of people who contribute least to the economy. Such expectations often are frustrated. For example, in many instances Terramedians were encouraged by Europeans to become educated, because the Europeans needed junior clerks, court messengers, and the like; but the Terramedian's opportunity for assuming really senior positions in the colonial government or domineering economy was quite limited.[31]

The acceptance or adoption of new values imported by the Europeans very often entails modification of the old order—change which is very obvious in urban surroundings in Terramedia, and relatively acceptable there, but which also feeds back change to the villages and rural areas where traditionalism tends to remain strongest. For example, if the Terramedian respects education, he must give some status to the schoolteacher in the community, although the schoolteacher by any traditional reckoning would most likely be a person without any particular status at all. Accordingly, if one gives status to the schoolteacher in a Terramedian society, and if this results from the people's desire for a European-type of "modern" education, one almost invariably gets caught up in a value judgment about the relative importance of the schoolteacher and the traditional authorities, the elders or the chiefs. That is to say, mere addition of the teacher's knowledge to traditional knowledge can work only so far as the new teachings do not directly clash with the older knowledge and beliefs. When that occurs, the Terramedian will either take sides (that is, in a specific matter, substitute old knowledge for new knowledge, or refuse to accept the new knowledge), or he will practise the accommodating behavior which can be called double-think—the acceptance of both sides of a contradiction in belief or behavior.

THE ELITE

Through the forces unleashed by colonialism, European-type economic activities, and missionary efforts, the growth of new cities, migration to cities and mines, and the formation of new voluntary social structures or associations, a relatively small corps of Terramedian people became pronouncedly more able to assess the relative merits and defects of change, and to use this knowledge to their advantage. They soon constituted a new elite who could individually, or in cooperation, wield sufficient power and authority to influence the direction and nature of socioeconomic change. Being products of various tribal groups, institutions, and associations, but able to intercommunicate because of the vehicular (usually colonial) language, they projected a heterogeneous front—partly traditional, partly modernistic. Some had received their "enlightenment" from missionaries, others from experience during military service, still others from living and studying overseas. It was through the reactions of this group—the new elite, recognized as legitimate or not—that the drastic alteration in political control was to be realized; and it has been through this same group, consisting of conservatives, moderates, and radicals, that present-day manifestations of change are recognized or not as social problems.

Throughout the long period of resistance to colonial rule, which resulted at times in prophetic movements, labor unions, or mass political parties, the evolue or elite assumed an obligation to lead and to effect social change. And with independence they continue to direct change, even at the risk of being severely and sometimes justly criticized. It has been observed that, "unlike other elites in Western societies who control capital or land, the Terramedian elite controls government jobs." That they themselves are aware of this is suggested by a member of the elite who opined that "we who call ourselves an elite may have professional qualifications, but we do not have the spirit and drive our country needs. We must rid ourselves of the city intellectual's mentality that looks at the peasant with contempt. Our first battle then is with ourselves." It is this recognition that stimulated Rene Dumont to attempt an objective evaluation of the direction being pursued by those "who believe that political independence is sufficient, who underestimate the importance of economic development, or who simply sit back to enjoy their privilege."[32] The significance of the elitist problem is equally revealed in the following assessment by Manfred Halpern:

> To the great illiterate majority of the Middle East's population, the civil servant, however lowly his rank, is a remarkable man. He can read and write, he makes more money than most, and he is in daily contact with the powerful. To his peers outside, he is an object of envy and criticism. But for the first time in Middle Eastern history, the bureaucracy no longer has a near monopoly of literacy and education, but must make its actions acceptable to an ever-growing number of people who resemble bureaucrats in all but their frustration.
>
> The Middle Eastern bureaucrat remains vulnerable in his status and incomplete in his skills, but his role has never been as important in history as it is today. In the past, his task was to maintain an empire. Today it is to alter both society and the body politic. To fit himself for such work, he must simultaneously reform himself and his world.[33]

Yet not in all areas did the elite maintain a city mentality and contempt for the peasantry. Such leaders as King Faisal, Abdel Nasser, Kwame Nkrumah, Julius Nyerere, and Sekou Toure—to name a few—used their personal charisma and political authority to direct change in manners not always popular with their countrymen. In some instances, such as the overthrow of Kwame Nkrumah, his imposition of necessary, although unpopular, austerity programs was successfully challenged. In other cases, however, political leaders managed to maintain a specific posture: Sekou Toure maintained vigilance against neocolonialism and the formation of a "colonial mentality" among Guineans, while Nasser and Nyerere effected profound reforms in land tenure and fiscal institutions in Egypt and Tanzania, respectively.[34]

There are romanticists today who grieve the passing away of traditional Africa and the Middle East. But it must be realized that change is inevitable, that the clock cannot be turned back, and that one cannot ignore the problems of which social change has made us aware. In Terramedia, there can no longer be a stoic acceptance of illiteracy or blind resignation to the lack of skills (technical, managerial, administrative) necessary for an effective and rewarding participation in the modern world. That people in Terramedia migrated to industrial and commercial centers might have been merely a result of the target demands; but once incorporated into the new society, influenced by industrialism and urbanism, it is no longer possible for them to remain blind to the realities of their relative inadequacies; it is no longer easy for them to refer to social problems as merely "insoluble," "to be endured," or "God's will."

In various ways, social change has altered the nature and basis of human interaction. Change made it easier to connect sickness and physical causative agents, and to relate poverty to inadequate domestic capital and the manipulation of weaker compatriots by vested-interest groups. Social change has evoked, along lines more drastic and more immediate than ever thought possible, the sort of abilities required to guarantee the following: (1) the ability of the masses to protect themselves against suppressive elites through participation in unions, political parties, cooperatives, and education; (2) accessibility for a larger segment of the citizenry to a larger share of the national product, with higher wages and better working conditions; and (3) an effective diffusion of a sense of social justice. These are not easy goals to attain, but the consciousness of their significance is evident to any keen observer of Terramedian affairs. An example of such consciousness was revealed in the military coup in Sierra Leone which called for a "considerable change in attitude." In its April 4, 1967 broadcast to the nation, the National Reformation Council urged that people stop thinking of

> our job as "government woke," meaning that we are working for some impersonal organization to whom we are under no moral obligation to be honest and straight-forward and to give value for money. We must consider our jobs as an integral part of the state machinery working all the time for the good of Sierra Leone. Another change essential in our attitude is a change from the old maxim, "usi den tie cow nar day ee go eat grass." This must be eradicated entirely from our public life, and the Council will insist on honesty and devotion to duty.[35]

The comprehensive nature of change in Terramedia, with variations here and there, reflects the findings of an earlier study.[36] Not just in the copperbelt of Africa, but throughout Terramedia—including such nations as Saudi Arabia and South Africa—there has occurred a widening exposure to new, even "alien," ideals and goals, as well as interest in using history to determine self-enhancing courses of action. For good or bad, changing circumstances and reactions have altered the roles of the extended family, tribal groups, and traditional wielders of power. There is reason to believe, however, that Terramedians have the ability to shape such changes in terms of their own vested interests by relying on the flexible and additive character of their traditions. There is a great message in this regard to be found, for example, in the experience of the wise, but constantly flying, bird: "Men of today have learned to shoot without missing, so I have learned to fly without perching." The challenge for those guiding Terramedia is to ensure that the "birds" in their fellow-citizens find reliable "trees" on which to "perch," when perch they must!

NOTES

1. See Rivlin and Szyliowicz, *Contemporary Middle East* pp. 107-55. Cf. J. Spencer Trimingham, *Islam in West Africa* (London: Oxford University Press, 1959), pp. 200-25.
2. Yale, *Near East* pp. 4-5.
3. Cf. Colin Leys, *Politics and Change in Developing Countries* (London: Cambridge University Press, 1969), pp. 85-134.
4. See Manfred Halpern, *Politics of Social Change* pp. 79-112; and I. William Zartman, *Man, State, and Society in the Contemporary Maghrib* (New York: Praeger Publishers, 1973), pp. 439-92.
5. See Hallett, *Africa Since 1875,* pp. 704-46; and Landau, *Man, State, and Society,* pp. 245-311.
6. See Coser and Rosenberg, *Sociological Theory,* pp. 43-79.
7. Ibid., pp. 17-41.
8. Ibid., pp. 629-46; and see Amitai Etzioni and Eva Etzioni, *Social Change* (New York: Basic Books, 1964), pp. 403-10.
9. See E. A. Hoebel, *Anthropology, the Study of Man* (New York: McGraw-Hill, 1966), pp. 52-62.
10. See Wilbert E. Moore, *Social Structure and Personality* (Glencoe: The Free Press, 1957), pp. 78-111; and Talcott Parsons, *Order and Change.* (New York: John Wiley, 1967), pp. 171-16.
11. See Robert K. Merton, *Social Theory and Social Structure* (Glencoe: The Free Press, 1957), pp. 281-386.
12. Cf. Aidan Southall, "Problems of the New Morality," *Journal of African Studies* 1 (1974):363-89.
13. H. Miner, "Cultural Change Under Stress," *Human Organization* (Autumn, 1960).
14. See George O. Roberts, *Cultural and Social Differentials in Health Practices* (Ann Arbor: University Microfilms, 1961), pp. 177-81.
15. See Ira E. Harrison, "Health Status and Healing Practices," *Journal of African*

Studies 3 (1976):547-60.

16. See Mernissi, *Beyond the Veil,* pp. 99-109; and Christine Oppong, *Marriage Among a Matrilineal Elite* (London: Cambridge University Press, 1974), pp. 144-59.

17. See, for example, George E. Kirk, *A Short History of the Middle East* (New York: Praeger Publishers, 1964), pp. 129-230; and Robert I. Rotberg, *A Political History of Tropical Africa* (New York: Harcourt, Brace & World, 1965), pp. 190-243.

18. See Paul Bohannan and George Dalton, *Markets in Africa* (Garden City, NJ: Doubleday, 1965), pp. 35-179.

19. See Basil Davidson, *The African Past.* (New York: Grossett & Dunlap, 1967), pp. 171-263.

20. See Walter F. Afonagoro, "The Aro and Delta Middlemen of Nigeria," *Journal of African Studies* 3 (1976).

21. Cf. Charles Gallagher, *United States and North Africa,* pp. 30-115.

22. Lagos *Daily Express,* August 18, 1962.

23. See Ajayi and Espie, *West African History,* pp. 191-313.

24. See J. John Palen, *The Urban World* (New York: McGraw-Hill, 1975), p. 6.

25. See Sylvia F. Fava, *Urbanism in World Perspective* (New York: Thomas Y. Crowell, 1968), pp. 353-408.

26. See Palen, *Urban World,* pp. 354-92.

27. Cf. Kenneth Little, *African Women in Towns* (London: Cambridge University Press, 1973), pp. 15-28.

28. See Morroe Berger, *The Arab World Today* (Garden City: Doubleday, 1964), pp. 389-434.

29. S. O. Biobaku, "Historical Aspects of Acculturation," *Presence Africaine* 18 (1963):121.

30. See Hilda Kuper, *Urbanization and Migration in West Africa* (Berkeley: University of California Press, 1965), pp. 39-109.

31. See K. H. Silvert, *Expectant Peoples* (New York: Random House, 1963), pp. 77-94.

32. See Rene Dumont, *False Start in Africa* (New York: Praeger Publishers, 1969).

33. Ibid, pp. 345-346.

34. See Ali Mazrui, *Soldiers and Kinsmen in Uganda* (Beverly Hills: Sage Publications, 1975), p. 7.

35. This is a Krio proverb which can be translated as "a cow will consume hay only in the area where it is tied and confined." It means that the source of one's benefits (or, more particularly, gains not truly earned), derive from the specific work-place to which one is assigned.

36. See Hortense Powdermaker, *Copper Town* (New York: Harper & Row, 1962).

Chapter Nine

TERRAMEDIA IN AN INTERNATIONAL PERSPECTIVE

Image and Influence in the Modern World

Non-Terramedians in most parts of the world have retained, in large measure, the stereotypes of the area which prevailed prior to the period of modern independence. Most people still remember the crusades from their study of history, and remain unaware of the common origin of Judaism, Christianity, and Islam from the area. For others, Terramedia is identified with immoral barbarians, Moslems or pagans, who have survived their primitive existence only because of the humanitarian efforts of "white" administrators and missionaries. Seldom is the point emphasized that Terramedia has served as an important contributor to agriculture, philosophy, science, and technology. Writing about the Arab sector of Terramedia, for example, Mansfield has attempted a cogent reminder:

> By its union of Hellenic with Iranian and Indian scientific traditions, and by the transmission of Hellenic thought, Islam performed what is often regarded as its most important service to the world, though there are hardly any sciences to which it did not also make important original contributions. During the pre-Renaissance period in Europe it was to Arabic sources that Europeans turned in their attempts to rediscover the scientific heritage of Greece and Rome, and the improvement which the Arabs were able to introduce into

> mathematics by the use of a simplified system of notation of Indian origin was of critical importance in European intellectual development.[1]

Furthermore, not enough emphasis is given to the fact that substantial amounts of the resources necessary for maintaining the "civilization" of the "white" world continues to come from Terramedia which, incidentally, contains two-thirds of world oil deposits. A case in point is the international economic dilemma which accompanied the Arab curtailment and continued control of petroleum production and shipments, an act involving other Terramedian countries like Algeria, Libya, and Nigeria. From that experience has emerged the realization that oil could be used by Terramedia to resolve, at last, the question of persistent colonialism in Southern Africa. Unfortunately, this strategy has yet to prove successful. Of course, there are those like John Kenneth Galbraith who perceive a contribution, nonetheless:

> If the energy crisis forces us to diminish automobile use in the cities, stops us from building highways and covering the country with concrete and asphalt, forces us to rehabilitate the railroads, causes us to invest in mass transportation and limits the waste of electrical energy, one can only assume that the Arab nations and the big oil companies have united to save the American Republic.[2]

Modern independence in the area is now at least twenty years old, and there have been ample opportunity for the interaction between Terramedians and non-Terramedians to reveal that the area is one inhabited by people with desires, aspirations, and capabilities—subject to the fluctuating limitations posed by cultural and environmental factors—similar to those of people in other parts of the world. From the perspective of the ordinary outsider, however, Terramedia and Terramedians remain objects of condescension, paternalism, and apology. The argument which was once presented by non-Terramedians, that the area was unworthy of having its people determine and prescribe their own destiny, is still strongly supported, and it is a common expectation that time will prove, indeed, that such a cynical view is a valid and appropriate one.

The image of Terramedia is not a favorable one among most outsiders; at best, where positive attitudes are expressed, they are accompanied with doubt and apprehension. Despite these unfortunate impressions, however, sovereignty in Terramedia is a reality in law. It is to be noted, further, that the past two decades, particularly, have witnessed the evolution of greater significance for Terramedia, especially in regard to its impact on international relations and world politics. Other areas of significance have been in race relations, and the willingness to pursue economic equity on a universal scale.

In the area of race relations, the world has witnessed an increased sensitivity to racial and other forms of discrimination. (There is, of course, the unrealized goal of political justice for Namibia and Palestine, leaving one to question the sincerity of U.N. membership support.) This is not to say that racism and all its implications have been checked; rather it is to recognize that relations once considered "normal" when they involved persons or groups of different races are being modified to reflect a greater support for universal human dignity. The persistent discussion of the matter of apartheid, as well as the many legislative revisions that nations, including the U.S.S.R., have undertaken, give evidence of this fact. There is certainly much to be done to achieve the ideal situation. The Special Committee on Apartheid of the United Nations called attention to this matter in March, 1972, pointing out that components of "racial prejudice and discrimination, racial separation and segregation, economic exploitation and terror" persist in maintaining a system of racial containment. However, it was also observed that "the important thing was to push the progress, however, small, on all fronts." Toward this goal, Ambassador Tomeh of Syria, during the deliberations of the U.N. Special Committee, submitted the following suggestions:

(1) That racism and apartheid in all their manifestations be condemned;
(2) That the idea of dialogue with South Africa be rejected until majority rule is instituted in the country;
(3) That the policy of separate development be condemned and that the legitimate rights of the indigenous people in their land be recognized;
(4) That states collaborating with racist regimes, particularly those supplying arms and economic support, be condemned;
(5) That solidarity and support for those African majorities seeking self-determination and liberation be affirmed;
(6) That a program of study and action to combat apartheid and to achieve closer cooperation among all anti-apartheid organizations be initiated immediately.[3]

It is to be regretted that the debates and resolutions of the United Nations have as yet to produce any significant efforts at amelioration. In 1979, South Africa was still enjoying its membership in such influential interational agencies as the International Bank for Reconstruction and Development, the International Monetary Fund, and the United Nations Development Program. At the same time, South Africa was making a mockery of widespread condemnation of its human rights violations by asserting that "South Africa enjoys world-wide esteem in the judicial sphere." While acclaiming that "there is a great reservoir of goodwill between its Blacks and Whites," and that "happiness . . . is 40 winks in a wheelbarrow in the weak winter sun" for a laborer, South Africa continues to engage in atrocities against its citizens who dare protest, however peacefully.[4] Indeed, one would be foolish to believe that South Africa's attitudes toward external criticism today is different from that which characterized its police action in October, 1977:

> In raids, arrests and legal actions which began before daylight and continued all day, 18 black protest groups were outlawed, about 70 of their leaders and supporters detained or confined to their homes and South Africa's leading black newspaper, the World, was closed down. . . . A few prominent whites who sympathize with black campaigns for social and economic equality were "banned"–the legal term here for house arrest and strict isolation.[5]

Yet, such reaction, in the view of the South Africa government, need not have aroused as much consternation among outsiders; for "it is well known that since June 1976 there have been sporadic demonstrations and riotous incidents . . . instigated and carried out by a small minority."[6] After all, why was there no hue and cry when Idi Amin of Uganda decided that guns were preferable to rights and laws, and that intellectuals could be physically abused for thinking?[7]

In the area of humanism, developmental ideologies which promoted a concept of rugged individualism and survival of the fittest are being modified to satisfy or meet the persistent challenges regarding the adequacy of these ideologies to societies of the contemporary world. No longer are national ideologies (such as capitalism, communism, and socialism) kept pure, but modifications in all of them are being made to make room for the peculiar status of new nations, giving due regard to their relative inexperience in formal diplomacy. In effect, there is a shared willingness in international circles, to a greater extent than previously, to show more sensitivity to the conditions and differences of participants in international diplomacy.

With regard to economic equity, much has been done during the past three decades to improve the impoverished condition of Terramedia. Through various economic organs of the United Nations, as well as through bilateral agencies, traditionally exploitative nations–like Britain, France, Germany, and the U.S.A.–have become economic humanitarians with an interest in bridging the gap between the "haves" and the "have nots."[8] Given the paucity of indigenous technicians, a satisfactory industrial base, and the relevant social infrastructure in Terramedia, one must applaud the thrust and accomplishments of the various planning and volunteer groups (VISTA and Peace Corps, for example). Equally laudable is the extent to which the World Bank and the International Monetary Fund have assisted in promoting fiscal responsibility and capital formation. Some Terramedian leaders, of course, view such efforts as a modified form of the "grand larceny" which won European control over petroleum in Iraq and Saudi Arabia, copper in Rhodesia, the Suez Canal in Egypt, and lands in Palestine.

Whatever the motives for promoting economic equity among groups with in Terramedia and between them and groups outside Terramedia, the results have been beneficial. Not only are the resources of Saudi Arabia, Libya, and Nigeria being used to assist less privileged Terramedians of other nation states, but there is now more visible commitment to self-reliance as a supplement to, if not a substitute for, external "European" assistance and guidance. It would seem as if aspects of the force which compelled the founding of the Middle East Supply Centre, the Arab League, the Baghdad Pact, the East African Community, and the Central African Federation are now influencing Terramedian leaders also. At long last the remedy proposed (by the Clapp Commission) to solve the Arab refugee problem in 1949 is finding applicability to the wider question of hunger, poverty and economic inequity:

> An improved economy does not come in a neat package to be sold or given away in the market place. . . . The highly developed nations of the world did not make their way by wishing. By work and risk they forced the earth, the soil, the forest and the rivers to yield them riches. They pooled their energy and resources by taxation and mutual enterprise. . . . There is no substitute for the application of work and local enterprise to each country's own resources. Help to those who have the will to help themselves should be the primary policy guiding and restraining the desire of the more developed areas of the world to help the less developed lands.[9]

As for Terramedia, it is possible to delineate certain postures which have characterized the period of modern independence. Terramedians and their leaders, by and large, have emphasized support for nonalignment or positive neutralism; they have increased sensitivity to all forms of discrimination based on race or ethnicity; and they have emphasized an interest in the accelerated development of their societies involving all sectors simultaneously. Furthermore, through Terramedian leaders, there has evolved a greater indifference to the alleged imperialist character of communism, perhaps acceding to the reality that the bedrock of national development is self-interest.[10] In summary, the major objectives of Terramedian nations in the modern world have been:

(1) to build and maintain modern and respected states
(2) to offset the historical humiliation of foreign domination and exploitation
(3) to reduce dependence on the foreign importation of skills, goods, and funds
(4) to build the physical and social infrastructure necessary for sustained growth and modernization
(5) to increase agricultural productivity through vertical (better seeds, fertilizer, and so forth) and horizontal expansion (dams, irrigation, desalination)
(6) to gain equitable footing in international trade
(7) to enhance self-sufficiency through appropriate industrialization and economic planning;
(8) to protect their territorial sovereignty and integrity;
(9) to establish and maintain internal stability and a sense of true nationhood among the citizens;
(10) to rediscover and reassert the dignity and importance of their heritage and of their contributions to world civilization and thought[11]

Modern independence in Terramedia has been influential not only in the major areas of international relations cited above. These are certainly important, and have attracted the attention of international statesmen, bringing to the area a feeling of international respect. It should be noted, however, that the implications of Terramedian sovereignty and independence have gone beyond the impact they have had on the foreign policies and trade relations of the major powers; effects have been felt at lower levels of group interaction, influencing the lives and attitudes of ordinary people. While it is impractical to separate state deliberations, decisions, and attitudes from those of individual citizens, it is significant to observe that current Terramedia has aroused the passion of previously powerless individuals toward an interest in their own images as members of nation-states, as well as that of other territorial entities.

There is no denying the fact that the independence of Terramedia has influenced the lives of various national minority groups. In the United States, for example, the presence and utterances of Terramedian representatives in the United Nations, including their movements within the United States, had an accelerated influence upon the pace of promoting social equity in which there had always been interest. Although the U.S. Supreme Court decision regarding segregation was handed down in 1954, it took the sustained condemnation of Terramedian observers and the oppressed black Americans who came to find strength in Terramedian independence, to correct the vestiges of resistance to, and avoidance of, laws guaranteeing equal opportunity and access. Equally, in the U.S.S.R. and in the People's Republic of China (countries which had manifested very little interest in Terramedian peoples), the fact of modern independence has stimulated concern for, and pursuit of, knowledge about peoples and nations of Terramedia. Not only have Russians and Chinese proved to be rhetorical champions of Terramedian causes—especially when these provided an opportunity to condemn neocolonialism, imperialism, and racism—but they have been actively involved with Terramedians in many kinds of activities ranging from cultural exchanges and sporting events, to industrial, agricultural, and other forms of technical activities. One can, however, question the quality of such interaction between Terramedians and non-Terramedians, since visiting Russians and Chinese usually insist on living in their own closed, residential "colonies."

At still another level, Terramedian emergence into increased prominence in the mass media of various nations would seem to be an indication of the positive contribution of Terramedian sovereignty. Certainly, there is more media attention being paid to events in Terramedia. There is definitely a consciousness of the different cultural styles which characterize Terramedian people, and there is evidence of the transference of some of these cultural modes (such as artistic expressions, fashions, foods, and the like) to non-Terramedian countries.

Among intellectuals, philosophers, and industrialists, the presence of modern Terramedian sovereignty has been recognized. For intellectuals, this presence has been evidence in the increased and innovative attention being given to the area. Indeed, in history and the social sciences, Terramedian society has become a viable laboratory for testing traditional hypotheses and theories, as well as serving as a source for comparative studies of human affairs. It is significant to note, for example, that "oral tradition" has now received the clear endorsement of intellectuals and social scientists as a legitimate tool of analysis, hence offsetting the traditionally held view that nonliterate societies in Terramedia had nothing to offer to the understanding of human culture and its evolution. In addition, an examination of Terramedian realities has been intensified with the intention of enriching the available knowledge of discrete or generalized data pertaining to all disciplines, particularly anthropology, economics, history, philosophy, political science, sociology, and even art—especially that of southern Terramedia. According to William Bascom:

> African art has won its own place among the great art traditions of the world. Much has been written about the impact that African

sculpture made on Picasso, Derain, Braque, Matisse, and . . . of the great contributions that Africans have made to the cultural heritage of mankind. . . . Recent archaeological discoveries in Africa suggest the possibility of African contributions of far greater significance for man's cultural history: namely, the development of tool-making, fire-making, and language. Nevertheless, in the aesthetic sphere African sculpture is unquestionably a most important contribution, and its excellence is widely recognized today.[12]

Industrialists have also become prominent in Terramedian affairs. It was not too long ago that (aside from limited involvement in South Africa, Egypt, and a few other countries), most of the area of Terramedia was seen as one for investment in extractive enterprise—mining and plantation agriculture—and very little else. There has been a favorable shift of emphasis which has resulted in an appreciable diversification of activities by industrialists in Terramedia. Not only have the traditional extractive efforts been expanded, but these have been accompanied by a greater willingness to establish secondary and tertiary activities, entailing the use of local resources. At times, imports of essential components have had to be undertaken to advance the pace and quality of manufacturing and other industrial activities.[13] The consequence has been that Terramedia today, more than ever before, has facilities to provide significant amounts of consumer and other needs which—due in part to the disinterest or resistance by industrialists and entrepreneurs—had to be imported from developed nations. There are serious efforts being made to initiate and expand various manufacturing and assembly facilities, including materials for building construction, home furnishings, and machinery.

Terramedia's Role in International Organizations

Although Terramedians have been trying to make their needs and aspirations known to the world community for a long time (especially around the turn of the century, when foreign usurpation of their rights and resources became grossly unbearable), only since 1945 can it be said that they were concretely heeded. Both Pan-Arabism and Pan-Africanism had meaningful goals and vocal spokesmen before 1914, but it took World War II and the creation of the United Nations to bring constructive reactions from the rest of the world and from the mass of Terramedians themselves. One immediate development, even though this was done with the assistance of the controlling British, was the founding of the Arab League whose objective was to enhance the political integration of the Arab lands, and to coordinate the policies and activities necessary for safeguarding Arab needs and aspirations. In Africa south of the Sahara, even though the interest was on the continent as a whole (Arab north Africa was already closely identified with the Arab League), there developed a renewed interest in Africanism generated by Pan-Africanism and the Manchester Conference of 1945. It was at that conference, like the parallel Arab League which stimulated the "revolutionary mission" of the Free Officers of Egypt in 1952, that a core of Africans pledged themselves to the immediate liberation of Africa from the colonial yoke. It is useful to note that the creation of the United Nations, shortly thereafter, with a forum for expressing the concerns of oppressed peoples, offered an opportunity for African and Arab revolutionaries to express themselves. These sometimes audacious beginnings resulted in a clearer recognition of the rights of Terramedians to self-determination and to the promise of membership in a world community of nations. Terramedia and Terramedians were then able to operate in an atmosphere—thanks to the mood and promise of the United Nations—of security and confidence of support for their just complaints and aspirations.

By the early 1960s, a significant number of Terramedian countries, including the Arab countries which had enjoyed only nominal independence, became truly independent and acquired membership in the United Nations. There was an experience with divisiveness among Terramedians, as various nations debated whether to direct their attention to revolutionary or moderate programs, or whether to sever the relationships they had had with those nations which had previously dominated their affairs. The 1950s, a decade preceding the entry of most of the Terramedian countries into the fold of modern independent nations, witnessed the formation of several segmented and vested interest groups, such as the Baghdad Pact, the Union of Egypt and Syria, the Union of African States, and the formation of the Brazzaville and Monrovia blocs of nations. It was during this same period that the Arab League expanded its objectives to the point where it now included a strong anti-Zionist and anti-Israeli posture. A significant outcome of these divisive intra-Terramedian activities was the formation of the Organization of African Unity in 1963, whose membership included all those African nations who were also members of the Arab League. Both the Organization of African Unity and the Arab League, by 1965, were viable vehicles, effectively influencing the deliberations and policies within the United Nations; and these Terramedian countries constituted approximately two-thirds of the total membership.

As assessment of the image and influence of Terramedia can, perhaps, be enhanced by looking at the major objectives of the Arab League on the one hand, and the Organization of African Unity on the other. (Attention should be called also to the overlapping membership enjoyed by the north-African Arab countries in both of these organizations.) The following are the main objectives of the Arab League today:

(1) to effect the political integration of Arab Lands;
(2) to work together for the common good of all Arabs—to gain national identity, realistic independence, and to achieve ethnic and cultural unity
(3) to cooperate in affairs of mutual interest, such as financial and cultural affairs, communication and other infrastructural developments, health and social problems
(4) to counteract Zionism and check the expansion of Israeli nationalism (some would prefer the elimination of Israel as a nation)

As for the Organization of African Unity, with membership open to all independent African states except for South Africa and white-controlled Rhodesia, the following are the objectives:

(1) To promote the unity and solidarity of African States;
(2) To coordinate and intensify cooperation and efforts needed to achieve a better life for the peoples of Africa;
(3) To defend the sovereignty, territorial integrity, and the independence of all the African states;
(4) To eradicate all forms of colonialism and neo-colonialism in Africa;
(5) To promote international cooperation, having due regard to the charter of the United Nations and the universal declaration of human rights.[14]

Both the Arab League and the Organization of African Unity affirm the following general principles:

(1) the sovereign equality of member-states
(2) noninterference in the internal affairs of other states
(3) respect for the sovereignty and territorial integrity of each member state and for its inalienable right to independent existence
(4) peaceful settlement of disputes by negotiation and mediation
(5) unreserved condemnation of political assassination, in all its forms, as well as subversive activities on the part of neighboring states or any other state
(6) absolute dedication to the total emancipation of territories which are still dependent
(7) affirmation of a policy of nonalignment with regard to all blocs

In effect, an adherence to these principles guarantees the existing status of independent territories, while leaving open the possibility of economic, social, and political regionalism or federation. Indeed, recent developments have seen such viable entities as the Saudi Development Fund and the Mano River Union.

Through membership in the United Nations, and because of the increased security of the right of self-determination, Terramedia stands visibly in the arena of international relations. The area and its leaders must still endure the limitations of past neglect and the negative stereotypes of non-Terramedians (and even some Terramedians for that matter), as they continue to shape the destiny of Terramedia. More and more Terramedians have called attention to concerns whose resolution would accrue to Terramedian interests. Not only have Terramedians been able to have the major powers consider equitable arrangements regarding the petroleum industry, but they have applied sufficient pressure to encourage an ongoing discussion of commodity prices and the marketing arrangements of the developed countries for the products of the developing nations. Terramedians have also conveyed the view that financial aid and other assistance to them should transcend the tendency to see such aids as vehicles for satisfying essentially the donors' own vested interests.

A summary of the interaction of Terramedian nations in the international arena has been made by Miller. According to Miller,[15] one can draw the following generalizations about the nations of Terramedia:

(1) Contacts with neighbors are often what matter most;
(2) Connection with the former colonial powers remain quite strong, even in those areas like Zaire and Belgium, which have experienced hostility in the recent past;
(3) Great concern for persistent colonialism and neo-colonialism remain. Anti-colonialism has become an indispensable piece of equipment, a set of formulae without which a state may not be accepted in other Terramedian company;
(4) There has been a significant expansion and diversification of alliance involving all the major powers, U.S.A., U.S.S.R., and the People's Republic of China, and even both East Germany and West Germany;
(5) Policy making among Terramedian nations appears to be essentially provisional, flexible, and ad-hoc;
(6) Great emphasis is placed on "positive nationalism" rather than on "negative nationalism."

Recent developments regarding petroleum and gold supplies are likely to change Terramedia's role and importance in international organizations. Until about fifteen years ago, it was up to Terramedia–collective or otherside–to urge others to promote its interests and well-being: to support self-determination, to curb neo-colonialism, or to win respect for a posture of non-alignment. Currencies have been devaluated or been threatened with devaluation, as the international community faced the fluctuating dilemma of a gold standard. In the issue, South Africa, as the major producer of gold as well as a country within Terramedia, has won cautious treatment by many of the Western nations who developed a sense of apprehension regarding continuing access to South Africa's gold resource. Terramedian nations, on the other hand, have become increasingly disenchanted as these same Western nations ignored or attached less significance to matters of human rights and dignity which South Africa had been instrumental in thwarting.

Several conferences have been held among ministers and secretaries of national treasuries, and with concerned agencies such as the World Bank and the International Monetary Fund; in all of these meetings very seldom has the interest of the major segment of Terramedia been considered, given the prevailing notion that international monetary matters are best resolved by the major industrial nations. It is conceivable, however, given the increasing assertiveness of Terramedia and the accompanying confidence in Terramedian independence—particularly if gold continues to serve as the standard of value—that possible changes in power relationships could bring Terramedia into greater prominence in the debate. (Saudi Arabia, for example, now influences International Monetary Fund decisions.) For now, South Africa operates in the non-Terramedian orbit; yet there is nothing impossible about an ultimate change in such a relationship to bring South Africa into the Terramedian fold. If this occurs, and if gold remains a standard of monetary exchange, Terramedia could influence questions of great significance to international trade and monetary exchange.

Petroleum and the energy crisis have already brought renewed attention to Terramedia. During the past five years, some of the Arab nations have used their control of vast petroleum reserves and production as a lever for influencing attitudes toward, and involvement in, Terramedian affairs (especially the Arab portion) by some of the major world powers. The agreement between Mr. Sadat of Egypt and King Feisal of Saudi Arabia, in which Saudi Arabia expressed a willingness to support some of the needs and aspirations of the Egyptian nation, through the Gulf Organization for the Development of Egypt, has produced a climate of concern among the Western nations and the United States, if not in the U.S.S.R. and China. Of equal interest is the peace agreement recently formulated by President Sadat and Prime Minister Begin, and the boycott resulting from it. The current debate regarding petroleum distribution to "enemies" of Terramedia may result in still greater influence in the international arena for some Terramedian countries.[16] But one must still wonder about the potential for Terramedian divisiveness which the Egyptian-Israeli peace treaty portends.

Contemporary Manifestations and Prospects for the Future

It can be said that Terramedia has regained dignity and respect in world affairs, following the long period of national and regional subservience imposed by westernism. Terramedia has remained a vital source of primary resources required by non-Terramedian nations, and its coastlines and their relation to other land masses have revealed, further, the strategic advantage of Terramedia's "middleness." Whereas nations in the past used military and technological might to usurp Terramedia's endowments, delicate diplomacy is today the strategy being used to establish relations of cordiality and foundations for vested interests negotiations. It is to be regretted that the prolonged conflict engendered by the existence of Israel as a nation-state has hampered the progressive coordination and the common articulation of Terramedian goals. Indeed, as if to give support to the mirror image of Terramedia's climate and geography, Rhodesia, Namibia, and South Africa pose a similar obstacle in the southern sector. Nonetheless, there is reason to believe that a continuing appreciation of the commonalities which characterize all Terramedians, and a heightening awareness of having the shared responsibility in shaping Terramedia's destiny primarily to serve indigenous needs and interests, will bring about the minimal unity required for the maintenance of the area's sovereignty and integrity. Recent political modifications in Southern Africa are, indeed, cause for optimism.

Protecting the dignity of Terramedia in the international community is important. But efforts and vigilance toward that end may come to naught if a simultaneous endeavor is not made to uplift the spirits and respond to the hopes of the citizens whom recent events have aroused. In too many countries of Terramedia, the leadership has failed to apply the principles used in their international deliberations on justice, equity, and responsibility to their own citizens. It is a glaring inconsistency for Kenya, for example, to deplore racism in South Africa while failing to remove the vestiges of the same among its own citizens. Similarly, it is an abrogation of inherent responsibility for a King Hussein or a General Amin or a President Houphouet-Boigny or a President Khadafy to seek international esteem or personal luxuries while substantial numbers of his own citizens are denied access to the bounties of their own homeland. Equally unpalatable is the selective extension of privilege to citizens in which Prime

Minister Begin, President Tolbert, and many other Terramedian leaders are engaged.

In Egypt today, for example, many peasants are deprived of a relatively better standard of living, simply because the leadership has given the abstraction of ideological rectitude greater importance than human beings. And there is still the untenable feeling of superiority or indifference toward other Terramedians, especially those of "black Africa," which must be corrected if the bland brotherhood of which leaders speak is to find coordinated concreteness. There is a need to promote internally a sense of common destiny among all Terramedians, and the need to put an end to the prevailing stereotype that divisiveness and entrenched ethnocentrism are unavoidable and permanent attitudes which Terramedia must endure. As Claude Ake has correctly pointed out,

> Colonial politics was power politics in the most literal sense of the phrase. Those in power used their power with little or no restraint to maintain their privileges, and to repress those out of power who wanted to replace them. Those who were not in power sought power with the same indifference to restraints, and with the same indifference to the "rules of the game." The colonial political culture to which the nationalist leaders were socialized was one characterized by a lack of public-spirited restraint in the quest for, and the exercise of, power.
>
> To a very great extent the influence of the colonial experience persists. This is manifested in the statism of the new states, and in their political authoritarianism: the refusal to hold elections, the abolition of higher courts, the suspension of constitutions, the arrest and imprisonment of counter-elites. It is evident in the tendency to construe politics strictly as a struggle for rulership.[17]

Terramedia, however, must not nurture such a curse, and thereby corrode the moral superiority (vis-à-vis those nations with guns and bombs), which its relative defenselessness affords. Leaders must constantly demonstrate their responsibility to all citizens, and civil servants must use their privileged status in diligent service to the nation.

The potential gains of self-determination must not be curbed on account of citizens' skepticism or the failure to develop appropriate strategies for their attainment. Must public officials spend as much time and energy in international conferences while denying their talents to needs at home? Must Terramedian countries compete for superiority in military hardware against each other, or must their military "inferiority" be preserved as a moral shield to a troubled and self-destructive world community?

Constructive critics of Terramedian policy makers and administrators, even when they are themselves Terramedians, are at times condemned as obstructionists and wantonly imprisoned, punished surreptitiously by being prevented from engaging in their chosen professions, or limited in their power of influence through incorporation into, or submission to, the system. Instances are known of aspirants to political office being harassed, or being murdered for manifesting the "temerity" to stand up against an incumbent. There are instances of newspaper editors, or workers, being harassed into ceasing their criticisms of those in power. In fact, thugs have at times been used clandestinely to destroy the equipment of journalists who ignored such warnings. It is therefore no surprise that most of the newspapers in Terramedia today are under the supervision and censorship of the governments in power. In effect, through economic pressure, arson, or other threats, many conscientious Terramedians (with skills and the willingness to contribute to the well-being of their homelands), have been forced into voluntary and involuntary exile, or have retreated into silence while manifesting a facade of support for the actions of those in power. The brain and moral drain which Terramedia has been forced to endure since independence, in varying degrees, must not continue to be blamed on such ideological intangibles as neocolonialism, the colonial mentality, or historical accidents. Greedy politicians, military egomaniacs, spineless civil servants, indifferent educators, and callous citizens must share a major part of the blame. The future of Terramedia, after all, must include a guarantee of greater enjoyment by all of the right for which sovereignty was sought and gained: equity in the access to rewards, and in the assumption of responsibility essential to national integrity and stability.

NOTES

1. Peter Mansfield, *The Middle East* (London: Oxford University Press, 1973), pp. 35-36.
2. John K. Galbraith, "The Coldest Winter?" *Newsweek* December 3, 1973).
3. See U.N. Document A/AC 115/SR 201 (March 23, 1972).
4. See *This is South Africa* (Pretoria: Government Printer, 1976), pp. 24-27.
5. Los Angeles *Times,* October 20, 1977.
6. *A Ghetto in South Africa* (Pretoria: Government Printer, 1977), p. 13.
7. Cf. Mazrui, *Soldiers and Kinsmen,* pp. 45-46.
8. See Mohammed Reza Shah Pahlavi, *Mission for my Country* (London: Hutchinson & Co., 1961), pp. 293-98.
9. Cited in William R. Polk, *The United States and the Arab World* (Cambridge: Harvard University Press, 1975), p. 315.
10. Cf. Vernon McKay, *Africa in World Politics* (New York: Harper & Row,

1963); Jacob Landau, *Man, State, and Society* and John K. Colley, *East Wind over Africa* (New York: Walker & Company, 1965).

11. See Polk, *United States,* Gallagher, *United States and North Africa,* and William A. Hance, *Southern Africa and the United States* (New York: Columbia University Press, 1968).

12. William Bascom, *African Art,* pp. 3-4.

13. See Carl Widstrand, *Multi-National Firms in Africa* (New York: Africana Publishing Company, 1975).

14. Zdenek Cervanka, *The Organization of African Unity and Its Charter* (New York: Praeger Publishers, 1969).

15. J. D. Miller, *Politics of the Third World* (London: Oxford University Press, 1967), pp. 9-17.

16. Cf. Michael L. Lofchie, "Why Africa Turned Against Israel," Los Angeles *Times,* December 2, 1973.

17. "Explaining Political Instability in New States," *Journal of Modern African Studies* (September 1973): 358-359.

Chapter Ten

MAKING INDEPENDENCE A REALITY

Introduction

The experience of World War II, serving as it did to make all manners of men realize that justice and equity cannot be guaranteed if pursued only for oneself, evoked a regenerated interest in humanitarianism—comparable to what had been experienced during the second half of the nineteenth century. In place of the dispersal of missionaries to bring light where darkness had prevailed, a universal organ was created, the United Nations Organization, to promote brotherhood in both its dimensions of rights and responsibilities. The spirit of good will and manifestations of genuine concern that characterized the first decade of the U.N.'s existence—as it used multilateral teams and resources to combat poverty, ignorance, disease, prejudice, and discrimination—gave hope to those who had lived in cynicism and pessimism; and as more and more of the underdeveloped and colonialized territories achieved self-determination and sovereignty with U.N. support, a sense of well-being and a trust in the inevitability of justice for all emerged. Occasionally, however, developments threatened continuing trust in justice as the vested-interests of the economically and militarily

AUTHOR'S NOTE: This chapter, now slightly revised, appeared in *Journal of Black Studies* 9 (1978):15-44.

powerful reappeared to prove that their seeming support for universal justice had only been illusory.

The "wind of change" and its guarantee of self-determination in time ceased to blow over Terramedia, with large areas being left to suffer from the yoke of colonial denial. Even a country like Ghana, which had brought "black dignity" into the arena of international relations, soon realized that political control was no panacea for alien economic control; and the effort to find a key to unlock the unwanted handcuff of "neocolonialism" subscribed in some measure to the overthrow of Kwame Nkrumah by a people who once idolized him. In various parts of Terramedia, leaders found themselves confronted with the dilemma of choice, a choice of this or that "master" or "friend," or a choice of a specific ideology to guide the planning and execution of development. Some became strong adherents or advocates of "nonalignment," while others chose a system of "guided democracy" or socialism (African and Arab). None of these, however, adequately resolved the challenge of nation-building and rising expectations, given the magnitude of the problems. As Palen has aptly observed:

> Developing countries vary in their rates of development, but they all suffer in varying degrees from common problems such as low industrial output, low rates of savings, poor roads and communication, a high proportion of the labor force engaged in agriculture, insufficient medical services, inadequate school systems, high rates of illiteracy, poor diets, and sometimes malnutrition. The developing countries contain two out of three of the world's people, but they account for only one-sixth of the world's income, one-third of the food production, and one-tenth of the industrial output.[1]

Essentially, most of the leaders faced the pressure of choosing between capitalism (with its emphasis on individual initiative and control), and communism which emphasizes state planning and control. Ultimately, all Terramedian leaders, even while attracted to the capitalism with which they had become familiar and had a basis for detesting—in contrast to communism which was a new incursor, but without an absorptive infrastructure in the area—chose an ideological middle ground of democratic, theistic socialism which permitted selective, rather than absolute, state initiative and control.

Independence, unfortunately, did not bring with the ritual raising of a national flag a sense of common destiny and of shared responsibility among citizens in Terramedian nations. What had coalesced against a common object of rejection, colonial rule, was in fact a coalition of many vested-interest groups—educational, regional, religious, tribal, and so on.

Hence, once the nonindigenous and external imperial enemy disappeared, and no longer provided the bond which had united the disparate groups and blinded them to their differences, discrete and visible encampments emerged to pursue their individual self-interests. One was left to wonder about the sudden disappearance of the united and enthusiastic mass which had supported the independence movements, and which had shared in the celebrations of victory over colonial rule. From Syria to Iraq, Morocco to Egypt, Sudan to Zanzibar, Senegal to Zaire, there appeared glaring disagreements and divisions over the manner in which nationalism was to be manifested, as well as over the privileges and responsibilities that would be ascribed to, or assumed by, the various groups constituting the emergent nations. Some states soon came under the control of military dictators or one-party rule, while others became involved in tribal, class, or other forms of ethnic conflict and rivalry. Some of the conflicts were of such magnitude as to invite the incursion of external military intervention.[2]

Obstacles to Nationhood

One of the crucial problems which countries in Terramedia had to face soon after gaining their independence was that of developing an effective sense of nationhood.[3] Unfortunately, this problem has remained largely unresolved, creating a situation in which full "mastery over one's own household" has been lacking. Although national leaders throughout Terramedia have been aware of the problem, including those instances where some have pretended that they were in full control of their sovereignty, several obstacles have stood in the way of efforts to develop a realistic sense of nationhood. Among these obstacles to the building of nations in Terramedia have been the following:

FALSE EXPECTATIONS OF LASTING UNITY AMONG DISPARATE GROUPS

The imposition of colonial rule, direct and indirect, had assumed the unimportance of "ethnic" groups while stressing the significance of "territorial" or regional entities. That demarcated boundaries had within them historically distinct linguistic, tribal, and religious groups was of no importance to the British, the French, the Portuguese, the Germans, and the Belgians who created the Iraq, the Morocco, the Nigeria, and the Kenya that would ultimately secure independence as integral nations. The fact of Terramedian life, however, has always been one of localized loyalty and self-interest with minimal, if any, recognition of an equal or greater loyalty toward a pluralistic and larger social unit—such as the nation state which independence conferred. The consequence of this has been a "provincial" or "regional" notion that what is good for one's own region or province of a large national unit is all one need care about, because the people of other regions or provinces look out only for their own benefits. And even though it has sometimes been argued that education can reduce provincialism, and thereby increase concern for the affairs of the entire nation among the various groups which comprise the nation, the perspective imposed by tradition and long experience has not easily yielded to the nationhood compulsion which education can promote and foster.[4]

Traditional Terramedia lacked a social structure that revolved around a central authority, and which did not have to be in constant competition for a loyalty that was more freely displayed toward a local authority. The nations that attained independence after 1950, then, have had to face the reality of their artificiality, the result of superficial boundaries drawn by Europeans or their agents to satisfy imperialistic and commercial interests, and upheld by force (overt and covert). The exuberance over the possibility and reality of sovereignty blinded both colonialists and "nationalists" to the face of multiculturalism, leading them to believe, wrongly, that mere political control would suffice to uphold the artificial nations which colonial force and might had released to the Terramedians. Only the sudden disruption of the superficial harmony and "togetherness" which independence conferred lifted the blinders to reality, forcing leaders in various parts of Terramedia to grapple with tribalistic or irredentist aspirations (such as those which have undermined governmental stability in Iraq, Jordan, Kenya, Libya, Malawi, Mali, Morocco, Nigeria, Sierra Leone, and others).

THE ADHERENCE TO "WESTERN" VALUES AND STATUS SYSTEMS

The crisis of identity, which Black reformers or "revolutionaries" in the United States have seen as an obstacle to building an effective and loyal following, has long been recognized by Terramedian leaders. Some, like those in the United States who have promoted changes in attire, language, and personal names, have instituted comparable reforms—all intended to enhance or diffuse a sense of national consciousness. Nkrumah, for example, adopted the name *Ghana,* while lending greater dignity to the kente cloth than to the striped suit or tuxedo; Nasser retained the name, *United Arab Republic,* even when territorial facts no longer supported such identity; and other leaders introduced names (Azania, Kinshasa, Lesotho, Zambia, Zaire, and Zimbabwe), and advocated behavior patterns which would inspire a sense of rejuvenation and purposefulness. The intent, ranging from mere urgings to rigid compulsion, was to curb regional and tribal obstacles to nation-building. Relatively speaking, however, the intent has not produced the desired results; a "colonial mentality" persists among a significant number of senior and junior "executives" which finds them applying, oftentimes unconsciously, Western yardsticks in the performance of their tasks–in formulating or executing policy, or in reacting to grassroots needs and expectations.

It would be irrational to expect a sudden demise of the adherence to Western values among an elite whose formal socialization–lasting until the very eve of independence–impressed upon them the high esteem and dignity of Westernism, including the "proper" evaluation of artistic, educational, and occupational endeavors, as well as the socioeconomic characteristics appropriate for assignment to a specific rank in an inevitably stratified society.[5] Hence, the determination of priorities in the allocation of scarce revenue has often been influenced more by the designs of Westernism than by Terramedianism. Why, for example, should the structure of government retain the Western pattern of "ministries" or "bureaus" or "departments," along with the attached privileges and appurtenances of office once granted to Europeans under colonialism–free housing, telephone, automobile, and the like? And why must officials continue to expect the government to provide them with long, paid holidays in Europe, as was done for European officials? Were the funds rather expended for overseas holidays within Terramedia, a significant boost to services and to the local economy would be the result.

Many practices and facilities are maintained for national development, but in reality they are but prestige items deserving low priority in the Terramedian scheme of things. The curricula in most national universities continue to reflect Western aspirations and goals at the expense of a proper focus on Terramedian needs and realistic objectives; and instead of supporting programs for indigenous creativity in goods and services, a colonial mentality persists in directing the wind of understandable rising expectations toward European things and ideas. And even as leaders propagate their commitment to "nonalignment," to "Arabism," and to "Africanism," they simultaneously become agents of inconsistency and hypocrisy by driving around town in a Mercedes-Benz or in a Cadillac, and by using scotch and champagne in their lavish entertainments–official and private.

INFRASTRUCTURAL INADEQUACY OR SUPERFLUITY

No nation today is unaware of the significance of the quality of the infrastructure to the well-being of its citizens. Building nations and maintaining their viability, regardless of the specific ideology appealed to for guidelines, is known to depend on the prevailing infrastructural base and character. Because of the accident of history, however, the importance attached to infrastructure has not yielded optimum results for Terramedia, since the leaders have had to grapple with items whose objectives do not fit those necessary for rational nation-building in the modern world. Furthermore, major partners in contemporary building—including some of the Terramedian leaders—have been unable to recognize the obsolescence of approaches because of their enculturation in values irrelevant to nation-building outside a colonial framework.

The term, *infrastructure,* is often used to refer to material and non-material elements which may contribute to beneficial economic activity, especially in the major aspects of production, distribution, and consumption. These elements are, in turn, categorized as *physical infrastructure* (such as roads, power and electricity, banking and credit facilities, postal and telegraph facilities, and mass media), and *social infrastructure* (such as educational facilities, and health and welfare facilities). While the economic sector is often the one most immediately and directly influenced by the character of the infrastructure, other sectors, including the political, inevitably come under its sway in terms of the limitations which the infrastructure may impose on the attainment of goals generated from other than the economic sector. It is because of this interrelationship that politics and economics have usually shared the primacy in national affairs, with the government always assuming the responsibility for the design of economic plans even under capitalism. Thus it is that leaders of contemporary Terramedia must face the challenges posed by the problem of the infrastructure, both in those instances where the elements are inadequate for the demands of meaningful nation-building—including well-formulated "economic plans"—and in those where they are superfluous to the essential needs of the nation.

Looking at the existing infrastructure in both its physical and social dimensions, it is striking to note that its character has not been altered significantly so as to reflect the drastic change from a politics of colonialism to a politics of independence. This unchanged character has made most, if not all, Terramedian nations innocent victims of neocolonialism; for the infrastructural base designed to serve colonial interests has as yet not been satisfactorily modified to serve "independence" interests. In some instances, the pattern of roads and shipping have maintained a trade relation unfavorable to Terramedian nations; in others, the retention of Western procedures in education, banking, and journalism, for example, has blocked the attainment of necessary Terramedian goals. One of the urgent needs for making independence a reality, then, is that of promoting infrastructural designs which will serve essential independence interests primarily, rather than as adjuncts to "external" infrastructural interests.

DISTORTION OF NATIONAL PRIORITIES BY NON-TERRAMEDIAN "FRIENDS"

The normal scheme of things is for a nation and its citizens to determine their national priorities. In Terramedia, unfortunately, partly because of the difficulty in evolving an integrated perspective, and the persistence of a colonial mentality, however unconsciously held, these questions have often been influenced greatly by outsiders. Oftentimes, even skeptical Terramedian politicians have looked at the humanitarian or friendly basis of such external "guidance," rather than at the natural vested-interest stimulation that is involved. The consequence has been that the determination of development goals, targets, and timetables have not been free of non-Terramedian influences, thereby encouraging activities and policies that are not always in the best interest of Terramedian people.[6]

It is a fact that all Terramedian countries have emphasized what should be done to improve their existing social, political, and economic institutions. Most, if not all, leaders have been concerned with undertaking such projects, and with enunciating such policies as would uplift the nations and its citizens. In carrying out these interests, however, they have found themselves bound by the available advice and resources—material and ideological. Indeed some of these leaders have had no choice but to reason things out on the basis of their own experience, including the process of socialization and the type of personal and philosophical identity which they might have developed. Such influences, particularly when they are in large measure derived from values external to traditional Terramedian values, often result in the adoption of formulas not in tune with the realities of the social and physical environment, i.e. faulty calculation of pain and meaning.[7] There are many instances of building factories and roads when Terramedian interests clearly indicated that they were unnecessary. In situations where there is need for improving agricultural productivity, it becomes questionable when resources are committed instead to prestige items such as wider roads or air-conditioned homes for cabinet members. It is equally questionable when a minister of education exhorts the population to pursue indigenous interests, and then have the director of education formulate such rigid standards as would make it difficult for a local educational board to implement a village school and curriculum. Even today, one is left to ponder about the continuing interest among many of the young people in Terramedia for higher education abroad, rather than at the local universities. Certainly something is out of whack when fifteen years after independence, given the high investments in education that have been made by most Terramedian countries, prospective professionals and nation builders feel that they must go abroad to become qualified.

It is reasonable to conclude that the continuing reliance on external educational designs will only prolong the influence of non-Terramedians—who understandably will retain a different perspective of Terramedian needs and aspirations—in the unfortunate distortion of national priorities. The same can be said of a leadership that fails to check the increasing exodus of citizens from rural communities, to add to the pool of unemployed, while basic food commodities remain insufficient. A close look ought to be given to the charge against civil servants that the exercise of their roles—as police officers, teachers, inspectors, and administrators—have been more in the pursuit of their own selfish interests than in contributing toward viable nation-states.

Remedial Responses

The dilemma facing Terramedian countries, in striving to make independence a reality, has led to an appreciable degree of reevaluation of posture on the part of leaders and citizens at large. In some cases, idle criticism and indifference have been manifested; in others, constructive efforts have been made by representatives of all levels of government and of all segments of society. Some of these efforts have resulted in improvement, however minimal, thus encouraging a positive attitude and hope for some ultimate improvement in individual lives and in the national image.[8]

A remedy has certainly been found in *syncretism,* a process by which individuals, groups, and even nations have pursued a meaningful blend of traditional views and tactics with those that have newly become known to them. Syncretism has shown its effect on the ideologies that have characterized most of the Terramedian countries, as well as the economic directives and political styles which have become prominent. Even a system as basic as that of stratification has succumbed to the influence of syncretism, in that traditional stratificational patterns have become sufficiently flexible to reward "achievements" in the face of ascriptive limitations.[9] In ideology, Terramedian leaders have resisted the temptation to pursue pure socialism or pure capitalism, relying instead on a guideline based on what they conceive to be the best of several options. In the political realm, even though most Terramedian countries had come up feeling that parliamentary democracy (even when it included a monarchy) was the normal pattern of government, most of them have succeeded in implementing one-party states.

Another response was *militarism.* It should be noted that in the attainment of independence, most of the countries of Africa and the Middle East did so with a mass support for the politicians who had gained prominence through their anticolonial appeal. These preindependence politicians had also given the impression of drastic changes once they came into power—changes that would improve the lot of the majority of the citizenry. In Zaire, for example, many peasants were given the understanding that the automobiles and comfortable homes of Belgians would become theirs with independence; while in many other countries the mood prevailed that indigeneous persons would gain access to the pleasures and comforts that were being enjoyed by the European masters. Unfortunately, independence failed to give reality to these expectations; indeed, in many instances, the experience of the common man became one of disappointment as the cost of living increased, as job opportunities declined, and as aspirations for betterment fell short of attainment. One consequence of this feeling of disappointment was that the military, which had the only organized ability to use force or the threat of force, removed the civilian government and its representatives who had not only failed to promote betterment for the majority, but had become involved in pursuing their own personal interests. There was reason to believe, inasmuch as these politicians were able to maintain a standard of living far superior to that of the rank and file, that they "ate with both hands"—that they were involved in corruption and bad management of the affairs of state.

It should be remembered that when Europeans became involved in Terramedian affairs toward the end of the nineteenth century, not expecting that the people who had been subjugated would ever be capable of ruling themselves, they furnished little or no help to aspiring native politicians, who as a group were distrusted. Even in those instances when Europeans recognized the legitimacy and authority of indigenous rulers, this was done with an attitude of superiority, leaving the former free to manipulate these leaders in the interest of Europe. The people who succeeded in politics during the colonial or pseudocolonial era, indeed, went through the process of survival of the fittest, ranging from some who were very able, to those who were merely weak, egotistical opportunists. Politics during the colonial regime consisted less of modes of rational social control than of means of succeeding, of getting elected so that one would make money, gain prestige, and get rid of colonialists. With the withdrawal of the colonial regime, all too often, the persons who had won political recognition and some measure of power had no more altruistic a goal than self-aggrandizement.

Unlike the indigenous politician, the individual in the military was not left to his own devices. The colonial officials by and large ignored indigenous politicians, since they hardly expected them to attain any success in replacing the Europeans who were then in power. By the same token, since the Europeans did not intend to leave Terramedian countries to their own devices, and, in fact, needed to protect their own commercial and other interests, they maintained armies in all of the colonies, or some kind of defense facility in those areas where they were not formally in control. The military forces that were established, in most instances, were controlled by European officers. Most of the indigenous people who became part of such military forces represented a variety of ethnic groups, and were often those persons who found it impossible or difficult to succeed in other endeavours. The fact is that the military was not an attractive profession, perhaps because opportunity to advance to officer rank was very limited. On the other hand, those Terramedians who were given the opportunity to become officers (and such opportunities expanded during and after World War II) received the best military training in such European institutions as Sandhurst and St. Cyr. It should be noted that the character of military training and experience, unlike the nature of politics which encouraged the ethnic and tribal identity of individual politicians, gave military personnel a feeling of belonging to an integrated nontribalistic entity. In effect, the military in Terramedian countries became the least tribal conscious and the most nation-conscious group.

There have been many coups d'etats in Africa and the Middle East since independence, although not with the frequency and neglect of national interest that occurred in Latin American countries. As the pains of independence became more difficult for civilian politicians to handle, the military was able to enter the political arena as one of the few relatively stable and organized groups. Enter they did in many countries, in Egypt and Iraq, in Lebanon and Algeria, in Zaire and Mali, usually citing as reasons for toppling the existing civilian regimes the following:

(1) that the existing government had done nothing to stop unemployment, to maintain justice in the treatment of political opposition, to end corruption, and to halt neocolonialism
(2) that the government had operated on too narrow a "tribal" foundation and thus had not properly represented the people of the whole "nation"
(3) that the government had been inefficiently structured, with resulting duplication of services and waste
(4) that most civilian politicians had been reluctant to allow the people to fairly express their confidence or lack of confidence in their regimes, making it impossible for inefficient leaders to be voted out of office

All military regimes have, upon overthrowing the civilian governments, asserted their intention to establish the feeling of true nationhood and to end tribalism by marshalling all the national abilities and forces needed for the task of realistic national, economic, and social development. Unfortunately, despite the normally nonpartisanship of outlook and disciplines among the military, many officers have turned out to be not much different from civilian politicians, as they too succumbed to the arrogance of power and the comforts of authoritarian rule. In most instances, then, whether it be in Uganda or Iraq, in Ghana or in Algeria, the fundamental problems of national identification and nation building have persisted. The so-called "nation" has remained an artificial entity in which the majority of the citizens have developed little faith, and in which the masses have continued to suffer from the depravation of poverty, ignorance, and disease.

Another reaction in making independence a reality has occurred in *education.* Education was seen as one of the principal vehicles by which development of necessary manpower could be pursued, not only to promote economic betterment, but to enhance the sense of national unity. Unfortunately, Terramedian educational systems, at the eve of independence and since, tended to be less adaptable to such a good end. For one thing education of children remained localized, keeping together children of the same ethnic and language background. Associated with this tendency for promoting tribal in-grouping, has been the fact that role models have been chosen from among one's own ethnic group. The appreciation of other Terramedians was thus not promoted in a way that would minimize the normal inclination toward ethnocentrism. Such a state of affairs would have proved relatively unimportant had not independence forced upon disparate groups the need to become members of one nation.

But there were other faults with the educational systems and curricula inherited by Terramedia from the colonialists and their European "protectors." One of these was the inappropriateness of much of the educational substance needed for effective participation in the local milieu, and the irrelevance of most of the content of Terramedia experience. Frequently textbooks that were used, except for those instances where indigenous literature such as the Qur'an and Arabic were used, contained illustrations of an Anglo-Saxon experience not readily identifiable with that of the Terramedian child. One can now easily see the silliness of teaching Terramedian children in the tropical zone to recite a statement like "I am sad because it is snowing" or "Our ancestors, the Gauls, did so and so." Furthermore, the economics studied was European; the constitutional laws were either French, British, or German; and the history and literature to which Terramedians were exposed, by and large, were of European vintage. It was as if education in Terramedia was designed to prepare one for a European lifestyle!

Even more important than the foregoing was the status level attained by certain areas of studies. Most of the colonialists and "protectors" with whom the Terramedians had contact were representatives of the military, medical, clergy, education, or civil service personnel. Hardly any contact, in a formalized teaching and learning situation, was had with technicians, engineers, industrialists, and administrators. Furthermore, the means of achieving higher status were very limited to Terramedians, so most were attracted to studies enabling them to obtain the sort of employment and status to which their experience with the Europeans had directed them. Because the civil service offered the greatest number of jobs as well as respectable status, and because many, if not most, European civil servants had arts degrees rather than technical degrees, the arts, and to a lesser extent the sciences, attracted most of the Terramedian students. Medicine, of course, attracted an appreciable number, particularly in the earlier period of colonial rule when very few civil service opportunities existed, and when politics and law were not widely considered as paying professions. Engineering and other technical education tended to lag behind, simply because these areas offered fewer jobs and did not carry the prestige of an honors degree in the arts field.

The circumstances of history have, in fact, continued to influence adversely the curricula in most of the Terramedian universities. While it is true that there were very few formal universities in Terramedia prior to 1950 (exceptions would be the Fourah Bay College founded in 1827, University of Khartoum in 1898, University of Algiers in 1909, University of Cairo in 1927, University of Ibadan in 1948, and University of Ghana in 1948), the majority of the universites sponsored by the independent governments have retained curricula that reflect the attitude to education and professional choice which developed during the colonial period. A cursory examination of the approximately sixty universities in Terramedia reveals minimal provision for studies in agriculture, dentistry, engineering, medicine, nursing, social work, and vocational and industrial education. It is further to be observed that in only a very few of these universities are there provisions for pursuing degrees in Islamic African studies, and in African languages.[10]

Significant changes have occurred in Terramedian education during the past ten years, sometimes with the assistance of United Nations personnel or those from various European, Latin American, and Asian nations. It is a fact that the curricula in the various faculties have been expanded in most of these universities, thereby reducing the necessity of sending persons to universities outside of Terramedia. A significant development in education has been the assumption of leadership and top-level administration by Terramedians themselves, and the increasing localization of the faculty and staff. Related to this matter of localization has been the development of a more diversified faculty, in terms of national origin, as most universities now employ nationals other than those of the excolonial powers. Textbooks have been rewritten, and significant research is being pursued to provide relevant teaching materials for Terramedians. The study of the Qur'an and Arabic has increased in the Middle East in particular, whereas indigenous African languages such as Edo, Hausa, Ki-Swahili, Twi, and Yoruba have become subjects in many of the sub-Saharan universities. Schools of engineering and technology, of nursing and medicine, of archeology and geology, of agriculture and home economics, have been established, and increasing job opportunities have been developed for technicians.

Much has in fact been done, but there is still a residue of European mentality that resists a hastened pace toward a more relevant Terramedian curriculum. In most Terramedian universities, for example, admissions standards and pedagogical methods are still an imitation of the European. Only a very few of these universities have responded to the changed needs of their societies by making admissions standards flexible enough to meet the needs of varying applicants.

There is no question but that a desire for change, for improvement in the quality of life, is held throughout Terramedia. Kings and Presidents in Algeria and Uganda, in Morocco and Kenya, in Saudi Arabia and Jordan, have at times given reality to this by invoking drastic reforms in the patterns of social relationships and in the rules governing access to opportunities. But much remains to be done, especially on the part of the existing high-level manpower sector (including cabinet ministers and educational administrators), to reach the needed goal espoused by the late Kwame Nkrumah:

> The intelligentsia, the workers, the farmers, and peasants, all people must pull together in one great effort to liquidate and abolish all the remnants of the evils of colonialism—illiteracy, disease, poverty, hunger, malnutrition, and squalor. All the people must work together, for our interests are one and inseparable and our destiny is one and single.[11]

It is not enough to place in positions of authority indigenous persons who act as if they are reluctant to pursue Terramedian interests on the basis of Terramedian values and aspirations. There is need for looking within the nation (without necessarily ignoring the techniques which have proved beneficial to non-Terramedians) for guidelines whereby independence can be hastened into reality. It means nothing to nationalize foreign industry and to restrict foreign control in banking, commerce, and education, if such acts are not supplemented by concrete designs to bring in Terramedians as actors in national transformation—as participants ready to shoulder their share of the responsibility for national transformation, with the confidence and trust that their share of benefits and privileges will not be usurped by an entrenched and privileged oligarchy.

Proposals for Realistic Independence

It is ironic that Terramedia falls in the category of "underdeveloped," despite the fact that significant amounts and kinds of resources needed to maintain the "highly developed" character of the major world powers come from Terramedia. While Terramedia has contributed its petroleum, copper, diamonds, iron ore, and bauxite toward the development of other nations, the region itself has remained predominantly agricultural, with most of its citizens forced by the neglect and denial of colonialism (overt and covert), to live at a subsistence level. The short experience with modern independence has not changed the glaring backwardness in agriculture, education, industrial energy, manufacturing, and the quality of living.

An essential expectation in Terramedia has been that living conditions and opportunities will be better than they were during the colonial period. Even those whose material well-being was always satisfactory, have derived a sense of dignity from knowing that they can now enjoy, in addition, a psychological satisfaction of no longer being judged socially inferior to the "powerful outsiders within their gates." In the long run, however, once the euphoria of being free has worn off, it becomes normal to measure the real gains of independence to self and to others. The category that then receives the closest scrutiny is the *economy,* which can most clearly reveal whether there has been an increase in aggregate real income or in average real income per head. For the ordinary citizen this is a simple matter; for Terramedian leaders and decision makers, however, it calls for comprehensive attention to many details having not only economic, but social, political, and psychological implications as well. It is they who must analyze, marshall, and sustain such growth ingredients as the level of capital investment, the quality of the labor force, the plan for economic, educational, and manpower use, and the system of commodity and trade relations.[12] It is they who must determine when, and at what pace, to:

(1) Restrain consumption to support capital formation and investment;
(2) Change the traditional agricultural and industrial activities;
(3) Control the proper mix of rugged individualism and socialism which shall characterize economic, social, and political behavior;

(4) Raise the share of personal taxes toward local and national programs;
(5) Prescribe standards of occupational competencies and the levels of compensation;
(6) Restrain external influences upon the lifestyles of the nation.[13]

To attain these goals, especially in a world community impressed with the "miracles" of modernity, Terramedian leaders must come to grips with their own cultural and societal limitations. They must anticipate the obstacles that are bound to emerge (as have been manifest in many instances already) from the clash between traditional and modern values—in religion and in family life; in status and in authority; in attitudes toward work, economic options, and discipline; in the notion of loyalties appropriate to the tribe or the nation. They must grapple with the unsolved question of which sector—agriculture or industry—deserves priority, while remaining fully aware that change for betterment must be pursued.

The following suggestions have often been made by analysts of Terramedian affairs as relevant for true independence:

(1) seriously adapting education to the needs of Terramedian countries
(2) using education, both formal and informal, to promote civic and community responsibility
(3) promoting a realistic pattern of adult education that would help to combat illiteracy, ill health, malnutrition, disease, unemployment, and poverty—with emphasis on inculcating personal discipline, initiative, productivity, and problem-solving attitude
(4) improving the lot of women in society
(5) encouraging a pattern of socialization of the young—both at the primary and secondary levels—to make them better prepared for effective participation in the pluralistic relation that nationhood requires
(6) encouraging educational research that would enhance a realistic expansion of primary and secondary education, with emphasis on:
    (a) the quality of primary and secondary instruction and learning
    (b) expanded access to institutions of higher learning
    (c) expanded access to occupations and professions for which one is educationally qualified

In an attempt to propose directions for development and growth, Hunter has urged that the following factors be given serious consideration: Capital intensity, labor cost, size of demand, and consumption incentives.[14] Hunter has also presented arguments in support of initial investment in, and expansion of, the agrarian sector, including the reminder that "if there is a place in the world in which 'human investment' can be harnessed to cut shorter the road into the modern world, it is to be found in the villages of Africa." Hunter supports his contention by pointing out that:

(1) The history of industrial countries shows that, given the resulting population growth from improved medical services and living standards, an increased demand for food arises. Hence it follows that "an agrarian revolution must both precede and accompany an industrial revolution."
(2) African unemployment or underemployment, because it is highly nonmechanized and illiterate, can only be solved in the rural sector. This relative abundance of labor will find less use under mechanization that often results in reduced need for human labor.
(3) "It is the primary occupations—agriculture, mining, fishing—which really give diversification; the secondary industries will follow, to process the products and in due course to supply equipment."
(4) High mobility of labor—often wasting time, energy, and earnings—could be reduced by agricultural development in a relatively stabilized community.
(5) Developing the agricultural sector would prevent the "burden of European salary levels and social costs. . . . Conditions which no government can long tolerate arise very quickly when poor country folk flood into towns—overcrowding, total lack of sanitation, neglect of children, gross undernourishment, and frequently a breakdown of moral and cultural disciplines under the pressure of poverty, competition, and the absence of social sanctions of village life."
(6) "The development of rural life and production from the land . . . is likely to harmonize best with the deeper emotional and cultural instincts of Africans."[15]

Whether Terramedian leaders pay a greater attention to agriculture or industry, or tackle both simultaneously, there is common agreement about certain technical and social dimensions of development. There is a general awareness of the need to introduce new crops and methods, to improve facilities for irrigation, the control of water, and environmental sanitation, and to provide relevant energy and machinery. Further, it is necessary to promote adult education, undertake relocation and settlement schemes, enhance the efforts of cooperatives and marketing boards, induce or force local savings, modify the system of land tenure, and undertake realistic manpower development and "localization." In effect, making independence a reality—given both the historical and contemporary forces which will influence the ultimate shape of Terramedia—requires a recognition of the multifaceted nature of priorities. Precise selectivity and ranking is a luxury that Terramedian planners and decision makers must continue to resist; for the problems are complex and overlapping, and demand a simultaneous attention to many areas at once. Even the separation of essentially "national" from "international" priorities becomes difficult, since concern with one often affects what can, or should, be done with the other. The conditions of life and the aspirations of all Terramedians demand, after all, that certain general pursuits be included as priority items if independence is to become a reality:

(1) *Reasonable modernism,* entailing access to the benefits of science, must be pursued to help erase the image of backwardness or inferiority. It has been argued, at times, that the relative lack of modern scientific paraphernalia in Terramedia has saved it from the moral decay and environmental pollution being experienced today in the highly developed nations. This may be true; but there is no reason why a large number of Terramedians must continue to suffer from malnutrition and ill-health, from poverty and ignorance about themselves and others, when the universal pool of knowledge can be applied to provide remedies in keeping with the Terramedian environment and culture.

(2) *Political independence* needs to be given concreteness and viability by erasing neocolonialism. The experience of most Terramedian nations indicates that the conditions of life and the aspirations of societies have remained under the influence of the major world powers, including the excolonialists, inasmuch as these "foreigners" have remained highly influential in charting the course of events in the economic and political life of the people. Even the psychological realm is not unaffected, since many Terramedians are forced to see that the anticipated benefits of independence (in terms of living standards, occupational opportunities, and compensation), have remained unrealized. The fact of the matter is that indigenous politicians have assumed the offices of responsibility and decision-making, but have continued to behave as if their preference is for an alien style of conduct and of thinking, rather than a style that pursues the well-being of those over whom they now exercise control. In the visible areas of banking and commerce, in education and developmental planning, the views of outsiders as well as the roles such outsiders play have remained dominant.

(3) There is an urgent *need for eradicating white supremacy and racism,* especially within the borders of Terramedia. In the early 1960s, it had been assumed that the wind of change which had brought independence to most of Terramedia would continue to blow favorably. Unfortunately, the 1970s have made it clear that in the southern area of Terramedia the old notion of white suprem-

acy and racism has stimulated a retrenchment of forces to the disadvantage of Terramedians. It may be that within the national boundaries to the north, there exists the confidence that independence is real. As long as other Terramedians remain subjected to white masters, being denied the opportunity to enjoy personal and social advancement in their countries—and this oftentimes with the overt support of nations which pose as friends to individual Terramedian nations—no nation in Terramedia ought to consider its independence secure and worthy of pride. Faith in the United Nations has failed to bear the fruit of equity and justice, for the conditions in Namibia, Rhodesia, and South Africa have remained unpalatable to nonwhite Terramedians.

(4) *Ethnic partisanship,* personality conflicts, and power struggles continue to pose obstacles to harmonious relations among Terramedians. There is so much to do with so few top level, experienced personnel, that genuine brotherhood—allowing for constructive criticism of each other's viewpoints and a commitment to the national good—should be deemed a virtue. In this regard, politicians, educators, and top administrators can play a vital role in encouraging their segmented followers to realize that the good of the whole nation can be better pursued through a sense of common nationhood, rather than through an adherence to localized loyalty.

(5) *Inter-Terramedian Cooperation* in various developmental activities needs to be promoted with vigor. Too much time has been spent talking rather than doing. It is sad to observe that many of the existing vehicles for regional cooperation—agriculture, aviation, education, and commerce—have deteriorated since independence, as each nation sought its own interests. The resulting "balkanization" of activities has produced mediocre results, to the benefits of non-Terramedians.

Outlook for the Future

Many areas of Terramedian affairs have experienced encouraging developments since independence. The two decades since 1960 have witnessed a positive assertion of Terramedian independence in the responses to crucial national and international questions. There have been some nations which have acted with extreme aversion toward preindependence relationships, whereas some others have seemed very unwilling to modify their relations with the excolonial powers. Ideological postures and developmental plans have been taken in some cases, seemingly to portray a rigid anticolonial and anti-imperialistic stance, rather than to enhance the national situation. The events following independence in Guinea, Mali, Iraq, Algeria, and Egypt are examples of extremism which show the need for prior consideration of the potential impact of revolutionary decisions on the infrastructure and mass attitudes which colonialism had nurtured.

It is true that the development of new friendships with nations that were once strangers—and may, in fact, still be because of the relative unfamiliarity with each other's culture—has opened new avenues of contact and benefits, as well as reduced the dependency upon the old, but sometimes distrusted, colonial relations. Terramedians may have increased their options regarding sources of advice, emulation, trade, education, and assistance—both technical and financial. But these options have, in turn, demanded costly eliminations or substitutions in providing the necessary accommodative infrastructures. Students raised in a French- or English-speaking tradition, for example, will gain more readily from a learning or other relationship that is familiar, than from one involving less familiar Russian- or Chinese-speaking persons. It is to be noted, however, that the flexible attitude in Terramedia toward "arrangements" has not resulted in a drastic change in relationships. Development in the major sectors of commerce, education, and cultural interaction reveal the persistent strength of the old relationships, even as wider diplomatic exchanges have occurred. In most of Terramedia, most assistance and consumer goods, and most of the arrangements for manpower and resource development have continued to come from, and have been made with, the excolonialists.

Many Terramedians have recently come in contact with Russians, Chinese, and East Europeans as they engaged in the construction of new school buildings, new highways and bridges, new irrigation and agricultural projects, new stadia and recreational projects, or as Terramedians have engaged in studying abroad in universities, or participated in international conferences and cultural events. From these contacts, Terramedian leaders and ordinary citizens have enriched their perceptions, even to the point of being able to recognize that their living styles and aspirations are not always as "backward" as some would want them to believe.

In view of all that has been said, what significant developments have taken place in Terramedia to enhance national consciousness and pride? *First,* most of the countries in Terramedia have experienced actual civil war or threats of ethnic divisiveness. From these experiences, even when they have resulted in the overthrow of the existing regime by military or political action, the center of attention has always been the nation. The result has been the diffusion of a greater awareness of the nation's existence and an appreciation of the dignity to which it is entitled. In the end, hostility brought about a keener sense of nationhood; energies were expended toward protecting a concrete sovereignty within a clearly delineated boundary. Civil wars and coups d'etats have occurred in Algeria,

Ghana, Jordan, Mali Nigeria, Sudan, and Zaire, to name a few; in all of these cases, however (including the prolonged hostility in Sudan, Zaire, and Nigeria which witnessed the creation of new states in territories known to be part of existing states), the original national boundaries were ultimately retained and kept intact. One contributing factor to the prevention of further fragmentation of Terramedian states has been the unwillingness of the Organization of African Unity to violate its own principles, to wit, to respect the inalienable right of each nation to its territorial integrity and sovereignty; and to pursue the peaceful settlement of disputes by negotiation, mediation, conciliation, or arbitration.

Second, the area has witnessed the emergence of a significant number of persons with managerial and administrative skills. Furthermore, the fact that the government has been able to select persons for professional training in keeping with designated national priorities has brought into being a pool of highly trained professionals and technicians. Now that the political sphere has proved incapable of absorbing all these persons, including even those with less training who had been made to see political involvement as the most prestigious and rewarding, attention is being given to other important sectors of national life requiring talent and energy. It is also a fact that the increased assertion of sovereignty has opened up occupational opportunities that were once enjoyed by foreigners only. The ambitious Terramedian no longer is forced to limit his ambition to the medical and legal professions, nor to restrict his investments to real estate or savings accounts. There is now a real opportunity for diversified participation in all areas of economic, political, and social affairs, and the visible evidence has been that a respectable and oftentimes comfortable living can be pursued outside of politics and government service.

Third, there has occurred a heightened international respect for the right of Terramedians to manage their own affairs, including the freedom to enter into varying international alliances. Gone are the days when expulsion or arrest of a European would result in gunboat diplomacy. Indeed, Terramedians have been able to assert their sovereignty by nationalizing foreign enterprises, by proscirbing the rights and responsibilities of noncitizens, and by insisting on being pro-Terramedia rather than pro-West or pro-East. Qatar, for example, decreed a complete nationalization of all petroleum activities between 1974 and 1977. All these actions have not resulted in any visible attempt to "punish" the Terramedian nations, even though there have been occasions when such behavior stimulated discussions of foreign aid curtailment or the severance of diplomatic representation.[16]

Fourth, there is evidence of increased pride among Terramedians in their own traditional values, and a reduced tendency—especially among the new elite—to be like Europeans. More and more Terramedians are showing satisfaction with being trained in their own universities and being proud products of their environment and traditional culture. The fact that no less than fourteen percent of the national revenue has been allocated for education has been a significant stimulant in most Terramedian countries. Equally significant has been the interest in rediscovering and reinterpreting Terramedian history to offset the distortions, limitations, and inadequacies portrayed in some of the colonialist renditions.

The future of Terramedia is fairly bright, given the advances that have been made to date, and considering the handicaps imposed by colonial exploitation and "other-directedness." Countries like Libya and Tanzania, for example, have shown how "African socialism" and "Arab socialism" can improve the national condition and image. Vast natural resources remain untapped or under utilized as far as Terramedian interests are concerned, and the fruits of Terramedian interdependency and mutual assistance have yet to be harvested. In addition, the agony of persistent colonialism must be endured, even as Terramedians create a climate conducive to constructive criticism. Too many necessary human talents have been lost to nation-building because of personal and political conflicts which have exacerbated hostility and resulted in the imprisonment or exile of one brother by another. But if the posture of dignity and respect for the brotherhood which all Terramedians share continues to be nurtured and diffused, then an ever-bounteous experience shall be Terramedia's reward.

As sovereigns of circumstance, policy-formulators and decision-makers must realize, as did Spinoza, that "a sovereign has right insofar as he has might, and he has might insofar as he rules in such a way that his subjects regard rebellion as a greater evil than obedience." Let it not be said of Terramedia that its trusting and patient citizens are the only introspective saints, while its leaders are but burly sinners. Instead, let a subsequent reckoning show that in the face of challenge, with a will to make independence a reality for all Terramedians, the admonition of William Dewitt Hyde was kept in constant perspective:

> Who would we rather be—a man who by successful manipulation of dishonest financial schemes had come to be a millionaire, the mayor of his city, the pillar of the church, the ornament of the best society, the senator from his state, or the ambassador of his country at a European court; or a man who in consequence of his integrity had won the enmity of evil men in power, had been sent in disgrace to a state prison, a man whom no one would speak to; whom his best friends had deserted, whose own children were being brought up to reproach him?

Current events in countries like Kuwait, Qatar and Saudi Arabia, especially in using their superfluous petroleum revenue to enhance the quality of health, education, and housing of ordinary citizens, provide a basis for believing that some Terramedian leaders know who they would rather be.

NOTES

1. Palen, *Urban World,* p. 322.

2. See D. M. Condit, et al., *Challenge and Response in Internal Conflict* (Washington: Center for Research in Social Systems, 1968); and Waldermar Nielsen, *The Great Powers and Africa* (New York: Praeger Publishers, 1969).

3. See Landau, *Man, State, and Society*; Nielsen, *Great Powers*; Silvert, *Expectant Peoples*; and Kwame Nkruma, *Dark Days in Ghana* (London: Panaf Publications, 1968).

4. See George Dalton (ed.), *Economic Development and Social Change* (Garden City, NJ: Natural History Press, 1971); and L. Gary Cowan et al. (eds.), *Education and Nation-Building* (New York: Praeger Publishers, 1965).

5. See Ake, "Political Instability," pp. 347-59; A. L. Adu, *The Civil Service in New African States* (New York: Praeger Publishers, 1965); and Jason Finkle and Richard Gable (eds.), *Political Development and Social Change* (New York: John Wiley, 1966).

6. See Peter Berger, *Pyramids of Sacrifice* (Garden City, NJ: Doubleday, Anchor, 1976), pp. 121-44.

7. Ibid., pp. 149-204.

8. See Zartman, *Contemporary Maghrib*, pp. 93ff.

9. See Celia S. Heller, *Structured Social Inequality* (New York: Macmillan, 1969); and Gerhard Lenski, *Power and Privilege* (New York: McGraw-Hill, 1966).

10. African-American Institute, *African Colleges and Universities* (New York: The African-American Institute, 1970); see also, Adam Curle, *Educational Problems of Developing Societies* (New York: Praeger Publishers, 1969); and Taman Golan, *Educating the Bureaucracy in a New Polity* (New York: Teachers College Press, 1968).

11. Ken Post, *The New States of West Africa* (Baltimore: Penguin Books, 1964), p. 109. Cf. T. Peter Omari, *Kwame Nkrumah* (Accra: Moxon Paperbacks, 1970).

12. See E. R. Rado, "Manpower, Education and Economic Growth," *Journal of Modern African Studies* (1966):83-93.

13. Paul G. Clark, "Development Strategy in an Early-State Economy," *Journal of Modern African Studies* (1966):47-64.

14. See Guy Hunter, *The New Societies of Tropical Africa* (New York: Praeger Publisher, 1964), pp. 65-69. Cf. Landau, *Man, State, and Society.*

15. See Guy Hunter, *Modernizing Peasant Societies* (New York: Oxford University Press, 1969).

16. *U.S. Overseas Loans and Grants* (Washington: Agency for International Development, 1969); and Commission on International Development, *Partners in Development* (New York: Praeger Publishers, 1969).

Chapter Eleven

IN PURSUIT OF RELEVANT LIFESTYLES

The Nature of a Unique Lifestyle

The term "lifestyle" has gained popular usage among blacks in the United States, particularly those who find themselves in the compelling socializing grip of higher education. These blacks, as an aftermath of the affirmative action thrust of the 1960s and 1970s, were recruited into higher education essentially because of their blackness—whether as students, staff, or faculty—and encouraged, if not compelled, to assert their difference. After all, their inclusion in the educational institutions demanded rationalization, inasmuch as other than traditional standards had been employed: Unlike athletes, these new members had yet to justify why their usually low scholastic achievement and socioeconomic status should suffice. The same held true for faculty and staff who, in most cases, assumed positions above those for which, on the basis of the prevailing traditional guidelines, their qualifications and experiences would make them competent. A self-fulfilling prophecy attitude soon developed among "legitimate" and "illegitimate" members alike, to explain away inadequacies, as well as to confer the badge of acceptability upon once unacceptable phenomena—speech, comportment, values, and so forth.

The consequence of all this was the search for differences and, ultimately, the creation of attributes to satisfy the need to be different. At times, these attributes derived from glaring biogenic and sociogenic characteristics, including those which had been suppressed in order to gain acceptability. The integrationist inclination now became unattractive, and blackness, for example, became an attribute of pride rather than of inferiority. The "dashiki," "corn row," "self-reliance," and "communal segregation" (not to discount the adoption of Swahili, Islam, and a conspicuous hand-shake), became symbols of a different identity—all parts of an evolving lifestyle. There was even a detection of arrogance in the myth that the new lifestyle had no connection with the common phenomenon of culture possessed by all groups. It was assumed, for example, that soulness was unique to blackness! In reality, however, use was being made of a people's heritage, and a syncretistic construct was the vehicle by which the real and the imagined, the past and the present, coalesced into an identifiable lifestyle.

A lifestyle is a way of living. It is a comprehensive system of norms and values that influence the nature of responses and reactions to situations involving natural phenomena. Lifestyle is akin to habit and culture, and reflects distinctiveness and behavior patterns. Except for the fact that some active and articulate Blacks in the United States have given prominence to the term, there would appear to be no reason for not using *culture* or *subculture* instead. The latter terms, however, might have proved less important in a movement (or mood) which sought separation from one membership group in order to promote incorporation into another distinct group. Proximity of persons requiring such separation and ultimate incorporation made for enough difficulty without having to use the same language. Success in proving that one "belonged" elsewhere would depend, after all, on showing apparent differences in speech, thoughts, and deeds, as well as in ideals and emotions.

Although there are many arguments to prove that blacks have a unique lifestyle—some imposed, others adopted or inculcated through socialization—the depth and consistency of modern acculturation makes such uniqueness difficult to maintain. This is the experience of all groups which seek to be unique in lifestyle, as well as those groups which are pressured into remaining unique by "unlike groups" whose "superior feeling" require acknowledgement by an "inferior" group. What, after all, would sustain stratification and pluralism (persistently cherished ideals), if not unequal access and differences? Yet, modern acculturation remains a threat, through such factors as easy mobility, changing and flexible group identifying criteria, easy access to opportunity, assimilation, centralized power and authority, individualism and universalism.

Despite these threats to uniqueness, however, the insistence on manifesting a unique lifestyle had benefitted a group—the blacks in the United

States—whose lives had been marred by prejudice, the limited realization of the potential for a good life, deprecating perceptions, and rootlessness. Many Blacks now possess a positive image of self and confidence in their ability to shape their lives and the destiny of black people. One wonders what the application of such positivism would have wrought within a nation of their own to control! In the black American experience, in a colonial context, lies a lesson for Terramedians to learn and to apply in a national context. For unlike black Americans who have had to adapt to an alien and domineering society, Terramedians have been relatively free to maintain and nurture peculiarly Terramedian lifestyles. The dent made by the colonial period was, on record, minimal in the successful alteration of lifestyles, and most traditional values survived into the modern postindependence period. A pressing problem for Terramedian leaders and decision makers is resolving the extent to which alien lifestyles (introduced during the colonial era and still pursued to enhance vested alien interests), should be allowed to influence the responses of life which Terramedians must evolve to build viable nations for themselves.

Challenges to Lifestyles—Intranational and International

No society in the modern world is capable of ignoring the alterating influence of acculturation, and fewer still are those whose members can escape the pressures of syncretism or assimilation. Given the widespread adherence to universal and multilateral responsibility and obligation, there is a readiness to intervene (as well as to condone intervention) in the affairs of others—individuals, groups, nations, and regions—to ensure their access to the bounties of modernity. Partly because of the decisions and assigned roles of the United Nations and other international agencies, there has developed a commitment to correct glaring anomalies in incidences of hunger, poverty, sickness, illiteracy, mass communication, and territorial defensive capability. And with each intervention by these international teams of experts (promoted either by humanitarianism or vested interests or both), there is the accompanying introduction of new elements requiring reaction from the host culture.

Inasmuch as Terramedia provokes the greatest amount of these "altruistic" interventions, seen as rightful remedies, if not compensation, for the abuses and ravages of colonial rule (direct and indirect, overt and covert), Terramedians are faced with the highest incidence of culture invasion. The consequence of this is the introduction of added obstacles to efforts aimed at maintaining the integrity of indigenous value systems and lifestyles. Hence the seeming oversensitivity toward incidences of marginalism, detribalization, and urbanism that have occurred among only a minority of the total population. In essence, therefore, Terramedians possess a vast reservoir of traditional pillars with which to face the pressures of intervening modernity, including a cherished capacity for addition rather than for substitution. Such an attribute, exercised rationally, can prevent the undue dislocation of values and response patterns which might otherwise occur. It is for the wielders of power and the policy formulators to recognize that these traditional pillars–*communalism, the coordination of the spiritual and temporal in religion, emphasis on the extended family, gerontocracy, respect for legitimate authority, and self-reliance*–can, and must, serve as the norms of conduct and relationships, and as perspectives from which to correct existing infrastructural and other inadequacies. Obsession with "other-directedness" must not distort the virtue of "inner-directedness."

The reality facing Terramedia is that the traditional pillars cited above, which influence the character of lifestyles, cannot ignore the inevitable incursion of alien values and lifestyles. Knowledge exists, however scanty among most Terramedians, that conditions of living can be improved. A disparity exists, however, between the urgency and perception manifested by the traditionalist mass, on the one hand, and by the shapers of Terramedian destiny, on the other, toward alteration and change. There is a postulate of misunderstanding, if not of ignorance, demanding resolution; and there is the need for a keener calculation of pain and meaning in an arena of traditional-modernistic clash.

The maintenance of appropriate lifestyles, as well as the alteration of traditions to suit prevailing conditions and the expectations of Terramedians, face challenges from within and without. The external challenges can more easily be controlled by the simple act of closing the borders of Terramedia to non-Terramedians, or by selective strategies of isolation. There is ample historical evidence for this in China, Egypt, Guinea, Japan, Saudi Arabia, the Soviet Union, Tanzania, and Uganda, entailing severance of diplomatic relations, nationalization of all means of production and distribution, censorship, harassment and intimidation of aliens, and the like. Such acts have often produced a level of noninterference in efforts at nurturing unique lifestyles devoid of "destructive" alien influences. It would be inadvisable, however, for Terramedia to pursue a course of isolation and the rejection of alien intervention. Indeed, such a course of action might prove impossible given the "alienness" that is already present in the Terramedian environment–economic, political, psychological, and social.

Furthermore, Terramedia possesses natural resources whose availability and accessibility are vital to the well-being of nations militarily and technologically more powerful than Terramedia even as a collectivity. Of course, there is recent experience to suggest that these militarily powerful nations (The United States, the Soviet Union, the United Kingdom, and France) need not be feared in invoking an isolationist and rejectionist posture. The deliberate curtailment of human rights in Rhodesia, Israel, Namibia, and South Africa, for example, has evoked no more than verbal outrage on their part. Equally significant has been the inaction toward a "violation" of the human and economic interests of these powerful nations in Uganda, Ethiopia, Libya, Saudi Arabia, and Iraq. Perhaps because of a desire to adhere to the popular notion of respect for territorial sovereignty and noninterference—at least overtly—the more powerful nations have adjusted to the disadvantageous decrees and actions of these Terramedians. Would the actions by the Oil Producing and Exporting Countries (OPEC) to drastically increase the price of petroleum have been possible under Foster Dulles and Dwight Eisenhower? Would the pronationalist stances of Nyerere, Kadafi, and Amin have been ignored in the absence of a United Nations? Or is the reality that these seemingly delimiting actions toward the interests of powerful nations are not so perceived by them, and that those who lose most by these actions are Terramedians themselves?

Apart from the residue of influences among Terramedians who have been educated outside Terramedia—many of whom occupy executive and managerial positions—there is the ongoing acculturative incursion by a variety of foreign aid experts. Where they are not situated within Terramedia to dispense food and advice (educational, ideological, military, and technological), they are visible in the international agencies to which Terramedian executives go often for grants and loans. A continuity of alien impressions is, therefore, made possible equally by the local United Nations Development Program office as by the International Monetary Fund and Food and Agricultural Organization offices in Washington and Rome. The process involved in the exploration and mining of minerals and petroleum, for example, not only exposes Terramedians to foreign technicians and managers, but demands of them alterations in their prevailing postures toward land tenure, management of resources, and familial designation of economic activities. The resulting mobility and heterogeneity of populations, along with the relative individualism and formalization of sanctions, ultimately generate a significant impact on traditional values and norms—personal adornment, food preferences, and social responsibility, for example. Equally significant is the consequence when, with the involvement of aliens, Terramedians engage in such secondary and tertiary industries as milling, transportation, commerce, building and construction, packing and distribution, and food processing; or when Terramedians are drawn into social welfare services, health clinics, cooperatives, labor unions, adult education programs, and recreational clubs.

Terramedia is faced, indeed, with a dilemma as to whether lifestyles should be retained with minimal alien incursion, or whether to admit that modernity is impossible without a drastic transformation in prevailing lifestyles. A determination of this serious challenge rests, in large part, on a Terramedian calculation of the necessity and relevance of the many activities in which alien agents are involved, both by planned invitation and by subversion. It might seem prestigious, for example, to acquire military equipment (armored cars, fighter planes, automatic rifles, and gun boats), but one must doubt their effectiveness in territorial defense vis-à-vis that possessed by the external suppliers. Would Somalia and Ethiopia, for instance, have had to fight against each other if Cuban arms and military advisers (presumed to be agents of the Soviet Union) were not available to each of these countries? Would the peace deserved by Terramedians in the Middle East have been deferred, in favor of incessant tension and periodic military clashes, had not the military incursion of aliens been tolerated by Terramedians themselves? One can reasonably surmise that the level of human suffering and interethnic tension experienced in Algeria, Israel, Nigeria, Sierra Leone, Tanzania, Uganda, Zaire (to name only few countries) have been caused, in great measure, by a faulty calculation of Terramedian pain and meaning in the matter of territorial security and defense. From the perspective of the masses of Terramedia (their lifestyles entailing values, norms, and expectations of an improved living condition), leaders now have a responsibility to prevent the negative impact of foreign involvements. Because of the potential, if not the reality, of maleficence, the shapers of Terramedian destiny must examine keenly the appropriateness of designs involving technology, education, food and medicine, communication, administration, housing, migration, ideology, and trade relations, for example.

One admirable characteristic of Terramedia, despite the constant challenge posed by alienating incursions, is its emphasis on the extended family. From this flows the Terramedian acceptance of communalism and self-reliance, and an attitude capable of minimizing the segmentary influence of urbanism. To continue in a path which fails to tap the strengths embodied in tradition (to transform Terramedia in a manner advantageous to an overwhelmingly rural area), would be to invite most of the negative influences of increased urbanization—the stimulant for the desire to retreat into suburbia or small towns being manifested by more and more urbanites in the Western world. As Lofland has observed,

> The transformation from the world of personally-known others to the world of strangers has been, and continues to be, an emotionally painful one. It is one thing to make abstract statements about the

great changes that have taken and continue to take place in the world: about the massive growth of population and urbanization, about increasing spatial mobility, about the growing numbers who put down their roots not in a place, but in a profession. It is quite another thing to talk about these changes in terms of their emotional meaning for, and effect on, the day-to-day lives of human beings. The tribalist does not easily become a cosmopolitan, and the cosmopolitan, having been transformed, looks back wistfully to a life that will not come again.[1]

Terramedia has an opportunity to prevent such an inevitably painful and fragmentary transformation, for there is still time to direct change from the perspective of known experiences. Let indifference not lead to the pains of marginalism, detribalization, and normlessness which have already been experienced in the slum communities that have evolved in such national capitals as Addis Ababa, Cairo, Freetown, Lusaka, and Nairobi! There are still solid traditional pillars in Terramedia—if only the leaders and shapers of destiny would heed them—to respond to the challenge of invading urbanization noted by Doxiadis:

> We must face the fact that modern man has failed to build adequate cities. In the past his problems were simpler, and he solved them by trial and error. Now human forces and mechanical ones are mixed and man is confused. He tries and fails. We say he will become adapted. Yes, he is running the danger of becoming adapted, since adaptation is only meaningful if it means the welfare of man. Prisoners, too, become adapted to conditions! For man to adapt to our present cities would be a mistake, since he is the great prisoner. Not only is man unsafe in his prison, but he is facing a great crisis and heading for disaster.[2]

Alien incursion alone must not be blamed for the challenges imposed on Terramedian lifestyles; for there are many internal challenges which influence individual nations and the whole of Terramedia. There is the factor of mininations, for instance, entailing small territories or low populations in most of the Terramedian countries. With few exceptions, such as Nigeria, Egypt, Ethiopia, South Africa, and Morocco, none of the countries has a population close to 15 million. Even the petroleum-rich nations—Saudi Arabia, Iraq, and Kuwait—follow this pattern. Indeed, it would be accurate to state that ninety percent of all Terramedians are citizens of countries with populations of 10 million or less (see Map 8). Equally significant is the fact that mininations exist even in some territories that are geographically vast, such as Saudi Arabia, Chad, Libya, Botswana, Mali, Niger, and Zambia. The consequence of their smallness is

Figure 8.1 Population Distribution

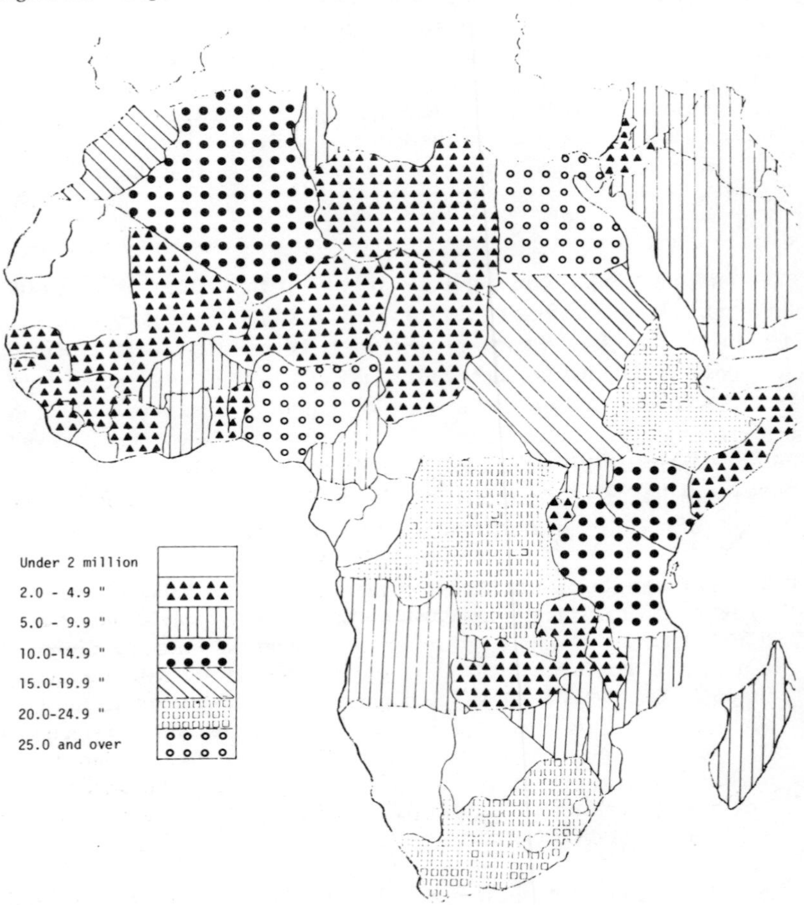

that the vast majority of Terramedian nations have to wrestle with the problem of viability and the creation of a level of self-sufficiency compatible with de facto sovereignty. A rich nation such as Kuwait and a poor nation such as Gambia, in short, face the same challenge of viability! Nkrumah, with admirable foresight, warned in vain against this regrettable consequence of balkanization.[3]

While, as members of the Organization of African Unity or of the Arab League, Terramedian nations persist in their commitment to territorial integrity, the reality for meaningful sovereignty is that "mininess"—even in the context of territorial vastness, if not sparse population—requires attention and remedy. Markets for Terramedian industry would not need to be sought in Europe, nor efforts at capital formation and manpower development be duplicated, if a concern for the Terramedian mass could be seen as a matter of greater priority than that of maintaining a multiplicity of parliaments and national flags. Is it right for the petroleum-rich countries to wantonly invest in foreign items of luxury, while their less fortunate Terramedian "cousins," if not "brothers," are forced to take "begging bowls" to neocolonialists outside? Is the reliance on the International Bank for Reconstruction and Development and the European Economic Community, for instance, rather than on the expectation of Terramedian self-reliance, not evidence that Terramedian leaders are prominent contributors to neocolonialism? Why the lack of support for the indigenous virtue of charity at home, or responsible behavior toward the deprived and the dispossessed?

How serious the question of "mininess" is can be adduced from the current strategies for nation building. Secondary and tertiary industrialization are processes to which most, if not all, Terramedian nations are strongly committed. Even those whose infrastructures and resources make such a commitment unrealistic adhere to the view and expect, at least, an accelerated diversity in the limitations placed on them by primary industrialization and subsistence agriculture. They remain hopeful that necessary capital, manpower, and technology will evolve to correct the colonial patterns of production, distribution, and consumption that have proved inconsistent with sovereign independence in the modern world. In striving to satisfy these expectations, national universities and technical institutes have been established, along with investments in a variety of projects—aviation, electricity, health and sanitation, highway construction, housing, insurance and banking, manufacturing, telecommunications, and the like. In most cases, however, the markets and the size of clientele involved seem disproportionate to the required outlay in resources. Because of "mininess," therefore, overinvestment becomes the common experience for Gambia, Sierra Leone, and Libya—to cite only an example—when each insists on having its own elegant diplomatic corps! To look at the matter from the viewpoint of opulence, Terramedian well-being is equally transgressed when Kuwait and Saudi Arabia are "forced" to invest their extremely surplus capitals on armaments and other "luxury" items in Europe and the Americas because of the feeling that investment opportunities within Terramedia are lacking.[4]

The patterns of commitment referred to above suggest an internal challenge to the statesmanship of Terramedian leaders. The obsession with impressing the leaders of the highly developed and industrialized nations (forgetting that the "superiority" of these nations was possible, in large measure, to the exploitation and expropriation of Terramedia's natural resources), has created what can reasonably be termed an aura of "statesmanlessness" among Terramedia's wielders of power. One must not blame the Central Intelligence Agency of the United States for Zaire's de facto subservience to the United States and Belgium, but President Mobutu for ignoring his moral responsibility toward his own people. One must not blame the international petroleum cartel for the inferior status of women in some oil-producing countries, but the ruling oligarchies for their arrogant abuse of the responsibilities of leadership in nations of coterminus wealth and poverty. One must not blame the callousness of foreign industrialists for the inhumanity with which Rhodesia and South Africa have been accursed, but Prime Ministers Smith, Vorster, and their cabinets for their immoral lack of statesmanship and stewardship. Indeed, with few exceptions such as President Nyerere of Tanzania, most Terramedian leaders behave much more irresponsibly toward their fellow-citizens than did the colonial imperialists whom they replaced!

As political leaders have acted irresponsibly, so have senior civil servants and judges. Even executives in the private or semiprivate sector have, in large measure, shown a lack of stewardship in the management of their affairs. These "servants" of the people, a privileged elite, have often subscribed to an atmosphere of corruption, despotism, and injustice by condoning or remaining aloof to actions which run counter to the nation's best interest, lending continuing credence to Yale's assessment: "Corruption is a social phenomenon observable both in the past and present, prevalent in monarchies and republics, empires and kingdoms, autocracies and democracies, wherever the organization of society favors the exploitation of the many by the few."[5] Waste, miscarriage of justice, illegal arrests and incarceration, misuse of public trust, and professional incompetence become visible elements of the cancer of "statesmanlessness" and irresponsible stewardship. That one observes a weak judiciary and the semblance, if not the reality, of a police state might be the consequence of events that have entrenched power in the hands of a few, while increasing the powerlessness and helplessness of the masses. It is surprising that one hears an occaional cry for violent revolution?

Regrettably, the withdrawal of colonial rulers, or the overt neutralization of their influence and power, has not put an end to colonial class consciousness and elitism. Nor has the assumption of decision-making responsibility by Terramedians curbed a propensity for emulating alien values. Accepting the fact that culture exchange is impossible to check in an age of mutual assistance and "benevolent" interaction among nations, one can still question a situation which encourages a blindness—especially among legitimate power wielders—toward one's own cherished traditions.

The objective of modern independence ought to be the pursuit of the well-being of Terramedians in the context of Terramedian realities, rather than the creation of carbon-copies of what colonialists intended. Or is it that Terramedia's destiny is to remain a colonial conglomerate with indigenous rulers? Certainly, this could remain Terramedia's fate if the search for guidelines does not include an internal, situational one. For, as Clecak has observed, even the ideologies being contested have proved wanting among "advanced" practitioners:

> Whatever becomes of democracy (and its fate seems unclear at best), economic and social life will be affected more and more by political decisions. Politics will intersect personal life in more decisive ways, even though public cynicism may be expected to persist at disappointingly high levels.
>
> Socialism, liberalism, and conservatism break down at crucial points. None of them is sufficient—indeed, any one of them pursued exclusively very probably would yield disasterous results. But each remains indispensible. None furnished materials for resolving the cultural crisis, especially its deepest religious aspects, though each contains important (if generally negative) clues to its amelioration.[6]

Toward Meeting the Challenges to Meaningful Lifestyles

While recognizing that traditional lifestyles will undergo transformation (and must face an inevitably changing environment—internal and external), certain steps can be undertaken by the wielders of power to prevent malevolent developments. The point at issue is that Terramedians have a right to their just and reasonable aspirations, as they do to a major control over shaping their lives. In the exercise of such deliberate participation, leaders and the masses alike must retain the security of reliance on cherished traditional values and the lifestyles that experience has shown to be meaningful. These must serve as the foundation to make adaptations to present challenges, and upon which to build for the future.

There are several remedies or courses of action which can be pursued. First, seriousness can be given to the need to translate official utterances for self-reliance into reality. Even though to do so would be consistent with Terramedian traditions, leaders have often adopted a contrary posture. Many, in their own lifestyles, strive to live like Westerners in their food, clothing and relational choices, creating a frustrated sense of false expectations among the rank and file. It might have been proper for Shah Pahlevi of Iran to dine on cavier and champagne, but doubtful whether President Senghor of Senegal ought to do so. It might be harmless for King Khalid, for example, to maintain a fleet of Rolls-Royce automobiles, but questionable whether a civil service dentist ought to display—at the expense of the poor citizens he is obliged to serve—a comparable level of ostentatious consumption in dwellings, clothing, and personal transporation. These acquisitions often entail a drain on scarce foreign currency reserves which might be applied toward the development of infrastructures beyond the scope of internal resources. The faulty examples set by many members of the elite—politicians, professionals, and civil service executives—conspire against the possibility of the greater self-reliance repeatedly verbalized by Terramedian leaders.

There is also a need to integrate the rural and urban sectors in the interest of nationhood. By retaining, relatively intact, the colonial centers and procedures of operation, the majority of the population is encouraged to conclude that independence from colonial rule is inapplicable to them. They are left to wonder, indeed, whether the unchanged mannerisms and interests of the new rulers are not evidence that it is the alien rulers who have assumed masks to continue their control over powerless Terramedians. The gap between those who manage Terramedian affairs from the few urban centers—in ministerial buildings, parliamentary chambers, and executive mansions—and those who remain in the many rural communities, has become wider since independence. The withdrawal of a significant number of aliens has opned up vacancies for Terramedians to fill, but these increased opportunities have not reduced the social distance that needs to be bridged. Significantly, even the unpretentious guest houses that once sufficed for colonial rulers have been replaced with luxurious official villas in the rural districts, making still more glaring the distance between the few "brothers" who have and the many who have not. It would seem prudent to transfer these "colonial" seats of administration and decision-making into the undeveloped hinterlands, thus reducing the propensity to look outwards rather than inwards. Minimally, some effort at reasonable decentralization of operational facilities and manpower would not only enhance the accesibility to life-enriching opportunities, but would in addition extend mere "categoric knowing" into the realm of "personally knowing" each other.[7]

The limited knowledge (categoric knowing) of "brother" by "brother" might have been advantageous to colonial rulers who controlled the lives of their subjects by dividing; who differentiated between those who were "primitive" agrarians and those who had become "civilized" or assimilated. Seventy years of alien control and influence proved adequate to create an acceptance of alien yardsticks by which Terramedians could judge their position along a superior-inferior continuum. Certainly, a principle which saw entrenchment over such a long period cannot be expected to lose its endearing, if not its acquiescing, appeal overnight. This is why its continuing influence must be curbed by the political engineers of Terramedia and their appointed agents of secondary socialization. Nations needing urgent integration of sectors previously kept apart, sectors previously denied adequate coordination, must see to it that fragmentary actions and ideals move toward a level of integration appropriate to the demands of national viability. The reluctance of trained personnel—teachers, doctors, bankers, and so forth—to serve in rural districts, or even for young students to accept scholarships not tenable in urban or foreign universities, is one evidence of the persistent threat to integration. Equally intolerable is the heightening level of selfish individualism and disrespect of authority among the young, who gravitate to urban centers rather than assisting in improving the living quality of the rural sector from which they seek escape, and which needs their vitality and support.

The proliferation of educational facilities and opportunities has not produced persons with the attitudes, skills, and priorities necessary for an independent and viable Terramedia. Many of the new nations have set the modification, if not the transformation, of their economic systems as a matter of high priority. Nonetheless, the allocation of manpower and resources toward this end has often undermined the overriding objective. Many are the trained technicians and farmers, for example, who are misemployed in the few urban centers, while rural projects needing their skills—food production, processing and other industries, adult education centers, health and welfare clinics, for example—go begging. Even those who qualify for executive and professional positions, in relatively large numbers, opt for politics, thereby increasing the ranks of national consumers at the expense of national producers.

There is ample evidence to suggest that educational reforms, entailing not only knowledge and skills conferral, but the development of nation-building attitudes as well, have been ineffective. Leaders must reexamine the situation to offset the seeming persistence of inappropriate and possibly unintended consequences. Efforts at manpower development must not endure the continuing embarrassment of reliance on alien experts because of the inefficient performance or inappropriateness of the indigenous personnel constituting the manpower pool. Indeed, for sovereign independence to attain viability, Terramedia must produce and utilize effectively its own developed manpower in consonance with its realistic needs. Values will certainly be warped if citizens persist in ignoring their responsibility to produce and serve, even as they pursue their right to consume and be served in return.

Moving beyond the serious challenges of a localized nature, there are internal Terramedian challenges of a wider scope requiring attention as well. The challenge of "mininess," for example, can be met only by taking a perspective which focuses on a transnational well-being. Stronger inter-Terramedian ties and recognition of the potential for a more pervasive betterment would lead to a viable system of regionalism, if not ultimate federalism. It is already clear throughout Terramedia that the resources with which the land mass is endowed are unevenly distributed, creating a situation of disparate pockets of opulence and poverty. Until it is realized that such disparity only diffuses unnecessary spiritual poverty among those who have escaped the material poverty of their other Terramedian "brothers," aliens will remain the beneficiaries of the bounties which rightfully must go primarily to Terramedians. Indeed, it is time, at last, for Terramedians to heed the appeal of Dubois shortly before the wave of modern independence:

> China after long centuries has arisen to her feet and leapt forward. [Terramedia] arise, and stand straight, speak and think! Act! Turn from the West and your slavery and humiliation for the last 500 years and face the rising sun. Behold a people, the most populous nation on this ancient earth which has burst its shackles, not by boasting and strutting, not by lying about its history and its conquests, but by patience and long-suffering, by hard, backbreaking labor and with bowed head and blind struggle, moved up and on toward the crimson sky. She aims to "make men holy; to make men free." But what Men? Not simply the rich, but not excluding the rich; not simply the learned, but led by knowledge to the end that no man shall be poor, nor sick, nor ignorant; that the humblest worker as well as the sons of emperors shall be fed and taught and healed and that there emerge on earth a single unified people, free, well and educated.[8]

Possibilities of Extraterritorial Fraternity

I spent a few hours on the streets of Watts (Los Angeles) recently, observing the sights and chatting with people as they were introduced to me. From a distance one could feel the wind of bitterness and frustration, the hopelessness and helplessness, that blew from block to block, through parks, streets, houses, and shops. There were forlorn gazes which seemed to seek hope from an unknown nothingness, but which managed, nonetheless, to cast glares of icy suspicion and distrust on strangers and cops alike. A depressing experience indeed, until one begins to interact and to share in the zest for living that has been so carefully concealed from the view of the casual observer. One is forced to realize that the pimp or dope pusher, the bookie or informant, the organizer or preacher, the lonely or disabled, the local businessman or politician, are all manifestations of transitory modes of adaptation designed to achieve ultimate human dignity and well-being. And to many, even as they envy the luck of those who have escaped the milieu to become students and members of the "system," such dignity and well-being are expected to emerge from black unity throughout the world.

The seemingly hopeless and forlorn retain a belief in the ultimate unity of peoples, based on the clearly recognizable characteristic of skin color. Skin color is an affinity which the history of dominant-minority relations has enforced; and because it stems from external pressures of negation and of denial, skin color has not provided an easy basis for cohesion. The result is that whereas nonblacks have found it easy to accept generalized stereotypes about "blacks," the latter—inasmuch as their collective views of such commonality need time to evolve—have had to be forced into "seeing" that the lot of all "blacks" is the same. It is this forced recognition, and acceptance, that brings about unattainable goals and false or distorted images. In turn, the boundaries of "blackness" on which "unity" is to be built for "salvation" and relief become blurred and ill-defined, causing surprise among many adherents (forgetting that they have really been pressured into expressing a belief in an all-encompassing blackness), when they are made to see that "blackness" does not automatically make for sameness in values and aspirations. This fact of life allows one to pass judgment on occasion on the failure of the leaders of "black unity," or even of Terramedian unity, to uphold the ideals of their followers and to persist in a progressive path toward the attainment of the goal for total unity.

In the recent past, Ron Karenga and Huey Newton have come under questioning, and persons such as Julian Bond, Stokeley Carmichael, and John Lewis have become heroes of an archaic past. No longer is the universal oneness in blackness once promised by identity with a Sukarno, a Ben Bella, and an Nkrumah visible, for the reality of diversity—compounded by loyalty to an ideology based on the pressures and definitions of "outsiders"—has revealed the futility of expecting a homogeneity of goals and aspirations. It would seem, therefore, that the direction which black unity is to take if it is to succeed, is one that emphasizes the common denominator of humanhood which all persons share—pigment becoming unimportant—and their equal subjugation to particular processes of socialization and culture. Acceptance of such a view diminishes surprise when "black" is good rather than bad, or when "white" is poor rather than rich, thus opening the doors to a human bond with room for diversity and a search for dignity which all human beings can share.

Yet, to espouse such a viewpoint without noting the difficulties for its acceptance is to be unrealistic; for history and the psychosocial experiences which individuals and groups have had, have created attitudes and emotions which uphold rigid and irrational perceptions that make some persons "a-persons" or "non-persons." Even when glaring physical similarities exist, men have been known to succumb to this malady of prejudicial discrimination, and to behave and make judgments toward "others" accordingly. For too long, focus has been on injustices transmitted by a "white" perpetrator on a "black" victim. Revolutionaries and "liberals" alike have, in turn, found such entrenched focus advantageous in encouraging unity, and in so doing have tended to forget that one who has been oppressed and victimized by another is not necessarily incapable of oppressing and victimizing others—even others that had been identified as one of his own kind. An unfortunate violation of humanistic ethics is often the result, to wit, that shortcomings within a union of those previously oppressed are made light of. It is, thus, equally condemnable for a Stokeley Carmichael to threaten the life of another black man with a gun (as he once did in West Africa), while advocating black unity against white oppression, as it is for a John Schmitz to advocate the rights of his Birchite constituents while trampling those of his constituents who happen to be non-Birchites. Similarly, it is immoral of a Saika Stevens to advocate self-determination for "blacks" in Namibia, while seeming blind to the suppression of those rights for "blacks" within his own country.

Man, regardless of color, religion, or ethnic origin, has shown a capacity for exploiting or of being unjust to his fellow man. Hence, there is danger in being blindly loyal to a unity which presumes that membership in an "in-group" assures protection from abuse by one's own kind. If it is true that physical appearance does not confer distinctive accursedness or purity—despite historical impositions by various social grops to the contrary—black unity (including those Terramedians who refuse to acknowledge their "blackness") must seek its rationale for existence in those universal verities which it cannot, like any other color-based group, escape. Black unity must accept the inevitability of individual manifestations of vices and of wrong judgments within its ranks, and realize that the denials which the history of man have made the lot of "black people" do not provide grounds for wanting to release them from shared responsibility in evolving a human condition that shares commonly in a system of universal rectitude and equity.

One of the slogans of those concerned with "black liberation and dignity" has been, "It's nation time!" In an effort to realize the idea implied, some groups in the United States have tried to establish independent communities in the Southern United States; others have tried to establish an effective control over communities already established through restrictive patterns of housing and other forms of discrimination and deprivation; and still others have undertaken designs to reestablish an ancestral identity in Black Africa and Israel. Among the last group, some have instituted "religious" or economic communes, while some individuals have taken their skills or capital as instruments for their participation in the building of Terramedian nation states. By and large, these various manifestations of nationhood—in Alabama or Mississippi, in Liberia or Ghana, in Tanzania or Kenya, for example—have proved disappointing. In turn, one has been left to ponder why European and Asian "nationalists"—such as Italian-Americans with regard to Italy, Japanese-Americans with regard to Japan, and Jewish-Americans with regard to Israel, for example—have been successful in an endeavor that Black-Americans have found unsuccessful. An answer to the dilemma, it seems, lies in the varying perceptions of nationhood and nationalism by the persons involved.

It is possible to delineate several groups, each with a unique view of the character of nationhood and nationalism vis-à-vis Black Africa especially. There is, first of all, the black African leaders themselves who have assumed the responsibility and (for some) the sole right of expressing and charting the nature and direction of nationalism for Black Africa. With very few exceptions, these leaders adhere to a European definition with its rigid observance of territorial containment and the incidence of birth. To them, therefore, an appeal to an ancestral commonality involving persons born in different territories, and imbued by circumstance with different sociocultural values, becomes irrelevant. Foreigners are foreigners even if they are black, and must be subjected equally to the restrictions of entry, property rights, and job opportunities applicable to all aliens.

The second group comprises the black militants who feel that Africa is their home and it is they alone who are enlightened and dedicated enough to define the applicable imperatives of nationhood and nationalism. They see the duly elected leaders of Black Africa as mere tools of neocolonialists, even as they wrongly profess Ki-Swahili to be the true language of Black Africa. They seek to usurp the rights of the indigenous people to a culture and a system of values different from those enunciated by an ideological plan based on their experiences outside of Black Africa. The same would apply to Westernized Muslims who lack a full and comprehensive appreciation of the primacy and vitality of Islam in Middle Eastern societies.

A third group consists of Americans of Negroid ancestry who are just now beginning to feel comfortable with the label, "black." Even as they strive to identify with the "Negro Renaissance" which used the rhetoric of "Black Power" to evolve into "Black and Proud," the characteristic orientation of this group remains traditionalist and "Americanist." For members of this group, the past deprivation (and even that which still persists) engendered by American racism, does not evoke in them a desire for "separatism" and full identity with Black Africa and Terramedia generally. They retain a belief in the glorious United States Constitution and look forward to continued "progress" in civil rights and human relations—and would say, if pressed, that "this is my country; and I ain't going no where for nobody."

A final group comprises the rank and file of Terramedians—the masses who adhere to the traditional African way of life, even as they respond to the stimuli of the modernism evoked by their interaction, in varying degrees, with bearers and proponents of European culture. Members of this group recognize the material comforts possible with technology and scientism; yet, they retain a loyalty and commitment to the traditional values and modes of behavior adopted and evolved by the generations that preceded them: acceptance of polygyny; kinship responsibility; gerontocracy; love for, and attachment to, their land; respect for, and obedience to, legitimate authority; and generosity toward strangers.

Having all these groups with varying perspectives and orientations, it is no wonder that meaningful manifestations of nationhood and nationalism, as far as Terramedia is concerned, have been inconsistent and difficult to sustain. Instances of enthusiastic migrants to Black Africa, for example, reveal a disappointment with Africa, with realities negating expectations: A group of nationalists who went to settle in Liberia, for example, were disappointed in being unable to identify with the realities of Liberia's political, economic, and social priorities; teachers who went on a summer trip to Africa with great expectations, had to admit to their own cultural shock, and to their amazement in seeing the strong influence of westernism that exists throughout the environment; and even reflective artists such as John Williams, despite a desire for strong identity with Africa, have returned from Black Africa feeling proud of being "Americans." Furthermore, within Terramedia itself, there is a constant contest for power and authority among "brothers," and a willingness to submit to the wiles and whims of external benefactors and humanitarians—all designed to show that this faction, rather than that one, is more able to protect the ideals of Terramedian nationhood and nationalism. Guinea, Israel, Lebanon, South Africa, Syria, Uganda, and Zaire provide vivid examples of such divisiveness and persistent dissension. One ought to be encouraged, however, by the call for reform issues recently by President Sekou Toure: "Being leaders or achieving one party status does not mean getting rich, driving in Mercedes Benz cars and accumulating wealth at the expense of the masses . . . leaders must be honest, truthful and hardworking . . . in the interest of their peoples."[9]

Is there any hope, then, for a reconciliation of these varying perspectives and aspirations to assure the well-being of the actual or imaginary

Motherland, Terramedia? The answer ought to be yes. The basis for such optimism derives from the possibility of understanding the historical roots from which these perspectives have arisen, and to undertake actions that would curb their obstructive confrontations. In short, there is room for empathy on all sides to be accompanied by the realization that some groups and individuals are in a better position—by virtue of exposure to a wider intellectual and territorial experience—to initiate such reconciliation. Black Americans, for example, should acquire sufficient basic knowledge of Terramedia—especially the values various localized groups hold dear, and the relative material limitation—before attempting to invoke "plans" which may prove untenable or impossible to effect. One does not make a favorable impression, for instance, with a micro-mini skirt among a people with a penchant for physical modesty and inhibition. Terramedians leaders and masses alike, on the other hand, must strive to eradicate the remnants of the colonial experience which evoke an unnecessary preference for the European style. They must realize the importance and dignity of their own traditions, and act seriously to restructure the psychological and social modifications and destructions wrought by colonialism. Institutions must be rejuvenated to promote genuine and realistic Terramedian needs and aspirations, and it may very well be necessary to find guidelines for instituional policies that are anti- or nonEuropean or Western. The examples of Saudi Arabia, Libya, and Tanzania are, in this vein, worthy of emulation.

There is certainly much to be gained by Terramedians and their non-Terramedian cousins and brothers who derive their right to an identity (especially with Black Africa) from a historical ancestry. The adaptions which the latter have had to make to survive and succeed when hostility and prejudice threatened such basic desires, have resulted in their acquisiton of skills and insights which a different "cultural base" has denied to a proportionate segment of Terramedians. Terramedians, on the other hand, have had the advantage (although with some exception) of a consistent personal and social identity which is now being enhanced still further by the fact of independence. Inasmuch as a careful analysis would show that this independence has limitations, corrective measures could be achieved from a union of interests among those who have enjoyed identity with a nation that is truly theirs, and those who have learned how to make nations "comfortable" even while suffering from the scars of being denied a piece of the land. Physical contact on a permanent basis is not necessary to bring about such mutuality. Terramedians, and those of the diaspora who would identify with them, must acknowledge at last that even though an individual stands in flesh alone, he is but a symbol of human interdependence. They must together contribute toward providing a check against persistent indifference which ignores interdependence with others. Indeed, Terramedian fraternity, if not nationalism, can be advanced from the roots of genuine empathy to the point where these partners on both sides of the Atlantic Ocean can, in the words of Professor Rupert Emerson, "feel that they belong together in the double sense that they share deeply significant elements of a common heritage and that they have a common destiny for the future."

NOTES

1. Lyn Lofland, *A World of Strangers* (New York: Basic Books, 1973), p. 178.
2. C. Doxiadis, "The Coming Era of Ecumenopolis," *Saturday Review* (March 18, 1967), p. 11.
3. Kwame Nkrumah, *Neo-Colonialism: The Last Stage of Imperialism* (New York: International Publishers, 1966).
4. Cf. Samir Amin, *Neo-Colonialism in West Africa* (Middlesex: Penguin Books, 1973), pp. 155-266.
5. Yale, *Near East*, pp. 22-23.
6. Peter Clecak, *Crooked Paths* (New York: Harper & Row, 1977), pp. 143, 147.
7. See Lofland, *World of Strangers*, pp. 15-16.
8. W.E.B. DuBois, *The World and Africa* (New York: International Publishers, 1965), pp. 311-12.
9. *West Africa* (April, 1979), p. 649.

BIBLIOGRAPHY

Abraham, W. E. *The Mind of Africa.* Chicago: University of Chicago Press, 1959.

Adu, A. L. *The Civil Service in New African States.* New York: Praeger Publishers, 1965.

Afonagoro, Walter F., "The Aro and Delta Middlemen of Nigeria," *Journal of African Studies* (Summer, 1976).

African-American Institute. *African Colleges and Universities.* New York: African-American Institute, 1970.

Ajayi, J. F. Ade, and E. A. Ayandele. "Emerging Themes in Religious History." *Journal of African Studies* (1974): 34-35.

Ajayi, J. F. Ade, and Michael Crowder. *History of West Africa.* 2 vols. London: Longman Group, 1971.

Ajayi, J. F. Ade, and Ian Espie. *A Thousand Years of West African History.* Ibadan, Nigeria: Ibadan University Press, 1966.

Ake, Claude, "Explaining Political Instability in New States," *Journal of Modern African Studies* (September, 1973).

Amin, Samir. *Neo-Colonialism in West Africa.* Middlesex: Penguin Books, 1973.

Anderson, J.N.D. *Islamic Law in the Modern World.* New York: New York University Press, 1959.

Arensberg, Conrad M., and Solon I. Kimball. *Culture and Community.* New York: Harcourt, Brace & World, 1965.

Arkhurst, Frederick S. *U.S. Policy Toward Africa.* New York: Praeger Publishers, 1975.

Armstrong, Robert P. *The Affecting Presence.* Urbana: University of Illinois Press, 1971.

Atiyah, Edward. *An Arab Tells His Story.* London: John Murray, 1946.

Awoonor, Kofi. *The Breast of the Earth.* Garden City, NJ: Doubleday, Anchor Press, 1976.

Banton, Michael. *White and Coloured.* New Brunswick: Rugers University Press, 1960.

Bascom, William. *African Art in Cultural Perspective.* New York: W. W. Norton, 1973.

Battuta, Ibn. *Travels in Asia and Africa.* London: Routledge & Kegan Paul, 1929.

Beckford, George L. *Persistent Poverty.* New York: Oxford University Press, 1972.

Beier, Ulli, and B. Gbadamosi. *Yoruba Poetry.* Ibadan: Ministry of Education, 1959.

Bell, Wendell, and Walter Freeman. *Ethnicity and Nation Building.* Beverly Hills: Sage Publications, 1974.

Bellah, Robert N. *Emile Durkeim on Morality and Society*. Chicago: University of Chicago Press, 1973.

Berger, Morroe. *The Arab World Today*. Garden City, NJ: Doubleday, 1964.

Berger, Peter. *Pyramids of Sacrifice*. Garden City, NJ: Doubleday, Anchor, 1976.

Bewkes, Eugene, et. al. *The Western Heritage of Faith and Reason*. New York: Harper & Row, 1963.

Biobaku, S. O., "Historical Aspects of Acculturation," *Presence Africaine* (1963).

de Blij, Harm J. *A Geography of Subsaharan Africa*. Chicago: Rand McNally, 1964.

Bohannan, Paul, and George Dalton. *Markets in Africa*. Garden City, NJ: Doubleday, 1965.

Bosman, William. *A New and Accurate Description of the Coast of Guinea*. London: Cass, 1967.

Buell, Leslie. *The Native Problem in Africa*, vol. 2. New York: Macmillan, 1928.

Buxton, Thomas F. *The African Slave Trade and Its Remedy*. London: Dawsons of Pall Mall, 1968.

Cairns, H.A.C. *The Clash of Cultures*. New York: Walker & Co., 1962.

Caplan, Gerald. *Emotional Problems of Early Childhood*. New York: Basic Books, 1955.

Cervanka, Zdenek. *The Organization of African Unity and Its Charter*. New York: Praeger Publishers, 1969.

Chambers, Robert. *Settlement Schemes in Tropical Africa*. New York: Praeger Publishers, 1969.

Clark, Paul G., "Development Strategy in an Early-Stage Economy," *Journal of Modern African Studies* (May, 1966).

Clecak, Peter. *Crooked Paths*. New York: Harper & Row, 1977.

Clements, Frank. *Rhodesia*. New York: Praeger Publishers, 1969.

Colley, John K. *East Wind over Africa*. New York: Walker & Company, 1965.

Commission on International Development. *Partners in Development*. New York: Praeger Publishers, 1969.

Condit, D. M., et al. *Challenge and Response in Internal Conflict*. Washington: Center for Research in Social Systems, 1968.

Coser, Lewis, and Bernard Rosenberg. *Sociological Theory*. New York: Macmillan, 1976.

Coulson, N. J. *A History of Islamic Law*. Edinburgh: Edinburgh University Press, 1964.

Cowan, L. Gray. *Education and Nation-Building*. New York: Praeger Publishers, 1965.

Crone, G. R. *The Voyages of Cadamosto*. London: Hakluy Society, 1937.

Crutcher, John. "Pan-Africanism: African Odyssey." *Current History* 50(1963).

Curle, Adam. *Educational Problems of Developing Societies*. New York: Praeger Publishers, 1969.

Dalton, George. *Economic Development and Social Change*. Garden City, NJ: Natural History Press, 1969.

Davidson, Basil. *Black Mother*. Boston: Little, Brown, 1961.

——— *The African Past*. New York: Grosset & Dunlap, 1964.

——— *The African Genius*. Boston: Little, Brown, 1969.

Davidson, Robert R. *Philosophies Men Live By*. New York: Henry Holt, 1952.

Doxiadis, C. "The Coming Era of Ecumenopolis," *Saturday Review*, March 18, 1967.

DuBois, W.E.B. *The World and Africa*. New York: International Publishers, 1965.

Duffy, J., and R. Manners. *Africa Speaks*. Princeton: Van Nostrand, 1961.

Dumont, Rene. *False Start in Africa*. New York: Praeger Publishers, 1969.

Du Toit, Andre. "Ideological Change," In *Change in Contemporary South Africa,* edited by Leonard Thompon and Jeffrey Butler. Berkeley: University of California Press, 1975.

Edwards, Bryan. *The History, Civil and Commercial, of the British West Indies.* 5 vols. 1793-1794. Reprint. New York: AMS Press, 1966.

Elkins, Stanley. *Slavery.* Chicago: University of Chicago Press, 1976.

Emerson, Rupert. *From Empire to Nation.* Boston: Beacon Press, 1962.

Etzioni, Amitai, and Eva Etzioni. *Social Change.* New York: Basic Books, 1964.

Fage, J. D. *An Introduction to the History of West Africa.* London: Cambridge University Press, 1962.

Falconbridge, Alexander. *An Account of the Slave Trade on the Coast of Africa.* London: J. Phillips, 1788.

Fava, Sylvia F. *Urbanism in World Perspective.* New York: Thomas Y. Crowell, 1968.

Finkle, Jason, and Richard Gable. *Political Development and Social Change.* New York: John Wiley, 1966.

First, Ruth. *Libya, the Elusive Revolution.* New York: Africana Publishing Company, 1975.

Foster, George M. *Traditional Cultures.* New York: Harper & Brothers, 1962.

Franklin, John Hope. *Color and Race.* Boston: Houghton Mifflin, 1968.

Frazier, Thomas R. *Afro-American History.* New York: Harcourt, Brace & World, 1970.

Friedrich, C. J. *Man and His Government.* New York: McGraw-Hill, 1963.

Galbraith, John K., "The Coldest Winter?" *Newsweek*, December 3, 1973.

Gallagher, Charles. *The United States and North Africa.* Cambridge, MA: Harvard University Press, 1963.

Gaudefroy-Demonbynes, Maurice. *Muslim Institutions.* London: Allen & Unwin, 1950.

Geiss, Imanuel. *The Pan-African Movement.* New York: Africana Publishing Company, 1974.

Gibb, H.A.R. *Modern Trends in Islam.* Chicago: University of Chicago Press, 1947.

——— and Harold Bowen. *Islamic Society and the West.* London: Oxford University Press, 1957.

Giddens, Anthony. *Emile Durkheim.* London: Cambridge University Press, 1972.

Golan, Taman, *Educating the Bureaucracy in a New Polity.* New York: Teachers College Press, 1968.

Greenfield, Richard. *Ethiopia, a New Political History.* New York: Praeger Publishers, 1965.

Grover, A. T. *Africa South of the Sahara.* London: Oxford University Press, 1967.

Hahn, Lorna. *North Africa: Nationalism to Nationhood.* Washington: Public Affairs Press, 1960.

Haley, Alex. *Roots.* New York: Dell Publishing Company, 1977.

Hallett, Robin. *Africa since 1875.* Ann Arbor: University of Michigan Press, 1974.

——— *Africa to 1875.* Ann Arbor: University of Michigan Press, 1974.

Halpern, Manfred. *The Politics of Social Change in the Middle East and North Africa.* Princeton: Princeton University Press, 1963.

Hance, William A. *Southern Africa and the United States.* New York: Columbia University Press, 1969.

Harrison, Ira E., "Health Status and Healing Practices," *Journal of African Studies* (Winter, 1976).

Heggoy, Alf A. "Arab Education in Colonial Algeria." *Journal of African Studies* (1975): 149-60.

Heller, Celia S. *Structured Social Inequality.* New York: Macmillan, 1969.
Herskovits, Melville J. *The Human Factor in Changing Africa.* New York: Random House, 1962.
Hitti, Philip K. *The Arabs.* Chicago: Henry Regnery Company, 1956.
——— *Islam and the West.* Princeton: Van Nostrand, 1962.
Hoare, Prince. *Memoirs of Granville Sharp.* London: H. Colburn, 1828.
Hodgkin, Thomas. *Nationalism in Colonial Africa.* New York: New York University Press, 1956.
Hoebel, E. A. *Anthropology, the Study of Man.* New York: McGraw-Hill, 1966.
Howard, C., and J. H. Plumb. *West African Explorers.* London: Oxford University Press, 1951.
Hunter, Guy. *The New Societies of Tropical Africa.* New York: Praeger Publishers, 1964.
James, C.L.R. *The Black Jacobins.* New York: Vintage Books, 1963.
Khadduri, Majid. *Islamic Jurisprudence.* Baltimore: Johns Hopkins University Press, 1961.
Kimble, George H. T. *Tropical Africa.* New York: The Twentieth Century Fund, 1960.
Kirk, George E. *A Short History of the Middle East.* New York: Praeger Publishers, 1964.
Klein, Herbert S. *Slavery in the Americas.* Chicago: University of Chicago Press, 1967.
Knight, Franklin W. *The Caribbean–the Genesis of Fragmented Nationalism.* New York: Oxford University Press, 1978.
Kuper, Hilda. *Urbanization and Migration in West Africa.* Berkeley: University of California Press, 1965.
Labouret, Henri. *Africa Before the White Man.* New York: Walker & Company, 1962.
Landau, Jacob M. *Man, State, and Society in the Contemporary Middle East.* New York: Praeger Publishers, 1972.
Laude, Jean. *The Arts of Black Africa.* Berkeley: University of California Press, 1971.
Leakey, L.S.B. *Olduvai Gorge.* 3 vols. London: Cambridge University Press, 1971.
Leakey, Mary D. "Footprints in the ashes of Time." *National Geographic* (1979): 450-456.
Legum, Colin. *Pan-Africanism.* New York: Praeger Publishers, 1962.
Lenski, Gerhard. *Power and Privilege.* New York: McGraw-Hill, 1966.
Lerner, Daniel. *The Passing of Traditional Society.* Glencoe: The Free Press, 1958.
Levy, Reuben. *The Social Structure of Islam.* London: Cambridge University Press, 1962.
Lewis, Bernard. *The Middle East and the West.* New York: Harper & Row, 1966.
Leys, Colin. *Politics and Change in Developing Countries.* London: Cambridge University Press, 1969.
Little, Kenneth L. *African Women in Towns.* London: Cambridge University Press, 1973.
——— *The Mende of Sierra Leone.* London: Routledge & Kegan Paul, 1951.
Lofchie, Michael L., "Why Africa Turned Against Israel," Los Angeles *Times,* December 2, 1973.
Lofland, Lyn. *A World of Strangers.* New York: Basic Books, 1973.
Lystad, Robert A. *The African World.* New York: Praeger Publishers, 1965.
Mabona, Mongameli. "African Spirituality." *Presence Africaine,* Fourth Quarterly, (1964): 158-62.

McCall, Daniel F. "Women in Gur Myth and Society," *Journal of African Studies* (1974): 280-84.

McKay, Vernon. *Africa in World Politics.* New York: Harper & Row, 1963.

Mair, Lucy. *African Societies.* London: Cambridge University Press, 1974.

Mansfield, Peter. *The Middle East.* London: Oxford University Press, 1973.

Mannoni, O. *Prospero and Caliban.* New York: Praeger Publishers, 1964.

Mazrui, Ali. *Soldiers and Kinsmen in Uganda.* Beverly Hills: Sage Publications, 1975.

Mbiti, John S. *African Religions and Philosophy.* New York: Praeger Publishers, 1969.

Mernissi, Fatima. *Beyond the Veil: Male-Female Dynamics in a Modern Muslim State.* Cambridge, MA: Schenkman Publishing Company, 1975.

Merriam, Alan. *Congo, Background of Conflict.* Evanston: Northwestern University Press, 1961.

Merton, Robert K. *Social Theory and Social Structure.* Glencoe: The Free Press, 1957.

Miller, J. D. *Politics of the Third World.* London: Oxford University Press, 1967.

Miner, H. "Cultural Change Under Stress." *Human Organization* (Autumn, 1960).

Monti, Franco. *African Masks.* London: Paul Hasulyn, 1969.

Moore, Gerald. *Seven African Writers.* London: Oxford University Press, 1962.

Moore, Wilbert E. *Social Structure and Personality.* Glencoe: The Free Press, 1957.

Mtewa, Mekki. "The Saga of John Chilembwa." *Journal of Black Studies* 8(1977): 227-48.

Nelson, Cynthia. *The Desert and the Sown.* Berkeley: University of California Press, 1973.

Neilsen, Waldemar. *The Great Powers and Africa.* New York: Praeger Publishers, 1969.

Nisbet, Robert. *Emile Durkheim.* Engelwood Cliffs, NJ: Prentice-Hall, 1965.

Nkrumah, Kwame. *Dark Days in Ghana.* London: Panaf Publications, 1968.

——— *Neo-Colonialism: The Last Stage of Imperialism.* New York: International Publishers, 1966.

Oliver, Roland, and J. D. Fage. *A Short History of Africa.* London: Collings, 1974.

Omari, T. Peter. *Kwame Nkrumah.* Accra, Ghana: Moxon Paperbacks, 1970.

Oppong, Christine. *Marriage Among a Matrilineal Elite.* London: Cambridge University Press, 1974.

Pahlavi, Mohammed Reza Shah. *Mission for my Country.* London: Hutchinson & Company, 1961.

Palen, J. John. *The Urban World.* New York: McGraw-Hill, 1975.

Parsons, Talcott. *Sociological Theory and Modern Society.* Glencoe: The Free Press, 1967.

——— *Social Theory and Social Structure.* Glencoe: The Free Press, 1967.

Peretz, Don. *The Middle East Today.* New York: Holt, Rinehart & Winston, 1964.

Perham, Margery. *Native Administration in Nigeria.* London: Oxford University Press, 1937.

Peterson, John. *Province of Freedom.* Evanston: Northwestern University Press, 1969.

Phillips, Thomas. *A Journey of a Voyage Made in the Hannibal.* London: Lintot & Osborn, 1746.

Polk, William R. *The United States and the Arab World.* Cambridge: Harvard University Press, 1975.

Porter, Arthur T. *Creoledom.* London: Oxford University Press, 1963.

Post, Ken. *The New States of West Africa.* Baltimore: Penguin Books, 1964.

Powdermaker, Hortense. *Copper Town.* New York: Harper & Row, 1962.

Preston, Ronald H. *Technology and Social Justice.* Valley Forge: Judson Press, 1971.

Quigg, Phillip. *Africa, a Foreign Affairs Reader.* New York: Praeger Publishers, 1964.

Rado, E. R. "Manpower, Education and Economic Growth." *Journal of Modern African Studies* (May, 1966).

Reisman, Paul. "The Art of Life in a West African Community." *Journal of African Studies* (1975): 39-63.

Rivlin, Benjamin, and Joseph Szyliowicz. *The Contemporary Middle East.* New York: Random House, 1965.

Roberts, George O. *Cultural and Social Differentials in Health Practices.* Ann Arbor: University Microfilms, 1962.

Ross, Jack C., and Raymond H. Wheeler. *Black Belonging.* Westport, CN: Greenwood Publishing Corporation, 1971.

Rotberg, Robert, and Ali Mazrui. *Protest and Power in Black Africa.* New York: Oxford University Press, 1970.

Rotberg, Robert. *A Political History of Tropical Africa.* New York: Harcourt, Brace & World, 1965.

Rustow, D. A. *Middle Eastern Political Systems.* Englewood Cliffs, NJ: Prentice-Hall, 1971.

Said, Abdul. *The African Phenomenon.* Boston: Allan & Bacon, 1968.

Schacht, Joseph. *An Introduction to Islamic Law.* London: Oxford University Press, 1964.

Sharp, Granville. *Tracts on Slavery and Liberty.* 1776. Reprint. Westport: Negro Universities Press, 1969.

Shelton, Austin J. *The African Assertion.* New York: Odyssey Press, 1968.

--- *The Igbo-Igala Borderland.* Albany: State University of New York Press, 1971. Press, 1971.

Shyllon, F. O. *Black Slaves in Britain.* London: Oxford University Press, 1974.

Silvert, K. H. *Expectant Peoples–Nationalism and Development.* New York: Random House, 1963.

Southall, Aidan. "Problems of the New Morality." *Journal of African Studies* 1(1974): 363-89.

Stamp, L. Dudley. *Africa, a Study in Tropical Development.* New York. John Wiley, 1953.

Stanley, Henry M. *Autobiography.* Boston: Houghton Mifflin, 1909.

Tempels, Placide. *Bantu Philosophy.* Paris: Presence Africaine, 1959.

Thompson, Leonard. *African Societies in Southern Africa.* New York: Praeger Publishers, 1969.

Trimingham, J. Spencer. *Islam in West Africa.* London: Oxford University Press, 1959.

Turnbull, Colin. *Man in Africa.* Garden City, NJ: Doubleday, Anchor Press, 1977.

Uya, Okon E. *Black Brotherhood.* Lexington: D. C. Heath, 1971.

Walker, James. *The Black Loyalists.* New York: Africana Publishing Company, 1976.

Warwick, Donald P. *Comparative Research Methods.* Englewood Cliffs, NJ: Prentice-Hall, 1973.

Watt, W. Montgomery. *Islamic Philosophy and Theology.* Edinburgh: Edinburgh University Press, 1962.

Widstrand, Carl. *Multi-National Firms in Africa.* New York: Africana Publishing Company, 1977.

Wylie, Kenneth C. *The Political Kingdoms of the Temne.* New York: Africana Publishing Co., 1977.

Yale, William. *The Near East.* Ann Arbor, University of Michigan Press, 1968.
Yinger, J. Milton. *Religion, Society and the Individual.* New York: Macmillan, 1957.
Zartman, I. William. *Man, State, and Society in the Contemporary Maghrib.* New York: Praeger Publishers, 1973.

INDEX

GEORGE O. ROBERTS is Professor of Comparative Culture and Social Sciences as well as Special Assistant to the Executive Vice Chancellor at the University of California, Irvine. A Mende Tribesman, born and raised in Sierra Leone, Roberts has first-hand knowledge of African culture, politics, languages, and lifestyles. He holds a Ph.D. in Sociology from the Catholic University of America and has taught in both the United States and Africa. That and his extensive professional travel in the Middle East and Africa make him exceedingly aware of the promise and problems of Terramedia. His publications include textbooks, articles, and papers on comparative culture, Africa, Sierra Leone, black Americans, mental health, and education.